IN THE MIND OF STALIN

IN THE MIND OF STALIN

JAMES GREENSMITH

PEN & SWORD HISTORY

AN IMPRINT OF PEN & SWORD BOOKS LTD.
YORKSHIRE – PHILADELPHIA

First published in Great Britain in 2022 by
Pen & Sword History
An imprint of
Pen & Sword Books Ltd
Yorkshire - Philadelphia

ISBN 978 1 39906 3 579

A CIP catalogue record for this book is available from the British Library.

Typeset in INDIA By IMPEC eSolutions
Printed and bound in England
By CPI (UK) Ltd.

Pen & Sword Books Ltd incorporates the Imprints of Pen & Sword Archaeology, Atlas, Aviation, Battleground, Discovery, Family History, History, Maritime, Military, Naval, Politics, Railways, Select, Transport, True Crime, Fiction, Frontline Books, Leo Cooper, Praetorian Press, Seaforth Publishing, Wharncliffe and White Owl.

For a complete list of Pen & Sword titles please contact
PEN & SWORD BOOKS LIMITED
47 Church Street, Barnsley, South Yorkshire, S70 2AS, England
E-mail: enquiries@pen-and-sword.co.uk
Website: www.pen-and-sword.co.uk

Or

PEN AND SWORD BOOKS
1950 Lawrence Rd, Havertown, PA 19083, USA
E-mail: uspen-and-sword@casematepublishers.com
Website: www.penandswordbooks.com

MIX
Paper from responsible sources
FSC® C013604

Contents

Author's Note

The following names are used in this narrative: Joseph, instead of Stalin's given first name of Ioseb; Dzhugashvili for Stalin's given surname. His middle name was Vissarionovich.

Stalin had many nicknames including Soso and Koba; the name Stalin first appeared in literature in January 1913.

The city of St Petersburg was renamed Petrograd in 1914, Leningrad in 1924, and St Petersburg again, in 1991. The city of Tsaritsyn was renamed Stalingrad in 1925 and Volgograd in 1961.

The Russian Social Democratic Labour Party (RSDLP) was founded in 1898. In 1903 the RSDLP split, and in early 1912 the RSDLP (Bolshevik) Party was created. In 1918 when the Bolsheviks became the ruling party of Russia, the name of the party was changed to the All-Russian Communist Party. In 1925 (after the founding of the USSR in December 1922) the Party was renamed the All-Union Communist Party (Bolsheviks). Finally, in 1952 the Party was renamed the Communist Party of the Soviet Union.

Introduction

In respect of Europe and Russia in the mid-twentieth century, two men top the gruesome list as having been responsible for the deaths of millions of people: Adolf Hitler, German Führer and an aggressive warmonger; and Joseph Stalin, Soviet leader who wilfully committed genocide against his own people and enforced policies such as the collectivisation of agriculture, regardless of human cost.

Hitler heard voices that no one else could hear, and it is virtually certain that he was suffering from schizophrenia. This was compounded by insanity, caused by syphilis, which affected him in his later years.[1]

What of Stalin – the name that he gave himself, from the Russian word 'stal', meaning 'Man of Steel'? He was General Secretary of the Communist Party of the Soviet Union from April 1922 to October 1952 and became Soviet dictator in January 1924 after the death of Vladimir Lenin, Chairman of the Council of People's Commissars of the Soviet Union.

Contrary to popular belief, Stalin was capable of great tenderness and kindness, as vouched for by his daughter, Svetlana. However, when she grew to adulthood, their relationship deteriorated and her father became unkind, indifferent, and even cruel towards her.

It is impossible to quantify the total number of deaths attributable to the policies of Stalin, but the 'Excess Mortality' (i.e., deaths over and above what would normally have been expected during the period in question) gives an approximate figure in excess of 40 million. They were murdered by the state, or died in purges in the Gulag prison system, or in famines as a direct result of agricultural collectivisation.

However, this is only part of the story of the amount of misery inflicted by the Stalin regime through torture, deliberate starvation, neglect, separation from loved ones, cold and hypothermia (e.g. in the prisons of Siberia) being unquantifiable and unimaginable.

Stalin was renowned for reacting violently to anyone whom he perceived to be a threat. But were these threats always real, or were they sometimes – often even – simply a figment of his imagination? In other words, was he paranoid? And if so, were his paranoid ideas his own, or was he being fed them by one or more of his henchmen who were anxious to exploit this defect in their leader's personality?

On 1 October 1939, Winston Churchill, First Lord of the Admiralty and soon to be the UK's wartime leader, described Russia as 'a riddle wrapped in a mystery inside an enigma'. The same can certainly be said of Stalin. How can this paradox of the loving father on the one hand, and the man who sent millions to their deaths on the other, be explained?

Stalin's daughter, Svetlana, confessed that she would never undertake to '"explain" what motivated all my father's actions, simply because I do not possess the psychological genius of [Russian novelist] Dostoevsky, who knew how to "penetrate" into another man's soul and "examine it from within"'.[2] Nonetheless, an attempt will now be made to unravel the enigma that was Stalin, and to discover what made this 'Man of Steel' tick!

Chapter 1

Joseph Stalin (Born 18 December 1878): The Early Years: A Cherished Child

Joseph Stalin was born in Gori in eastern Georgia in 1878. Georgia, a kingdom that existed during the medieval period, was annexed by the Russian Empire in the nineteenth century. Georgia is situated between the Black Sea to the west and the Caspian Sea to the east, in a mountainous region known as the Caucasus, including Armenia and Azerbaijan to the south and parts of southern Russia to the north. A sickly child of humble origins, Joseph barely managed to survive, and yet one day he would become both famous and notorious the world over.

Joseph's father, Besarion ('Beso') Dzhugashvili, 'a Georgian of peasant stock from the village of Didi-Lilo' 12 miles east of the Georgian capital, Tiflis (later named Tbilisi), was born in 1850. Besarion was 'a cobbler by trade, and later a worker at the Adelkhanov Shoe Factory' in Tiflis.[1]

Stalin's mother, Ekaterina ('Keke'), was born in 1858 'of a peasant serf named Geladze in the village of Gambareuli, on the outskirts of Gori. In 1935, Ekaterina wrote her memoirs, and it is therefore thanks to her that a first-hand account exists of the subject of this narrative, Joseph Stalin. Written in Georgian, the memoirs are preserved in the Archive of the Central Committee of the Communist Party of Georgia.[2]

Ekaterina recalled her time in Gambareuli, which is where she met Besarion. They were married on 17 May 1874.[3] Said Ekaterina, 'Beso turned out to be a good family man who made a good deal of money and provided the family with everything. He was a kind-hearted and pious man. He attended church on Sundays. Beso was proud of me and liked taking me along when he went to church. In short, we had a happy family, [so] that a lot of people would envy us.'

Besarion told Ekaterina that his ancestors had also been serfs and had come from Geri, in the Gori municipality. 'Our happiness had no limits,' she said. But sadly, this was not to last.

The couple's first child, Mikhail was born in 1876 but died two months later of measles. Their second child, Georgi, was born two years later, but he also died, unchristened, even before Keke 'was able to get up from bed after childbirth'. When Ekaterina became pregnant once again, there was much anxiety in case this baby too would not survive, and would also die unchristened.

Joseph, their third child, was born on 18 December 1878. Said Ekaterina, 'Although the baby remained alive, he was very weak in body, very tender and thin.' Furthermore, he became ill 'due to sitting in a draught'. However, he survived, and they nicknamed him 'Soso'. 'This illness urged Beso to take us to pray in Geri. We sacrificed a lamb and had the priest perform a thanksgiving service.' Surely, this was an example of both maternal and paternal love towards their son, Joseph, on the part of Ekaterina and Besarion.

Joseph's given name appears in the birth register of Gori's Church of the Assumption of St Mary as 'Ioseb Besarionis dze Dzhugashvili'.

'Soso learned to speak early,' said Ekaterina. 'I remember what names he called things in detail. I remember the joy and laughs it gave us. He touched every bright object, reaching out his hands and saying in a childish manner, "*nda, dundala nda*", meaning he wanted "*dundala*". Every glittering object was a "*dundala*" for him.

'He loved flowers, especially cornflowers and chamomiles [daisy-like plants of the family *Asteraceae*]. On seeing chamomiles, he would become impatient and start reaching out his hands and saying in his childish way: "*Zi-zi! nda zizi-zi*!". A chamomile was a "*zizi*" for him. He also loved music. My brothers Gio and Sandala played the duduk [woodwind instrument] very well. When they were in a good mood and played in unison, there was no limit to Soso's joy.

'Of birds, he liked the oriole and called it a "*gogia-gogia*". My mother carried him around and her arms hurt. She would often take him to the gardens and show him a "*gogia-gogia*" and let him enjoy a nightingale's songs.'

'But I was unhappy because Beso had started drinking more', said Ekaterina, and the outcome was that he 'lost the respect for both me and my mother. Beso, who had been a good family man, became useless and couldn't help drinking. His hands began trembling because of drinking and he could no longer perform his work so skilfully as before.

'Trying to find a solution, my brothers found me a room beside their home, with the hope that when I was near them, Beso would stop behaving badly. We moved there, which means I returned to the place which Beso had taken me from [presumably Gambareuli]. But it was a vain effort. He didn't give up drinking,' and, 'I moved further from that area, renting a room in the house of the village priest, Kristepore Charkviani with the hope that it would be a solution, but nothing changed. Beso still didn't give up drinking.

'My Soso was a very sensitive child. When he heard his father's voice and loud singing, he would immediately cling up to me and tell me to hide in a neighbour's house until dad had fallen asleep or else he [Besarion] would make me angry again. Soso was very worried about his father's behaviour; he became reserved and sad. He no longer went out to play with his peers; he even stopped to like being [i.e. pretending to be] Arsena.' (Arsena Odzelashvili, an outlaw fighting against serfdom, who was a popular hero in nineteenth-century Georgia.) Clearly Joseph was beginning to be adversely affected by Besarion's behaviour.

'I also wanted to take my child to school, but Beso had a different opinion. He said he wanted to teach his son his trade so that he would assist him. We were pulling in different directions.' But Besarion had his way. 'He started to teach the child his trade. He even taught it to him, but the child fell ill. Smallpox almost took his life.

'As soon as the child recovered a little, he [Joseph] asked me to teach him to read. My mother and I also wanted to take the child to school very much.' It was their hope that Joseph 'would study in the church school'. Both had 'dreamed of Soso's becoming a bishop many times'.

'Once I dared to speak with Beso about Soso's education. I complained that the child had reached the age of seven and still hadn't started school. He called me stupid, since he thought having an educated son was a disaster.'

When Kote, the eldest son of Gori priest Father Kristopore Charkviani, 'saw Soso's enthusiasm, he started teaching him diligently and taught the entire Mother Tongue [an ABC book for pupils of the primary school] in a week. Kote was surprised with Soso's talent and wondered how he had managed to catch up and overtake his [Kote's] younger brother and sister.'

With the help of Father Charkviani, Joseph was permitted to take the entrance examinations for the Gori Church School. 'He answered all the questions very easily. He retold the Mother Tongue very well and passed the exam in calculus. He also excelled in the prayers. The child was considered so well-prepared that he was admitted to the intermediate class. I was happy. My mother and I thanked Kristopore heartily.'[4] It was the autumn of 1888 and Joseph was now aged 9.

John Thomas Murphy was a British trade union organiser and member of the Communist Party of Great Britain from its formation in 1920 until he resigned from the Party in 1932. In *Stalin: 1879–1944* (published in 1945), Murphy stated that, 'Like every school in Russia, the Gori Church School conducted all lessons in Russian: Stalin had to learn his natural Georgian from his mother.'[5]

But instead of being pleased at the news, said Ekaterina, 'Beso got furious, telling me I was going to ruin his son. Time passed. My Soso passed to the next grade as the best pupil.' Meanwhile, 'with every passing year', Besarion 'was losing his ability to work because of drinking', until he gave up working 'and entrusted the workshop to a new, inexperienced apprentice'.

Once, Besarion 'came home very drunk. Soso was in the second grade then. He rushed towards me, but Sofio [mother-in-law of Gori priest Father Kristopore Charkviani] stood between us. He was telling me that I must give his son back to him or else I would ruin the child's life. He took Soso to the workshop by force and gave him a piece of leather to sew shoes.' Finally, under pressure from both Joseph's teachers and from Ekaterina's family, Besarion backed down. However, he 'considered this as a "disgrace" and, ashamed, left the family for good'. This was in 1890, when Joseph was aged 11.

In order to make ends meet, said Ekaterina, 'I started work. I performed all kinds of manual jobs. I was not even ashamed to do the laundry. Then I started sewing. In short, a needle and thread became my son's and my livelihood. I had no other source of income. Thanks to my diligence, I managed to provide the child with everything in time, so that he wouldn't feel disadvantaged and worry about living without a father.'

Soso had an excellent voice, said Ekaterina, and she 'liked to go to the church of the school and listen to my son's chanting'. Joseph 'graduated from the Gori Church School so well that he wasn't left in the same class even once.' He achieved 'fives' – top marks – 'and was considered the best pupil'.

In other respects, said Murphy, 'The years at the Gori School were not extraordinary. Young Soso played his games; learned Russian and (at home) Georgian; rambled with other boys into the mountain passes, the caves and woodlands, like any normal youngster of the district.'

He was still in this junior school when he read Darwin's *Origin of Species* and *The Descent of Man*.

The effect of these books on Soso was profound. They destroyed whatever religious ideas he had derived from his mother or his school training.'[6]

Chapter 2

How Stalin Became a Battered Child

Interviewed in the 1980s, Stalin's daughter, Svetlana, shed a more detailed yet disturbing light on her father's formative years. Relaxed and smiling for most of the time, she impressed with her dignity, poise, excellent command of English, thoughtfulness, and obvious intelligence. Her constant gaze betokened honesty and sincerity. Of her father, Svetlana said, 'Well, his origins are really humble, generations and generations of very poor peasants, peasants of Georgia, which means Asian people, Asian Christians for 15 centuries.

'His father became a worker, a cobbler in the factory. His mother was a purely peasant woman with a strong faith. I think he always had something of the peasant background, which was in his character: certain strength, certain rigidity, certain conservatism, and tremendous love for nature and land and fresh air.'

'When we revisited Russia three years ago with my teenage American daughter,' Svetlana continued, referring to Olga, 'we went to see the little shack [Svetlana had earlier described it as the 'poor cobblers hut'; 'the little hovel'[1]] where he was born, and then we went to see the school, the classroom with crude wooden desks where he sat, and my daughter asked how many languages he had to study and they told her that immediately in Georgia everybody had to know Russian; had to study Russian. He had also learnt Latin and Greek. He was a good student. His favourite subject was, as he himself admitted, mathematics. Not humanities, as a matter of fact.'

What was Joseph's mother, Ekaterina, whom Svetlana once met, like? 'I was brought to see her when I was a girl of 8 and my brother [Vasily] was 12. We didn't speak Georgian, she didn't speak Russian, and there were translators around. She was old, grey haired, with bright, light eyes, freckles, and she was crying, and tears were streaming down her face because she was happy to see us, her grandchildren.' On a plate, Ekaterina had placed 'some candies for us. That was the only communication between us which was possible because we couldn't really utter anything which was satisfactory. But she was pleased to see us. That was the only time I saw her.'

As for her father's childhood, said Svetlana, 'Well, as it is known and as he used to talk about it, it was rather a horrid childhood of poverty, with a father who was a drunk, who used to beat the rest of the household. It was a pretty rough childhood. However, he used to say that he loved his mother always, despite the fact that she 'used to beat him too. He admitted that, but that didn't obviously make any difference. He kept a certain reverence and a really very sincere admiration for her and her character into his late years.'[2]

In fact, according to Russian author Edvard Stanislavovich Radzinsky, a Georgian Jewish woman named Hana Moshiashvili, once a friend of Ekaterina, stated of Joseph that after his father Besarion left home, 'His mother was head of the family now, and the fist which had subdued his father was now applied to the upbringing of their son. She beat him unmercifully for disobedience.'[3]

In *Only One Year*, Svetlana elaborated further about her father. Said she, 'Sometimes he told me about his childhood. Fights, coarseness were not unusual in the poor, half-literate family in which the head of the household drank. The mother would beat the boy; her husband would beat her. But the boy loved his mother and defended her. One day he threw a knife at his father. The father rushed after him, screaming, and neighbours hid the boy. Both his parents were of peasant stock; the height of attainment for the father had been to work as a cobbler in a factory. The mother had more fantasy and ambition – she wanted to make of her only son a priest, thus raising herself from the lower depths in which her life was spent. She was truly and deeply religious, and having become a widow at an early age, she worked her fingers to the bone in order to give her son an education.

'The son was an ordinary village boy who fought, played naughty tricks. One day he dropped a brick down a chimney into an open hearth, frightening and burning the owners of the house. At school he liked arithmetic above all else; later mathematics. He drew a little. In his old age he still remembered Greek.

'His ambition, his aspiration to attain greater heights, to raise himself above others, must have come to him from his mother. Perhaps that was the reason for his being among the best pupils in the parochial school in Gori.'[4]

Ekaterina remembered stories told to her by Georgian physician Doctor Nikoloz Kipshidze, who treated her in her later years. For example, Kipshidze recalled a visit by Joseph to Ekaterina in October 1935, '"Why did you beat me so hard?", he asked his mother. "That's why you turned out so well," Keke answered. "Joseph – who exactly are you now?" his mother asked him. "Remember the tsar? Well, I'm like a tsar." To this, his mother retorted, "You'd have done better to become a priest."'

Kipshidze also declared, in respect of Joseph, that, 'One day when his father was drunk, he picked him up and threw him violently to the floor. There was blood in the boy's urine for days afterwards.'[5] (Radzinsky does not provide a reference for this statement, but in the context of Besarion's behaviour, and given that Radzinsky had privileged access to Russia's secret archives, there is no reason to doubt its authenticity).[6]

'Any tenderness and love [that her father, Joseph] remembered from his childhood days,' said Svetlana, 'was personified in his mother, whom in his own way he loved and respected all his life.' As for Ekaterina, 'From time to time [in her later years] she would send her son in Moscow some nut jam, which she had made. One day she sent in a blanket she had made with her own hands out of light, Caucasian wool.'[7]

A boyhood friend, Josef Iremashvili 'composed the first memoir of Stalin's childhood'. Said he, 'Undeserved, terrible beatings made the boy as hard and heartless as his father himself. Since all men who had authority over others, either through power or age, reminded him of his father there soon arose a feeling of revenge against all men who stood above him. From his youth, the realisation of his thoughts of revenge became the goal toward which everything was aimed.'[8]

Sofio 'loved and respected me very much', said Ekaterina. Every time Kote 'saw Beso coming home intoxicated, he would immediately run to my place. He knew that Beso would harm me and she [Sofio] hid my son and me in her home.'[9]

'When he saw his father intoxicated,' continued Ekaterina, 'tears filled his eyes and his lips became blue; he would cling to my chest and ask me with all his heart to avoid him [Besarion] and stay in a neighbour's house, mainly in grandma Sofio's house, until Beso had fallen asleep.'[10]

Josef Davrichewy was the son of a prefect of police who grew up with Joseph in Gori.[11] He too remembered Joseph as being a battered child. Davrichewy recalled how Besarion treated his son 'like a dog, beating him for nothing'.[12] Davrichewy described an incident when Besarion entered his parent's house, where Ekaterina and Joseph were staying, 'We heard the sound of plates and dishes breaking, the piercing cries of [Besarion's] wife, and little Soso, all covered in blood rushed towards us crying: "Help! Come quick, he is killing my mother!" My father and the neighbours had considerable difficulty subduing Beso who, foaming at the mouth and sitting astride Kato's [another nickname for Ekaterina] chest, was in the process of strangling her. In order to calm him down it was necessary to club him and to tie him up hand and foot. My mother took care of poor Soso, who had a wound on the top of his head and, since he was afraid to return home, he and Kato spent the night at our place, lying entwined on a mattress placed on the floor.'[13]

Said Ekaterina of her son: 'He became very reserved, frequently sat alone and didn't go out to play with other children anymore.'[14]

Besarion died on 12 August 1909.[15] According to Iremashvili, the death of his father 'left no impression upon the boy'.[16] This is hardly surprising. Joseph's senses would have been completely numbed by the treatment he had received at the hands of Besarion, and his only feeling would probably have been intense relief at his father's passing, which he was afraid to show for fear of upsetting his mother.

What was it that caused Besarion to change from being a loving and attentive husband and father to a murderous child batterer? Was it some kind of inherent personality disorder? This is unlikely. After all, Besarion was aged 28 when Joseph was born and such a tendency, had it existed, would most probably have manifested itself earlier. Was it because he was jealous of Joseph's close relationship with his mother, or because Ekaterina had prevented Joseph from joining his father and training to be a cobbler? Or was it the drink that made him aggressive and violent? In Georgia, a traditional home-made drink was Chacha brandy. Made by distilling pomace (the solid remains left over from wine making after the grapes had been pressed), it contained 65 per cent alcohol!

Whatever the reason, Joseph suffered what, in legal terms, would be termed 'assault and battery'; 'grievous bodily harm'; perhaps even 'attempted murder'! This would have grave repercussions in respect of the child's future, as will be seen.

Chapter 3

Was Besarion Stalin's Real Father?

Was it simply because of his drunkenness and irritation with his wife, Ekaterina, who had thwarted him in his designs to take his son, Josef, on as an apprentice that led Besarion to beat his son? Or was there a more profound reason?

There were rumours that Besarion was not Joseph Stalin's father. For example, Josef Davrichewy suggested in his memoirs *Ah! Ce qu'on rigolait bien avec mon ami Staline!* ('Ah! What we laughed about with my boyfriend Stalin'), that the real father was Yacobi ('Yakov') Egnatashvili, nicknamed 'Koba'.[1] Egnatashvili, a married man with children, was a wealthy merchant: a Georgian wine grower; owner of taverns, and also a champion wrestler. What evidence is there for this?

The close relationship between Egnatashvili and Joseph's mother, Ekaterina

Katerina was an employee of Egnatashvili, 'one of those who Keke [Ekaterina] worked for'.[2] Egnatashvili purchased machine tools in order that Besarion could set up as a cobbler in his own right with his own workshop.[3] Furthermore, Egnatashvili was best man (one of two), at Besarion and Ekaterina's wedding and after the birth of Josef, he was always referred to as 'Godfather Yakov', even though he was not the boy's godfather.[4] Egnatashvili welcomed Joseph and his mother into their family home. He also supported Josef financially, including during his years at school and at the seminary. Why, if he was not Joseph's father, would Egnatashvili have taken such a keen interest in the young Joseph Stalin, who was way beneath him in the social 'pecking order'.

Besarion's behaviour towards his son, Joseph

Besarion's brutality towards his son has already been described. Also, Besarion called Ekaterina 'a whore' and he referred to their son, Josef as 'Keke's little bastard'.[5] In other words, Besarion clearly believed that someone else had fathered his child.

Besarion's attitude towards Egnatashvili

Besarion is said to have vandalised a tavern owned by Egnatashvili,[6] even though the latter was his benefactor.

Children and their Step-parents

When a married person, e.g. Ekaterina (or one in a long-term relationship), has a child by someone other than their spouse, the spouse may forgive and accept the newcomer to the family, e.g. Joseph, unconditionally; or the spouse may become angry, and reject the child, as one who is not his or her flesh and blood, and instead as an outsider who is a constant reminder of their partner's infidelity. Finally, the aggrieved spouse may take his or her anger out on the child (or in Besarion's case, on both Joseph and Ekaterina).

If Egnatashvili (or some other person) was indeed Joseph's real father, then Besarion would, in effect, have been Josef's stepfather.

US-born British evolutionary psychologist and writer Satoshi Kanazawa posed the question, 'Why Are Stepparents More Likely to Kill Their Children?' and he quoted two Canadian psychologists: Martin Daly and Margo Wilson, who 'discovered, in their analysis of homicide data from Canada and Detroit, that stepchildren, those who live with a stepparent (usually, a stepfather), are anywhere from 40 to 100 times as likely to be murdered or maimed as those who live with two biological parents in the household.'[7]

Although there is no definite proof that Egnatashvili was Joseph Stalin's father, the attitude and behaviour of the parties involved strongly suggest that this was the case.

Chapter 4

Dr John Bowlby: The Importance of a Loving Childhood

Child Care and the Growth of Love by British psychologist, psychiatrist and psychoanalyst Edward John Mostyn Bowlby (1907–90) was first published in 1953. In writing the book, Bowlby drew on a wealth of scientific literature to back up his claims. For example, the 'List of Authorities' at the end of the volume runs to three pages and includes works and scientific papers by both men and women. Said Bowlby: 'Among the most significant developments of psychiatry during the past quarter of a century has been a steady growth of evidence that the quality of the parental care which a child receives in its earliest years is of vital importance for his [or her] future mental health.'[1] Joseph Stalin, of course, was an only child.

'For the moment it is sufficient to say that what is believed to be essential for mental health is that an infant and young child should experience a warm, intimate, and continuous relationship with his mother (or permanent mother-substitute – one person who steadily 'mothers' him) in which both find satisfaction and enjoyment. It is this complex, rich, and rewarding relationship with the mother in early years, varied in countless ways by relations with the father and with the brothers and sisters, that child psychiatrists and many others now believe … underlie the development of character and mental health.'[2]

'The child's relation to his mother', said Bowlby, 'is without doubt in ordinary circumstances by far his most important relationship' during the early years. However, 'fathers have their uses even in infancy. Not only do they provide for their wives to enable them to devote themselves unrestrictedly to the care of the infant or toddler, but by providing love and companionship, they support the mother emotionally and help her maintain that harmonious contented mood in the atmosphere of which her infant throne thrives.'[3]

In the case of Joseph, however, not only did his father, Besarion, come to epitomise all that a father ought not to be, in terms of loving his child, by his violent behaviour, but he also failed to provide support in terms of 'love and companionship' for his wife, Ekaterina, who, in turn, was doing her best to provide Joseph with a caring, stable and harmonious childhood.

Joseph suffered both physical and mental abuse from his father over a period of eleven years, until Besarion left home in 1890. However, even after that the child lived in constant fear that he might encounter his father once again. Not only that, but Joseph would have been traumatised emotionally by the fact that his parents were constantly at war, and often came to blows.

What are the likely consequences of such abuse for such a battered child and on his or her subsequent behaviour? Paradoxically, said Bowlby, 'some children may emerge from a deprivation experience with grave and permanent damage'. However, 'others may seem to escape any severe or lasting adverse effect'.[4] Which category would Joseph fall into? Only time would tell!

Chapter 5

The Tiflis Seminary (1894–99)

With the help of his teachers, Joseph was permitted to take the entrance examination for the seminary at Avchala in the northern suburb of the Georgian capital, Tiflis (subsequently renamed Tbilisi on 17 August 1936).

The Tiflis Theological Academy and Seminary, which trained young men for the priesthood, operated from 1817 to 1919 in the Georgian Exarchate (territorial jurisdiction) of the Russian Orthodox church.[1]

However, as the train approached the station, Ekaterina said, 'My son suddenly became sad, tears came to his eyes, and he started crying quietly. "Mum, when we get to the city, dad will find and capture me, and try to make me become a shoemaker. But I want to study. If he treats me like this, I would rather commit suicide than become a shoemaker." I realised what he was worried about. I kissed him lovingly and wiped the tears from his eyes.'

Priest Chagunava, a steward in the seminary who 'wielded considerable influence' there, 'kept a close watch on my son', said Ekaterina, and subsequently, 'sent word' that Joseph 'had passed the most difficult subjects so well that it had long been decided to admit him at the state's expense, though I had to buy a uniform for him. Who cared about the uniform? I was the happiest mother in the world. A month later, I saw Soso dressed up in the seminary uniform and I cried a lot with happiness.'

Joseph Stalin entered the Theological Seminary in Tiflis 'in September 1894', said British writer and politician David Tutaev.[2] He was 15 years of age.

In the seminary, said Svetlana, 'he no longer figured among the top students'. However, 'A church education was the only systematic education my father ever had.[3] When he was in the seminary at one time he worked at the astronomical observatory; he worked in some kind of capacity of writing down observations or something like that. He was a good student, as we know.'

'Soso studied well in the seminary,' said Ekaterina. 'I remember that when he visited me for Christmas for the first time, he even brought me sugar wrapped in his handkerchief. He had saved it from his portion. It was no more than a handful and a half, but I was so glad to receive this small present that I used it economically for almost a year.'

For Joseph, however, the restrictions imposed by the seminary were intolerable. Said Murphy, 'The regulations forbade them to belong to any public library or to hold meetings for any purpose outside the curriculum. The teachers spied on the pupils, searched their cupboards for forbidden books, and reported suspicious circumstances to the head of the college.[4]

'He had been in the seminary for about a year when the rector summoned him to his study. Joseph's tutors had reported their suspicions of his wider interests. He was duly lectured and warned. Soon there appeared in the Conduct Book this passage:

> It seems that Dzhugashvili has a ticket to the Cheap Library, from which he borrows books. To-day I confiscated Victor Hugo's *Toilers of the Sea*, in which I found the said library ticket.
>
> S. MURAKHOVSKY, ASS. SUPERVISOR;
> FATHER GERMOGEN, SUPERVISOR.

For this, Joseph was sentenced to a period in the punishment cell, as he had already been warned for being found with a copy of Hugo's *Ninety-Three*. On a later occasion he was caught with a copy of Letourneau's *Literary Evolution of the Nations*, and again was sent to the punishment cell. This was the thirteenth time books deemed subversive had got him into trouble.[5]

But all was not what it seemed. 'Little by little,' said Ekaterina, 'people started first whispering, and then telling me directly that Soso had become a rebellious man. I got very scared. I knew that rebellious men were always persecuted. I had expected my son to become a bishop and was wondering what demon had inspired him to become a rebel.' The answer, of course, was that the Orthodox Church was heavily invested in supporting what to Stalin was the hated Tsarist regime!

It was while Joseph was at the seminary, said Murphy, that he made 'his first contact with the Tiflis group' of Marxist revolutionaries. The membership introduced him to the works of Marx and Engels, of Plekhanov and Kautsky, of Adam Smith and Ricardo, of Buckle and Letourne, of Feuerbach and many more with which to supplement his already wide reading of Russian and Georgian writers. 'It was not easy to get some of the works of these writers,' continued Murphy. 'There was only one copy of Marx's [*Das*] *Capital* in the whole of Tiflis, and this was laboriously copied by hand and passed from group to group, section by section, and read aloud to its members.'[6]

In August 1898, Joseph formally enrolled as a founder member of the Tiflis branch of the Russian Social Democratic Labour Party: (RSDLP, also known as the Russian Social Democratic Workers Party).[7] He also 'joined that first Georgian Social Democratic organisation, known as the Messameh Dassy', which 'in the years 1893–1898, performed useful work in the propagation of Marxist ideas'.[8]

On 29 September 1898, the rector of the seminary received a report that informed him: 'At 9 p.m. a group of students gathered in the dining hall around Joseph Dzhugashvili, who read them books not sanctioned by the seminary authorities, in view of which the student was searched.'

On 29 May 1899, Father Dimitry proposed that the Seminary Council 'expel Joseph Dzhugashvili [sic]' on the grounds that he was 'politically unreliable'.[9] Joseph was now aged 20. Ekaterina had suspected that her son had a different agenda. Although 'Soso' denied it, she said, 'My neighbours' whispers turned out to be true. Soso had indeed, chosen a different path, for which he left the seminary.'[10]

Joseph himself said later: 'I became a Marxist, thanks, one may say, to my social position (my father was an operative in a shoe factory, and my mother too was a worker) and also because there was a stir of revolt in the *milieu* in which I moved, which was of the same social level as my parents: and finally, because of Jesuitic [Jesuit: a member of the Society of Jesus, a Roman Catholic Order of priests] repression and martinet intolerance of the Orthodox Church seminary where I spent some years. The whole atmosphere around me was saturated with hatred of tsarist oppression, and I threw myself whole-heartedly into revolutionary work.'

Did religion feature at all in Joseph Stalin's mind? According to his former fellow schoolmate at Gori Church School, Grigol Glurjidze, Joseph was 'a firm believer, punctually attending all the divine services'. He was also 'the leader of the church choir. I remember he not only performed the religious rites, but always reminded us of their meaning. But already in the third or fourth class [when Joseph was aged 13 or 14] he unexpectedly shocked me with clearly atheist declarations. We were lying in a meadow outside the city, talking about the rich and the poor. "You know, Grisha [Grigol's nickname]," suddenly Soso said softly after a short pause, "he's not unjust, he simply does not exist. They are deceiving us, Grisha." Soso then mentioned that he had a book for Grisha, which turned out to be by Darwin.[11]

'My father never had any feeling for religion,' said Svetlana. The endless prayers and enforced religious training could have brought out only contrary results: extreme scepticism of everything 'heavenly', of everything 'sublime'. The result was total materialism, a cynical realism of an 'earthy', 'sober', practical, and low view of life. Instead of a 'spiritual outlook', he evolved something very different: a close acquaintance with hypocrisy, bigotry, double-facedness, typical of a goodly number among the clergy, who only believe externally – in other words, do not believe at all. And as this youth did not possess the purity of heart and sincere religious feelings of his illiterate mother, at 19 he found himself prepared for a 'service' that was very different from the one she had wanted for him. He joined the revolutionary movement of Transcaucasia.[12]

To German journalist Emil Ludwig, Stalin said of his time spent at the Tiflis seminary, 'In protest against the humiliating regime and Jesuit methods that existed in the seminary, I was ready to become and actually became a revolutionary, an adherent of Marxism as a genuinely revolutionary teaching.'[13]

Svetlana attributed Stalin's subsequent 'lack of compromise', 'inflexibility', and 'inability to agree with an opposing opinion even if it was obviously a good one' to 'his experience at the seminary, where students had been imbued with fanaticism and intolerance. And, of course, this intolerance was only strengthened by an inadequate education, which my father never supplemented in later years.'[14]

According to Svetlana, her father's time spent at the Tiflis seminary achieved the opposite effect to that which was intended.

'For a time [Joseph] lived by giving [Marxist] lessons.' Later, in December 1899, 'he found employment at the Tiflis Observatory as a calculator and observer. But never for a moment did he cease his revolutionary activities.'[15]

Meanwhile, in 1898–00 a 'Social Democratic group' arose in Tiflis, which 'did an enormous amount of revolutionary propagandist and organisational work in forming a secret Social Democratic Party organisation. This group was headed by Stalin.'[16]

A strike by the horse-drawn tram drivers of Tiflis, organised by Joseph, took place on 1 January 1900, after which he was pursued by the police. He fled to Baku, capital of Azerbaijan (and 360 miles from Tiflis), but was arrested in late January and imprisoned in Tiflis's Metekhi Prison.

When Ekaterina went to visit Joseph in prison, 'Beso suddenly appeared from one of the cellars, saw me, ran after me, and stood in my way. He was intoxicated.' He told her angrily, 'I don't need a son who had been in prison. His father hasn't been a robber and why should he be one? I will kill such a son myself. I will take revenge on him because he has brought a disgrace on me.'

'They didn't allow me to see my son in the Metkehi Prison,' said Ekaterina, 'but anyway, Soso managed to send word through someone that he was alright. He asked me not to worry and informed me that he would soon see me.'[17]

Chapter 6

Stalin the Revolutionary: Exile

In *Twenty Letters to a Friend*, Svetlana stated that although Stalin had been born in Georgia, 'He was the one, I think, who cared about it least. It was Russia that he loved.'[1] His mother had wanted him to become 'a Georgian Orthodox priest … yet soon he embraced another "religion" with some zeal, and with that he lost his attachment to his native land, to his language. His love and obsession has become Russia.'[2]

Stalin, said Svetlana, 'chose the way of a revolutionary because in him burned the cold flame of protest against society, in which he himself was at the bottom of the ladder and was supposed to remain there all his life. He wanted infinitely more, and there was no other road open to him but that of revolution.' What is more, 'there lay in him a firm conviction that the precept about using any means to attain an end produced far greater results than lofty ideals ever could'.[3]

Furthermore, said Svetlana, Georgia at that time 'was on the outskirts. It was a place of quite a revolutionary ferment and the Social Democratic Party and social democracy was very popular, taking the minds of educated students from all classes. It always begins with the nobility and then comes to the lower classes, and many Russian revolutionaries were in exile in the Caucasus and of course, they brought Marxism in. So, I think he simply answered to what was rather very typical there. It was a sign of the times.'[4]

Said Murphy, 'Then came the day when he was permitted to take charge of a group of workers from the Tiflis railway workshops.' If the revolution was to succeed, it was vital that the revolutionary message be brought to the workers, and that the factories be flooded with revolutionary pamphlets! Stalin 'picked workers who were keen to learn the new teaching'. The teaching 'was fascinating work. He enjoyed it. It gave him tremendous satisfaction when he saw the light of pleasure in the eyes of his pupils as they grasped some new idea.'[5]

It was at a celebration (*Mayevka*) held on the outskirts of Tiflis on 1 May 1900 – 'May Day' – said Svetlana's maternal aunt, Anna Alliluyeva, and Anna's father, Sergei Alliluyev, that Stalin made his first public speech. And as the person 'in charge of the arrangements', it was he who 'invited one of our friends, an amateur painter, to make a red banner. On this banner the portraits of Karl Marx and Friedrich Engels were depicted, together with slogans written in Russian, Georgian and Armenian.' The celebration was attended by 'some five hundred people', including Anna and Sergei, and La Marseillaise [French national anthem] rang out and was echoed back in the distance from the surrounding hills.[6] More will be said about the Alliluyev family shortly.

In May and July 1900, 'Stalin and his [revolutionary] "cells" began to organise a wave of strikes.'[7] 'August 1900 witnessed a big strike at the [Tiflis] railway [work] shops and locomotive yards.'

On May Day 1901, a demonstration 'organised and led by Stalin' took place in Tiflis.[8] 'Cossack whips whistled through the air, sabres flashed: the workers replied with sticks and stones.'[9]

On 21 March 1901 'the police made a search of the observatory where Stalin worked and had his quarters. This search, and the warrant for his arrest which, as he learned, had been issued by the secret police, induced Stalin to go into hiding.'[10]

Stalin now asked Sylvestia Todria, a member of one of his 'study circles', to help him set up 'a little illegal printing plant'. Such plants were invaluable in ensuring that in every city each political faction had its own revolutionary newspaper. 'By September 1901 he and his group organised such a plant in Baku and published the first [illegal] Georgian Social Democratic newspaper, called *Brdzola* ('*The Struggle*'). The leading articles were written by Stalin and Ketskhoveli.'[11] This was Lado Ketskhoveli, a former pupil at the Tiflis seminary.

In November 1901 'the Tiflis Democratic organisation held its first conference of 25 delegates and elected its first leading committee of the

Russian Social Democrats in the Caucasus region. Stalin was elected to this committee and was promptly sent to Batum [Batumi] (Black Sea port of Georgia) to organise a similar movement there.' Batumi, said Murphy, 'was a big working-class centre where the Rothschilds, Nobels, Mantashevs and others had established large oil refineries. Here were opportunities which the youthful Stalin seized with both hands. He first organised workers' study circles in all the factories, then quickly followed this work with leaflets and the [revolutionary] newspaper.'[12]

On 9 March 1902, Stalin 'organised a mass demonstration of some 6,000 workers from the Batumi factories belonging to Rothschild and Mantaschev'. The workers 'had met to protest against the arrest of some 32 strikers the previous evening'. Said Murphy, 'The police arrested 300 of the demonstrators. Stalin avoided arrest and countered the police action by organising a greater demonstration the next day, when he persuaded dockers and railwaymen to join in. Carrying red banners, the demonstrators, with Stalin at their head, marched to the deportation barracks to demand the release of the arrested men. The police answered with rifle shots: 15 workers were killed and 54 wounded. How Stalin was missed by the fire neither he nor anyone else could tell. The demonstration was broken up, but not before it had secured the release of the arrested men. Stalin helped the wounded to get clear of the crowd.'[13] It was after this that Stalin was given the nickname 'Koba', which in Turkish means 'Fearless'.[14]

Stalin 'had changed his address many times and found place after place in which to hide his printing plant and papers'. But on 5 April 1902, 'during a meeting of the leading Party group', he and other strike leaders were arrested. Stalin was 'convicted of being the chief leader and teacher in the revolutionary movement of Batum [sic]'.[15] Stalin was first imprisoned at Batumi, then at Kutaisi in western Georgia, and finally at Batumi once more.[16]

Murphy pointed out that in Russia, political prisoners were segregated from those deemed to have committed 'other crimes'. For example, whereas most prisoners were imprisoned in the Gulag system, political prisoners were often billeted with local families, in so-called 'Special Settlements'.

'Special Settlements' were places of special exile (often called 'spetsposelki') to which 'problematic segments of the population' were sent 'as a repressive measure'. Such settlements existed from the early 1920s until the early 1950s. The system of Special Settlements was created as a precautionary, pre-emptive measure that was designed to thwart anti-Soviet demonstrations. In such settlements the exiled person was subject to 'severe restrictions' on his or her freedom of movement and was constantly supervised by local officials who, in turn, were under the supervision of the People's Commissariat of Internal Affairs (NKVD). (In July 1934 the OGPU merged into the NKVD. In March 1954 the NKVD was renamed the KGB – Committee for State Security.)[17]

'Areas of special settlement were most often located in the northern and eastern regions of the USSR. The largest regions of exile were Kazakhstan, western Siberia, the Urals, the northern stretches of European Russia, and Central Asia. The initial waves of deportees were directed to the North, the Urals, and western Siberia, but with time the focus broadened to include Kazakhstan and Central Asia.'[18]

In autumn 1903, Stalin 'was banished for three years to Novaya Uda, a village in the Balagan [Balagansky] District, Province of Irkutsk, Eastern Siberia. He arrived there on November 27 1903. While in exile he received a letter from Lenin.'[19] 'Novaya Uda is some 3,000 miles from the Caucasus and the climate is far more severe, though fortunately the journey was made in the summer months. Exiles were sent in batches. It was a long, long trail, partly by boat, partly by rail and many weary miles on foot. It was the first time Stalin, now 24 years of age, had been out of his native Georgia.'[20]

Paradoxically, said Svetlana, Stalin 'loved Siberia, with its stark beauty and its rough, silent people'.[21] This was despite the fact that he had been sent there as a punishment! 'Siberian exile looked to him as something inspiring,' she said, 'to join together with other revolutionaries'.[22]

Meanwhile, in the Alvlabar neighbourhood of Tiflis, a 'secret printing press', described as a 'remarkably bold enterprise of the Caucasian Union of the RSDLP and an outstanding example of the

Bolshevik technique of underground work' was established. Pamphlets by Stalin and Lenin were produced and also newspapers and leaflets 'in three languages' and 'in several thousands of copies'.[23]

On 4 January 1904, Stalin 'escaped and made his way through Siberia's snows, across the Urals and the Volga, and back to Georgia'. Six weeks later he arrived in Batumi.[24] From Novaya Uda to Batumi is a distance of 3,630 miles. Clearly, Stalin must have had help from Party sympathisers along the way. 'Between 1902 and 1913, Stalin was arrested seven times and exiled six times. Five times he escaped from exile.'[25]

In December 1904, under the leadership of Stalin and Prokofy A. Dzhaparidze, Bolshevik Party leader in Azerbaijan: 'there was a huge strike of the Baku workers, which lasted from December 13 to 31 and ended with the conclusion of a collective agreement with the oil owners: the first of its kind in the history of the Russian working-class movement. The Baku strike heralded a rise in the tide of revolution in Transcaucasia.'[26]

The Russian Social Democratic Labour Party (RSDLP) was founded in Minsk, the capital city of Belarus (which was annexed by Russia) in 1898, in order to unite the various revolutionary organisations of the Russian Empire into one party.

The Bolsheviks were a radical, far-left, revolutionary Marxist faction of the RSDLP. The Mensheviks, on the other hand, were members of the moderate non-Leninist wing of the RSDLP. The Bolsheviks differed from the Mensheviks in that the former advocated the immediate seizure of power by the proletariat (working-class people). Whereas the latter stated that social change must be achieved by co-operation with the bourgeoisie (middle-class people). In 1903, the Bolsheviks had split from the Mensheviks and formed a Bolshevik faction of the RSDLP, which was founded by Vladimir Lenin and physician, philosopher, and Bolshevik revolutionary Alexander Bogdanov.

The strike 'ended in a resounding victory for the workers, who secured a collective agreement with the owners: the first of its kind in the history of the Russian working class. This event reverberated throughout Russia. Hardly had its echoes died away than the workers of the Putilov works [steel mill] in St Petersburg went on strike over the dismissal of four men and the strike spread to the mills and factories of the great city.'[27]

On 9 January 1905, 'some 140,000 workers marched to the Winter Palace'. This was the palace in St Petersburg that served as the official residence of the Russian Emperors from 1732 to 1917. The demonstration was led by Russian Orthodox priest Father Georgy Apollonovich Gapon, 'with cross, and church banners, and the petition'.[28] However, unknown to the protesters, Gapon was a police informer. The marchers were 'greeted by machine-guns, rifle-fire, and a charge of the Cossacks. Blood flowed freely. According to police reports, 1,000 were killed and 2,000 wounded. The day has been called "Bloody Sunday" ever since.'[29]

In October 1905 there was a general strike 'which demonstrated the might and strength of the proletarian movement and impelled the mortally terrified Tsar to issue his Manifesto of October 17'. However, said Marxist philosopher and Soviet politician and statesman Georgy F. Alexandrov and colleagues, authors of *Joseph Stalin: A Short Biography* (published in 1949), 'Unstinting in its promises of popular liberties, this Manifesto was nothing but a fraud on the masses, a stratagem designed to secure a breathing space in which the Tsar might fool the gullible, gain time, and marshal his forces for a blow at the revolution. The Bolsheviks warned the masses that the Manifesto was a trap.'[30]

In November 1905, Stalin led the Bolshevik Conference of the Caucasian Federation of the Russian Social Democratic Labour Party.

On 20 December 1905, the Moscow Soviet (Soviet: an elected local, district, or national council), which was 'in the hands of the Bolshevik section of the Social Democratic Labour Party, called for a political general strike which commenced the following day. Two days later, barricades were in the streets and for nine days 8,000 armed workers resisted the Tsar's forces.' Finally, the rising was put down.

'Moscow's battle represented the high-water mark of the revolution of 1905,' said Murphy. It 'spread through a hundred cities and towns and a great section of the peasantry, into the Army and Navy and among the oppressed nationalities'. However, 'it is estimated that in these struggles 4,000 were killed and 10,000 wounded'.[31] In addition to the 'thousands dead and wounded', said Murphy, 'many more thousands filled the prisons of Russia or lingered in Siberian exile'.[32]

Stalin was not in Moscow during these eventful times, but mainly in the Caucasus. On 21 December 1905, he attended the First All-Russian Bolshevik Conference in Tammerfors, Finland, 'as a delegate from the Trancaucasian Bolsheviks. It was here that Lenin and Stalin first met. Stalin worked with Lenin on the political (drafting) committee of the Conference, to which he was elected, as one of the prominent leaders of the Party.'[33]

'In April 1906 the Social Democratic Labour Party held a conference in Stockholm – the first All-Russian Conference of the Party that Stalin had attended. It was called a "Unity Conference".'[34]

Chapter 7

Lenin and his Wife, Nadezhda

Vladimir Ilyich Ulyanov, pseudonym 'Lenin', was born in Simbirsk in Western Russia on 22 April 1870 'into a well-educated family. He excelled at school and went on to study law. At university, he was exposed to radical thinking and his views were also influenced by the execution of his elder brother, a member of a revolutionary group.' The brother's name was Alexander Ilyich Ulyanov.

'Expelled from university for his radical policies, Lenin completed his law degree as an external student in 1891. He moved to St Petersburg and became a professional revolutionary. Like many of his contemporaries, he was arrested and exiled to Siberia, where he married Nadezhda Krupskaya. After his Siberian exile Lenin – the pseudonym he adopted in 1901 – spent most of the subsequent decade and a half in western Europe, where he emerged as a prominent figure in the international revolutionary movement and became the leader of the "Bolshevik" faction of the Russian Social Democratic Worker's [Labour] Party.'[1]

Nadezhda Konstantinovna Krupskaya was born in St Petersburg on 26 February 1869. A Marxist activist, she met Lenin at a Marxist discussion group in 1894.

Nadezhda was arrested in August 1896 and sentenced in 1898 to three years in exile. However, she obtained permission to spend her term with Lenin, who was then in exile in Shushenskoye, Siberia, on the condition that they marry, which they duly did, on 10 July 1898.

In 1901, after serving her term, Nadezhda joined Lenin (who had finished his sentence in 1900) in Munich. She subsequently settled with him in several European cities, returning briefly to Russia to take part in the revolution of 1905, which was unsuccessful.[2]

As for Stalin, 'With equal vigour [he] supported Lenin's idea of armed insurrection as a means of overthrowing the autocracy and establishing a republic. The necessity for armed insurrection is exhaustively demonstrated in his [Stalin's] writings of 1905–1907.'[3]

At the Second Congress of the RSDLP, held in Brussels, Belgium, and London (30 July to 23 August 1903), the Central Committee was established with the power to decide all Party issues, except at a local level.

Chapter 8

'Tishka': Stalin's Beloved Companion in Siberia

In the early years of his relationship with his daughter, Svetlana, Stalin had shown that he was capable of showing great kindness. He also showed kindness to a dog, which he had befriended while in exile in Siberia. Referring to 'Tishka', Anna Redens (née Alliluyeva), Stalin's sister-in-law, said that Stalin 'loved talking about that dog', 'He used to keep me company during the long winter evenings – if I had any oil for the lamp – I would sit reading or writing, and Tishka would run in from the cold, and lie down, pressed against my legs, growling as if trying to say something. I'd bend down, ruffle his ears and saying [say] something like this: "Well, Tishka, are you frozen? Had enough running around? Warm yourself now. Warm yourself."'[1]

Chapter 9

Stalin's Marriage to Ekaterina Svanidze (15 July 1906)

Alexander Semyonovich Svanidze ('Alyosha') was born in 1886 'of a petty noble family in a small village of Baji in western Georgia, then part of the Russian Empire'.[1] Svanidze was educated at the Tiflis Seminary, where Stalin had helped him prepare for the entrance examination. However, in 1901, Alexander was expelled, together with 40 other pupils.[2] The seminary had become a breeding ground for revolutionaries. In that same year Svanidze joined the Russian Social Democratic Labour Party and 'worked in the Bolshevik underground'.[3]

In 1905, Svanidze was living with his three sisters and his brother-in-law in Soloaki Street, Tiflis, just above Yerevan Square, and immediately behind the South Caucasus Military District Headquarters. Alexander's sisters were Alexandra ('Sashiko'), who had recently married Mikheil Monoselidze, a fellow pupil of Stalin's at the Tiflis Seminary; Maria ('Mariko'); and Ekaterina ('Kato'). The sisters 'ran Atelier Hervieu, a prosperous couture house (named after its French couturier Madame Hervieu) making uniforms and dresses'.[4]

Sometime in the autumn of 1905, Stalin arrived in Tiflis. Whereupon, he 'asked his protégé Svanidze to find him somewhere to live', in other words, a 'safe house'. The outcome was that Stalin was invited to move in with the Svanidze family. Here he held political seminars.

Ekaterina, the youngest of the three sisters, was described as a 'ravishingly pretty brunette'.[5] Said Radzinsky, 'She was very handsome. And very gentle and docile. But nonetheless a revolutionary's sister.[6]

She was in Yerevan Square the day the Cossacks massacred students and workers there. Her sisters, fearing that she was dead, found her helping the wounded in a scene that resembled a minor battlefield.'[7]

In the summer of 1906, said US historian and author Stephen Kotkin, Ekaterina informed Stalin that she was pregnant. Whereupon, he 'agreed to marry her'.[8] Ekaterina 'wanted a church wedding and Soso [Stalin] agreed, even though he was an atheist.[9] However, because he 'had false papers and was wanted by the police, a legal marriage faced complications'. Finally, Kita Tkhinvaleli, another former classmate of Stalin's at the Tiflis Seminary who had become a priest, 'agreed to perform the ceremony'. This was 'in the dead of night' on 15 July 1906, at St David's Church.[10]

The newlyweds 'rented a room on the oil field' at Baku. Here, said Radzinsky, 'Ekaterina worked as a seamstress. Everything in their beggarly dwelling was sparkling clean, everything was covered with embroideries and lace of her making.'[11]

Said Monoselidze, 'I was amazed how Soso [Stalin], who was so severe in his work and to his comrades, could be so tender, affectionate, and attentive to his wife.'[12] However, this was not always the case. According to Ketevan Gelovani (cousin of Stalin's mother Ekaterina), said British historian and author Simon Sebag Montefiore, who interviewed her in Tbilisi, Soso behaved gently towards her except for flashes of temper: 'Soon after the wedding, he burned her hand with a cigarette in a fury, but she loved him, and he was mostly so kind and tender to her.'[13] Rage would increasingly become part of Stalin's make-up.

On 13 March 1907 Ekaterina gave birth to a son, Yakov ('Yasha') Iosifovich Dzhugashvili. After the birth, said Monoselidze, Stalin's 'love for [his] wife and child became ten times more'. He nicknamed the baby 'Patsana' ('Laddie'). Writing day and night, however, Stalin became 'irritated when the baby's crying disturbed his work. But as soon as the mother fed it and the baby stopped crying, he kissed him, tickling his nose, fondling him.'[14] Nine months later, on 5 December 1907, Ekaterina died aged only 22 years. Said Iremashvili of Stalin, Ekaterina 'died in his arms'.[15] But what had caused her death?

On 31 October 2005, Montefiore interviewed Mariam Svadnidze, 'another cousin still alive in Tbilisi'. Mariam was aged 109, but even so, she remembered the death of Ekaterina clearly. 'I was then nine years old. Kato [Ekaterina] and my father got typhus at the same time.' Typhus is an infectious disease characterised by purple rash, headaches, fever, and delirium, with a high mortality rate.

'Books say Kato died of TB [tuberculosis] but I can assure you it was typhus. Both got the red rash. We knew if the rash went black, they'd die. My father's rash stayed red. He lived, but I remember that Kato's turned black. Then all the family knew she'd die. And die she did.'[16]

Said Montefiore, 'Soso closed Kato's eyes himself. Stunned, he managed to stand beside his wife's body with the family for a photograph but then collapsed. "Nobody could believe Soso was so wounded," wrote Giorgi Elisabedashvili, whom Stalin coached for the Tiflis Seminary entrance examination. "He sobbed that he couldn't manage to make her happy."'[17]

Montefiore confirmed that, 'Soso was in such despair that his friends were worried about leaving him with his Mauser [pistol]. "I was so overcome with grief that my comrades took my gun away from me," he later told a girlfriend. "I realised how many things in life I hadn't appreciated. While my wife was alive, there were times I didn't return home at night. I told her when I left not to worry about me but when I got home, she'd be sitting there. She'd wait up all night."'[18]

What became of Yakov? Following his mother's death he was brought up by Mikheil Monoselidze and his wife, Alexandra. Stalin 'barely even visited' his son, said Monoselidze. 'Perhaps Laddie reminded him of the entire disaster.'[19]

Chapter 10

For Stalin the Work Goes On

In early 1907, said Murphy, Stalin was 'paving the way for another National Conference' of the Russian Social Democratic Labour Party, 'which would give the Bolsheviks control' over the Party.[1] 'Stalin took an active role in the work of the Fifth Congress of the RSDLP,' said Alexandrov.[2] The Congress was held in April and May 1907 in the Brotherhood Church, Islington, London, and was attended by virtually all the prominent figures of both the Bolshevik and Menshevik wings of the Party, including Lenin and Stalin. It was here that Stalin first encountered Leon Trotsky 'who was to cross his path so many times in future struggles'.[3] And it was here, that 'the victory of the Bolsheviks over the Mensheviks was sealed'.[4]

Trotsky was born Lev Davidovich Bronstein in the Ukrainian village of Yanovka in 1879 to a relatively prosperous Jewish farming family.

'From the age of 9 to 16 he lived in Odessa with his mother's nephew, journalist and publisher, Mossoi Filipovich Spentzer, who oversaw his education. The boy was strongly influenced by the intellectual atmosphere of the Spentzer home, where journalists and other writers frequently visited.

'Trotsky was sent to the nearby seaport of Nikolaev for his last academic year. There he met Russian socialists for the first time and joined a radical discussion group. One member of this group, Alexandra Sokolovskaya, considered herself a Marxist and Trotsky almost immediately opposed her ideology. He instead, preferred the populist view that education of the peasants was the best way to achieve social progress.

'Having initially sided with the Mensheviks rather than with the Bolsheviks, Trotsky soon "parted ways" with them.

"Suspended between both factions", Trotsky discovered Alexander Lvovich Helfand, a Russian Jew who had settled in Germany and was a Marxist theoretician who wrote under the pen name of "Parvus".'[5] The two men met in Vienna in 1904. According to Helfand, the concept of the 'nation state' was outdated. The Russo–Japanese War of 1904–05 (in which the Japanese were victorious), was: 'The start of a long sequence of wars in which the nation states, impelled by capitalist competition, would fight for their survival.'[6]

'Parvus revived [from Karl Marx] the concept-strategy of "permanent revolution". He communicated this philosophy to Trotsky, who then further expanded and developed it.'[7] In other words, the hope was that if every nation was rebuilt under the leadership of the proletariat, then there would be no more wars. Not only that, but if the revolution was spread to western countries, this would serve to prevent Russia relapsing into a bourgeoisie-dominated state:

'The perspective of the permanent revolution may be summed up in these words: The complete victory of the democratic revolution in Russia is inconceivable otherwise than in the form of the dictatorship of the proletariat basing itself on the peasantry. The dictatorship of the proletariat, which will inescapably place on the order of the day, not only democratic but also socialist tasks, will at the same time provide a mighty impulse to the international socialist revolution. Only the victory of the proletariat in the West will shield Russia from bourgeois restoration and secure for her the possibility of bringing the socialist construction to its conclusion.'[8]

It will not have escaped notice that there is a certain incongruity between the phrase 'Social Democracy' on the one hand and 'Dictatorship of the Proletariat' on the other!

Meanwhile, on 16 June 1907, Pyotr Stolypin, (3rd) Prime Minister of Russia and Minister of Internal Affairs, dissolved the Second Duma[9] after it refused to expel 55 socialist deputies.

The Duma was the legislative and advisory body in the ruling assembly of Russia. 'The first formally constituted Duma was the

Imperial State Duma introduced to the Russian Empire by Emperor Nicholas II in 1905. The Emperor retained an absolute veto and could dismiss the State Duma at any time for a suitable reason.'[10]

Fifty-three of the deputies were put on trial, accused of organising a plot to establish a Republic in Russia by means of an armed uprising. Found guilty, they were exiled to Siberia.

When Stolypin ordered the repression of revolutionaries and militant workers, executions increased to such an extent that the hangman's noose was dubbed 'Stolypin's necktie'. The outcome was a serious decline in the fortunes of the Social Democratic Labour Party.[11]

Stalin was undeterred. As organiser of partisan groups in the Caucasus region he had 'as his principal assistant a devoted friend of his boyhood days, one [Simon A.] Ter-Petrosian, whom Stalin affectionately nicknamed "Kamo". Kamo was a veritable Robin Hood of the Caucasus.'

'Kamo was the leading spirit of the group Stalin organised for the job of holding up the Treasury carriage carrying 250,000 roubles under escort from a Tiflis Post Office to the State Bank in another part of the city.'[12] The robbery occurred on 26 June 1907, and was successful.

On 22 November 1907, Stalin's wife, Ekaterina, died aged only 22.

On 25 March 1908, Stalin was arrested, yet again, and spent eight months in Bailov prison, Baku, Azerbaijan. Semya Verestchak, a fellow prisoner, stated that: 'The Stalin of these days was defiant; he submitted to no regulations. The political prisoners at Baku endeavoured to segregate themselves as much as possible from the criminals, and the younger among them were punished if they infringed this unwritten law. Openly flouting the custom, Koba [nickname for Stalin] was constantly to be seen in the company of bandits, swindlers, and thieves. He chose as his cellmates the Sakvadelidze brothers: one a counterfeiter, the other a well-known Bolshevik. Active people, people who did things, attracted him.'[13]

Stalin 'was regarded as the leading Marxist expert,' said Verestchak. 'Hence his very special hatred of Menshevism.'

Stalin was now exiled to Solvychegodsk in the Province of Vologda in north-western Russia, for a term of two years. 'But on 24 June

1909 he escaped and made his way back to Baku to continue his illegal work.'[14]

On 23 March 1910, said Alexandrov, Stalin was again arrested, and after spending another six months in Bailov prison, was 'conveyed back to Solvychegodsk'.

'In the latter half of 1911 began the St Petersburg period of Stalin's revolutionary career. On September 6 he secretly left Vologda for St Petersburg. He established contact with the Party organisation there; organised and gave directions for the fight against the Liquidators – Mensheviks and Trotskyites – and took measures to rally and strengthen the Bolshevik organisations.'

The Liquidators were a faction of the Mensheviks who left the party in 1905. They advocated the dissolution of the RSDLP on the grounds that it was an illegal party.

However, Stalin was arrested on 9 September 1911 'and sent back to the Vologda Province, whence he again managed to escape in February 1912'.[15]

'Meanwhile, in January 1912 a momentous event had taken place in the life of the Party. The Prague Conference, having expelled the Mensheviks from the Party, inaugurated a party of a new type, a Leninist Party – the Bolshevik Party.'[16] This was a conference of the RSDLP held in the Czechoslovak capital.

By now, said Murphy, 'Lenin had come to the conclusion that the time for further manoeuvring with the Mensheviks in the Party was ended. Henceforth, therefore, the Mensheviks and the likes of Trotsky were to be treated not as fellow-travellers, but as enemies of the Party and outside the ranks of organised revolutionary Marxism.'[17] The final split of the RSDLP into the Russian Social Democratic Labour Party (Bolshevik) and the Russian Social Democratic Labour Party (Menshevik) was now cemented.

At the Prague Conference, the Russian Bureau of the Central Committee was created, as 'a practical centre to direct the revolutionary work in Russia'. As for Stalin, he 'was elected to the Central Committee in his absence' and also 'on Lenin's proposal', was 'put in charge of the Russian Bureau of the Central Committee'.

'On Lenin's instructions, Sergo [Grigory] Ordzhonikidze went to Vologda to inform Stalin of the decisions of the Prague Conference.'[18] Stalin now 'became second-in-command' of the Bolshevik Party, after Lenin.[19]

On 29 February 1912 during a bitter winter, Stalin 'again escaped and made his way to St Petersburg, there to begin energetically to carry out the decisions of the Prague Conference'.[20]

On 12 April 1912 in the Lena goldfields of north-eastern Siberia, Tsarist soldiers 'opened fire upon strikers and hundreds were shot down. Immediately, in protest against the bloodbath, a spontaneous wave of strikes swept through the industrial towns and cities of Russia. The workers were on the march again.'[21]

On 22 April 1912 the first issue of the Bolshevik daily newspaper, *Pravda*, was published. 'It was founded according to Lenin's instructions, on the initiative of Stalin. It was under Stalin's direction that the first issue was prepared and the character of the paper decided.'[22]

On that same day, 22 April, said Alexandrov, Stalin was rearrested 'on the Streets of St Petersburg. After several months in prison, he was exiled again for a term of three years: this time to the remote region of Narym in Siberia. But on September 1 he once more escaped and returned to St Petersburg.' Here he edited *Pravda* 'and directed the Bolshevik campaign in the elections to the Fourth Duma. At great risk, for the police were constantly on his track, he addressed a number of meetings at factories. But the workers and their organisations kept close guard on Stalin and protected him from the police.'[23] In the event, six Bolsheviks were elected to the Duma.

'On two occasions Stalin went abroad to Cracow' in southern Poland, 'where Lenin was then residing: once in November 1912 and again at the end of December 1912 to attend a conference of the Central Committee [26 December 1912 to 1 January 1913] with leading Party members'.[24]

It was in January 1913, said Tutaev, that the name Stalin 'first appeared, in the magazine *Prosveschenie* (*The Enlightenment*)' which was 'devoted to a study of Marxism and the National Question'.[25] The 'National, or Nationalities Question' will be discussed shortly.

At a concert for the benefit of *Pravda*, held by the St Petersburg Bolshevik Committee in the city's Kalashnikov Hall, said Murphy, 'Stalin was again arrested. He had been betrayed by Roman Malinovsky, a member of the Central Committee. This raid was the beginning of a series in which Sverdlov, Kamenev, Spandaryan and the Bolshevik deputies in the Duma were finally rounded up and exiled to Siberia.'

Yakov Mikhailovich Sverdlov was a Bolshevik Party administrator and chairman of the All-Russian Central Executive Committee from 1917 to 1919.

Lev Borisovich Kamenev was a Bolshevik revolutionary and a prominent Soviet politician.

Suren Spandari Spandaryan was an Armenian revolutionary, literary critic, publicist and one of the founders of the Bolshevik faction of the Russian Social Democratic Labour Party.[26]

'This time the tsarist government exiled Stalin to the remote region of Turukhansk for a term of four years. At first, he lived in the village of Kostino but at the beginning of 1914, fearful lest he should escape again, the tsarist gendarmes transferred him still further north, to the village of Kureika [in northern Russia] on the very fringe of the Arctic Circle, where he lived for three years – right down to 1916. More severe conditions of political exile could scarcely have been found in all the remote expanses of the Siberian wilderness.'[27]

'In the remote hamlet of Kareika [Kureika],' said Murphy, 'amid the snowy wastes of the Siberian province of Yeniseisk, Stalin waited on events. Kureika stands on the banks of a river of the same name and consisted at the time of fifteen peasant huts. Stalin had a room in one of these, and Sverdlov a room in another. The owner of Stalin's hut lived with his family in another room and a kitchen.'[28]

'In December 1916, Stalin, having been called up by the army, was sent under escort to Krasnoyarsk [central Siberia].'[29] He later stated that in October 1916, all exiled men had been called up for the military, but 'they thought I'd be an undesirable element in the army, so they found fault with my arm'.[30] Stalin had suffered an injury to his left arm as a child, and it had become infected, 'and as there had been no one to treat the lad, blood poisoning developed and Stalin almost died'. Having been rejected by the army, 'Stalin was sent to Achinsk [in south-central Russia] to serve the remainder of his exile.'[31]

The Provisional Government – a coalition of Liberals and moderate socialists – was created on 2 March 1917 with Russian aristocrat and statesman Prince Georgy Lvov as prime minister. Of its 12 other ministers, two were Mensheviks and 4 were from the Socialist Revolutionary Party. There were no Bolsheviks: it being Lenin's aim to overthrow this government by force!

Political prisoners were now released from exile and on 8 March, Stalin 'bade farewell to Achinsk'.[32] Said Murphy: 'Without more ado the returned exiles resumed their leading positions in co-operation with the St Petersburg Committee of the Bolshevik Party.' On 12 March 1917, Stalin arrived at St Petersburg. 'Sverdlov arrived. Kamenev arrived. Kalinin arrived.'[33]

Mikhail Ivanovich Kalinin was an 'Old Bolshevik' revolutionary, and Soviet politician. He was known to the Alliluyev family as 'Uncle Mischa'. Old Bolshevik was an unofficial designation for a member of the Bolshevik faction of the Russian Social Democratic Labour Party before the Russian Revolution of 1917.[34]

Said Alexandrov, the Bolshevik Party now 'emerged from under ground. Many of its most prominent and active members were still on their way back from remote prisons and places of exile. Lenin was abroad and the bourgeois Provisional Government was putting every obstacle in the way of his return.'[35]

On 15 March 1917 the Russian Tsar Nicholas II was forced to abdicate the throne.

On 3 April 1917, said Alexandrov: 'After a long period of foreign exile, Lenin return to Russia. The news of the arrival of the beloved leader of the revolution was hailed with enthusiasm by the advanced workers of Petrograd [St Petersburg until 1914). Stalin, at the head of a delegation of workers, went to meet him at Byelo-Ostrov [Beloostrov, 23 miles north-west of St Petersburg]. The welcome accorded to Lenin upon his arrival at the Finland Railway Station in Petrograd turned into a mighty revolutionary demonstration. On the morrow of his arrival, Lenin announced his famous April Thesis, which provided the Party with a brilliant plan of action for the transition from the bourgeois-democratic to the Socialist revolution.'

On 24 April 1917, 'the Seventh (April) conference of the Bolshevik Party assembled'.[36]

The First All Russia Congress of Soviets of Workers and Soldiers' Deputies was held in St Petersburg from 16 June to 7 July 1917. Both Stalin and Sverdlov were in attendance, as was the Alliluyev family and, of course, Lenin.[37]

In that year of 1917, said Stalin, 'under Lenin's guidance, I became a master of the art of revolution'.[38]

On 21 July 1917, Lvov was succeeded by Alexander Fyodorovich Kerensky, Minister of War and the Navy. On 7 November 1917 the Provisional Government was dissolved.

On 22 July 1917, Lenin and Zinoviev left Petrograd (formerly St Petersburg) by train for Finland, the Central Committee having 'decreed that on no account' were they to 'be allowed to fall into the hands of the Government forces'.[39]

The Sixth Congress of the Bolshevik Party was held from 26 July to 3 August 1917 in St Petersburg. Stalin informed the conference that *Pravda* had now been replaced by a new newspaper, *Worker and Soldier.*[40] He proposed, 'obviously with the approval of Lenin, that Leon Trotsky and the Mezrayontsi' (a 'group consisting of former Bolsheviks and Mensheviks who, since 1913, had vacillated between the two divisions') be 'admitted to the Party'.[41] Said Murphy, Stalin 'was by no means a 'yes-man' of Lenin, but a convinced disciple, striving always to make Lenin's principles his own'.[42]

Said Alexandrov: 'Guided by Stalin and by Lenin's instructions, the Sixth Congress inaugurated the preparations for insurrection. The Congress headed the party for armed insurrection and for the establishment of the dictatorship of the proletariat.' Fast forward to 1924 when Stalin came to power and for 'dictatorship of the proletariat' read 'dictatorship of Stalin'!

In August 1917, said Alexandrov, General Lavr G. Kornilov, Commander-in-Chief of the Russian Army, 'launched his revolt with the aim of restoring tsardom in Russia. The Bolsheviks roused the massed to resist the attempted coup and Kornilov's revolt was crushed.' Meanwhile, 'When Lenin was in hiding, Stalin maintained a correspondence with his teacher and friend and kept in close contact with him. He visited him twice in his place of concealment near Razliv [24 miles north-west of St Petersburg]'.

On 7 October 1917, Lenin returned from Finland.[43]

On 28 October 1917 the Kremlin surrendered. In March 1918, the Bolshevik Party relocated its headquarters from St Petersburg to Moscow. Said Murphy of Stalin, 'For the first time since he left the paternal roof to embark on his underground political career, he secured a home. This home consisted of two or three rooms in a large block of buildings in the Kremlin which previously had been occupied by attendants of the Tsar.'[44]

In November 1917 the Council of People's Commissars was created with Lenin as chairman and head of government; Trotsky as Commissar for Foreign Affairs, and Stalin as Commissar for Nationality. There were thirteen other Commissars, all of whom were Bolsheviks and all of whom were selected from the Party's Central Committee. The Council evolved to become the highest executive authority of the government of the Soviet Union.

Little could these thirteen Commissars have guessed that between 1937 and 1940, no fewer than nine of their number would either be executed or assassinated on the orders of Stalin!

Stalin had proved that he possessed enormous courage, physical stamina and endurance, together with a deep knowledge of what the Party was about and what it stood for. He was also an indefatigable and able Party organiser and because of his knowledge and qualities of leadership, he became the Party's second most influential official, Lenin being the first. In his single-minded determination to overcome all obstacles, however great they might be – and the odds against him were great indeed – Stalin demonstrated almost superhuman qualities.

Chapter 11

The Revolution is Successful: Stalin's Dream Comes True!

'Early in the morning of October 24,' said Alexandrov: 'Kerensky ordered the suppression of the central organ [publication] of the party, *Rabochy Put* ['The Workers' Path'] and sent a number of armoured cars to the editorial and printing offices of the newspaper to effect the order. But by 10 a.m. a force of Red Guards and revolutionary soldiers, acting on Stalin's instructions, had pressed back the armoured cars and placed a strong guard over the printing and editorial offices. At 11 o'clock the *Rabochy Put* came out with a leading article by Stalin entitled, 'What do we need?' calling upon the masses to overthrow the bourgeois Provisional Government. At the same time, on instructions of the Party Centre, detachments of revolutionary soldiers and Red Guards were moved to the Smolny Institute.'[1]

The Smolny Institute of Noble Maidens was established in accordance with a decree of Catherine II (the Great), Empress of Russia in 1764. It was Russia's first educational establishment for women. The institute continued to function under the personal patronage of the Russian empress until just before the 1917 Revolution.[2]

'On the evening of October 25th the Second Congress of Soviets met and turned over the government power to the Soviets.'[3] Said Murphy, 'The insurrection had begun. Red Guards from the factories; Revolutionary soldiers from the Petrograd Garrison [who had mutinied], and the Kronstadt sailors moved into their pre-arranged positions and on to the attack.' The Red Guards were a Bolshevik force of paramilitary volunteers, created in March 1917.

Kronstadt was a naval base on Kotlin Island in the Gulf of Finland, about 18 miles west of Petrograd. In May 1917, about 3,000 sailors had joined the Bolsheviks. Now they were in Petrograd in aid of the Bolshevik cause.

'Railway stations, Post Office, Telegraph Office, the Ministries, the State Bank, were occupied. The cruiser *Aurora* moved up the [River] Neva and trained its guns on the Winter Palace. Lenin moved to the Smolny Institute and, with Stalin, took charge of the uprising.'

'At 2.35 p.m. on the afternoon of November 7th, Trotsky, Chairman of the Petrograd Soviet and its Military Revolutionary Committee, announced to the assembled deputies: "I declare in the name of the Military Revolutionary Committee that the Provisional Government has ceased to exist. Some Ministers are arrested. The rest will be arrested in the next few days or hours."

'Trotsky was followed by Lenin; and while they were addressing the Petrograd Soviet, Stalin was directing the revolutionary armed contingents to all the decisive points of the city. He was not in the limelight, but in his hands were the reins which guided forces in accordance with the collective will. At 3.15 p.m. soldiers of the Pavlov Regiment held up the traffic on Nevsky Prospect. At 3.45 p.m. troops of the Military Revolutionary Committee occupied Kazan Square. At 6 p.m. thc Winter Palace was invested. At 10.45 the Second All-Russian Congress of Soviets opened in the Smolny Institute. At the call of the Presidium of the Congress, Lenin stepped onto the platform, facing the assembled deputies. When the seemingly never-ending ovation which greeted him had at last subsided, he began to speak: "We shall now proceed to construct the Socialist order …"'[4]

Thus, the first Soviet Socialist Government – the Council of People's Commissars, 'stepped onto the stage of history', said Murphy,[5] with Lenin as Chairman of the Council and Stalin, Commissar for Nationalities.[6]

An appeal for international peace negotiations to be commenced was now made, but it was rejected by the Allied Powers. 'The Soviet Government thereupon, decided to start its own peace negotiations with the Central Powers [German Empire, Austria-Hungary, Bulgaria, and the Ottoman Empire].' The outcome was that on 15 December 1917 an armistice was signed.[7]

For Lenin's wife, Nadezhda, the revolution was a work in progress. After the revolution she returned to Russia, where she 'spread Bolshevik propaganda and carried messages from Lenin to his colleagues while he was hiding in Finland (July–October)'. After the Bolsheviks seized power in October 1917, Nadezhda 'became a member of the collegium of the People's Commissariat of Education'. In 1924 she became a member of the Central Committee of the Communist Party of the Soviet Union.

Nadezhda was an enormous support to Lenin: serving as his 'personal secretary as well as editorial secretary for his Party newspapers and journals'.[8]

On 1 January 1918, after addressing workers at a factory in Moscow, Lenin was shot twice by Fanya Kaplan, a member of the Social Revolutionary party. Lenin was seriously wounded but survived the attack. This 'and the constant strain of overwork, undermined his health and from the end of 1921 he was forced to absent himself from his work more and more frequently'. In consequence, 'The main burden of the work of guiding the affairs of the Party fell upon the shoulders of Stalin.'[9]

In that year of 1918, the Party was renamed the All-Russian Communist Party.

Chapter 12

Civil War

Conflict arose 'between the newly formed Bolshevik government and its Red Army' on the one hand, and 'the anti-Bolshevik forces in Russia' on the other. The unfavourable Treaty of Brest-Litovsk concluded with Germany caused socialists opposed to Lenin to break with the Bolsheviks and join the right-wing Whites and their volunteer army under Anton Denikin (former lieutenant general in the Imperial Russian Army).[1]

The Red Army was founded by the Council of People's Commissars on 28 January 1918. From March 1918 to January 1925 it was headed by Trotsky.

The Brest-Litovsk Treaty was signed on 3 March 1918 between the new Bolshevik government of Russia and the Central Powers, and ended Russia's participation in the First World War.[2]

The White movement, also known as the Whites, was a loose confederation of anti-communist forces that fought the communist Bolsheviks, also known as the Reds, in the Russian Civil War.[3]

From March 1918, the Allies – originally the French Republic, British Empire and Russian Empire together, subsequently, with Japan, Italy and the USA – gave limited support to the Whites. The government 'responded to the growing anti-Bolshevik movement by expelling Menshevik and Social Revolutionary deputies' and 'began a campaign of "Red Terror" that gave increased powers to the secret police to arrest and execute suspects'.

'The Bolsheviks maintained control over the heart of the country, but the anti-Bolsheviks gained power in Ukraine and Omsk [south-western Siberia],' where former Imperial Russian Admiral Alexander

V. Kolchak 'and other dissident groups joined together to fight the Red Army. Confused by the struggles between communists, Russian Whites, and Ukrainian nationalists,' the Allies, by late September 1919, had withdrawn their support.[4]

Alexandrov paid tribute to Stalin's dedication to achieving a Bolshevik victory. For example, on 6 June 1918 he 'arrived in Tsaritsyn with a detachment of workers', having 'at once realised the importance' of the city 'as the point at which the counter-revolutionary forces were likely to deliver their main attack'.

Tsaritsyn, in southern Russia, was renamed Stalingrad in 1925 and has been called Volgograd since 1961.

'Thanks to Stalin's iron will and masterly foresight, Tsaritsyn was saved and the Whites were prevented from breaking through to Moscow.'[5] In late 1918, Stalin arrived at the front in Perm, a city in western Russia, which was being threatened by Kolchak's army, together with British troops.

He 'acted swiftly and drastically, and soon had the situation in hand'.[6] When Petrograd was threatened in May 1919, 'the Central Committee chose Stalin to organise the repulse of the Whites'.[7] Said People's Commissar for Defence of the Soviet Union, Kliment Y. Voroshilov, 'Wherever alarm and panic might at any moment develop into helplessness and catastrophe, there Comrade Stalin was always sure to appear.'[8]

'After early military successes against the Red Army, the White forces under Kolchak were defeated by early 1920.' Hostilities ended on 25 October 1922 with victory for the Red Army.[9] Meanwhile, said Alexandrov: 'Guided by Lenin and Stalin, the workers and peasants began to turn the tsarist colonies into Soviet republics. There is not a single Soviet republic in whose organisation Stalin did not take an active and leading part. He directed the fight for the creation of the Ukrainian Soviet Republic, the Belorussian Republic, and the Soviet republics of Transcaucasia and Central Asia, and he helped the numerous nationalities of the Soviet Land to set up their autonomous republics and regions. Lenin and Stalin were the engineers and builders of the great Union of Soviet Socialist Republics.'

'In January 1918, on the instructions of the Central Committee, Stalin arranged a conference of representatives of the revolutionary wings of the Socialist parties of Europe and America, which was an important step towards the formation of the Third Communist International.'[10]

The Communist International ('Comintern', also known as 'The Third International') was an international organisation founded in 1919 that advocated world communism, controlled by the Soviet Union. The Comintern held seven World Congresses in Moscow between 1919 and 1935.

On 10 July 1918 the first Soviet Constitution was adopted.

The First All-Union Congress of Soviets was a congress of representatives of soviets of workers, peasants, and Red Army deputies, held on 30 December 1922 in Moscow. 'On the motion of Lenin and Stalin [the Congress] passed the historic decision on the voluntary amalgamation of the soviet nations to form the Union of Soviet Socialist Republics – the USSR.'[11]

In 1925 the Party was renamed the All-Union Communist Party (Bolsheviks).

Chapter 13

Stalin and the Alliluyev Family

'It was to Moscow in 1919,' said Murphy, that Stalin brought Nadezhda ('Nadya') Alliluyeva, 'the daughter of his old friend' Sergei Alliluyev 'of early Bolshevik days', who had 'now grown into a beautiful woman. Stalin was at this time 40 and she 17, but for her he was still the same hero who had once come from afar and taken refuge in her parents' home.'[1]

Nadezhda's father, Sergei Yakolvlevich Alliluyev, was born in 1866 at Voronezh in south-west Russia and her mother, Olga Evgenieva Fedorenko, was born in 1875 in Tiflis, Georgia. She had three older siblings: Pavel ('Paul') Alliluyev (born 1894); Anna Alliluyeva (born 1896), and Fyodor ('Fedya') Alliluyev (born 1898).

A Travelled Path, by Sergei, and *Reminiscences*, by his daughter Anna, were published separately in 1946, and as a compilation, *Memoirs*, in 1968. The memoirs provide a unique insight into the life of the family. (Sergei died in 1945 and Anna in 1964.)

The Alliluyevs 'originated from a family of serfs in central Russia', said Svetlana.[2] In *Memoirs*, Anna explained how the lives of Stalin and the lives of her family of fellow revolutionaries became deeply entwined; how her family were immensely supportive of and loyal to Stalin; how both Stalin and her father, Sergei spent time organising revolutionary activities; how they were both obliged to hide from the authorities; and how they were both arrested, imprisoned, and exiled for their pains.

'Everyone,' even the Alliluyev children, 'were involved in some "revolutionary work", said Svetlana.[3]

It was from her father, Sergei, a 'skilled machinist at the railway workshops at Tiflis',[4] the Georgian capital, said Anna, that she learned 'about the underground work at the railway depot. In those days the young revolutionaries: Stalin, Ketskhoveli, and Tsulukidze organised secret circles among the Tiflis workmen.' Lado Ketskhoveli and Georgian social-democratic revolutionary, journalist, and nobleman Prince Alexander Tsulukidze were fellow students at the Tiflis Seminary. 'The spirit of revolt spread amongst them.'[5]

On 1 August 1900, Sergei Alliluyev was arrested and imprisoned in the aforementioned Metekhi fortress prison at Tiflis. A few days later, Mikhail Kalinin ('Uncle' Misha), a friend of the family, 'suffered the same fate'.[6] In November 1900, Sergei was released.

Following a general strike in October 1905, Sergei Alliluyev 'was arrested again, together with some thirty other persons.[7] Four months after his arrest, said Anna, her father was 'sentenced to exile'.[8] This was in Archangel, from October 1906 to April 1907.[9] Meanwhile, when the strike came to an end in December 1905, Sergei's wife, Olga, and her family relocated to Tiflis.[10] When Sergei was released in April 1907 'he settled in St Petersburg where he was joined by his family'.[11]

'One day early in September 1911,' said Anna, after Stalin had escaped from Solovychegodsk, 'the front doorbell rang.' It was Stalin, 'the well-known revolutionary whom Father had already met in Tiflis and Baku'.[12] Because detectives were patrolling outside the Alliluyevs' house, Sergei took Stalin to hide in 'The Hole', a basement in the house of the shipowner Kolobov, where Konon Savchenko, a Bolshevik, worked as a porter.[13]

Following Stalin's arrest and exile in September 1911, said Murphy, 'Anna and her sister, Nadya [Nadezhda], busied themselves collecting money from Bolshevik sympathisers with which their mother bought food and clothes to be sent to Stalin, Y. [Yankel] Sverdlov, and I. [Iosif] F. Dubrovinsky, who had been banished to the remote north of Russia or to Siberia.'

In the winter of 1912, said Anna, Stalin again 'came to visit us'; this time in company with Sverdlov. 'They had run away together from the Narym Territory' of western Siberia.[14] Stalin was offered accommodation at the Alliluyevs' flat. However, 'As illegal persons [who were] on the run, both he and Sverdlov would flit from one place to another, crossing street after street to confuse the Okhrama, making their way through back alleys. The police pursued Stalin remorselessly,' said Anna. 'Every evening he had to think of some new place where he could spend the night.'[15]

Of her older brother Pavel, Anna declared, 'of course he was a member of a revolutionary cell'. Pavel's 'labours were finally rewarded when, in the summer of 1913, many factories went on strike'. However, Pavel 'was arrested and taken to prison' and placed in solitary confinement 'for a month'.[16]

Following Stalin's exile to Kureika, Siberia, in early 1914, Anna declared, 'We now have a new address to which to send parcels and letters.' Stalin 'often corresponded with Father', she said. 'From his letters which we all read, we received an impression of that distant place with its cruel winters. He lived in the hut of an Ostyak fisherman in a tiny hamlet lost in the gloomy, endless tundra.'[17]

In March 1914, from Kureika in the Arctic, said Anna, 'Stalin sent a manuscript of his work on the nationalities question to Father,' with a request that Sergei 'send it abroad to Lenin who was expecting the manuscript'.

The question of nationalities – that is, the oppression of nations and national minorities – which has characterised capitalism from its birth till the present time, has always occupied a central position in Marxist theory.[18]

'My sister Nadya and I took the manuscript to Comrade [Alexei Y.] Badayev,' said Anna, 'who sent it to Vladimir Ilych [Lenin].'[19]

Shortly afterwards, Stalin told the Alliluyevs, 'I should very much like to move in with you, but I don't think this is the right time. The flat could be put under police observation and you might get into trouble because of me.' To this, Olga replied, 'Please don't worry about us, Joseph, we're accustomed to such things'.[20]

As with the Svanidze family, the Alliluyevs had supported Stalin unstintingly over the course of many years; its members often putting their lives at risk for his sake. One day he would repay them in a way that they would least expect.

When Lenin arrived at St Petersburg on 6 July 1917, the Alliluyevs offered him accommodation at their home in Torhdesvensky Street, as a 'safe house'.[21] 'On the first day that Lenin came to stay in our flat,' said Anna, Stalin 'visited him' with fellow revolutionaries Sergo Ordzhonikidze, Viktor Nogin, and Yelena Stasova. 'They discussed whether Lenin should give himself up to the Provisional Government. Both Stalin and Sergo were against this because it was quite clear to them that Kerensky's promises could not be trusted. "The Junkers [military cadets] will kill him before taking him to prison," said Stalin.'[22]

Having shaved off his moustache and beard so as not to be recognised, Lenin left St Petersburg on 24 July 1917 and took the train for the long journey to Razliv.

On the very day that the Sixth Congress of the Bolshevik Party opened in St Petersburg, 26 July 1917, Stalin paid a visit to the Alliluyev family.[23] 'I had not seen him for four years,' said Anna, 'four years of cruel, lonely exile.'[24] There was much joy on this occasion. When Anna went into the dining room to lay the table, she said, 'the place' was 'alive with laughter. Father, Mother', Fedya [Fyodor, Nadya's older sister], and Nadya have surrounded Stalin. There are great gales of laughter.'[25]

Stalin described 'the North, the tundra with its endless snow horizons, and the frozen rivers where the sturdy, good-natured natives sit for hours on end at an ice-hole fishing. He lived in one of their modest huts and gained their confidence, so they came to like him.'[26]

Shortly after Lenin left for Finland on 24 July 1917 the Alliluyevs acquired a new apartment: Number 17, 10th Rozhdestvenskaya Street. Whereupon, Stalin asked them to put aside a room for himself.[27]

In October 1917 the Central Committee established a Politburo of five of its members to lead the Russian Revolution. The Politburo was the principal policy-making committee of the Communist Party.

What of Stalin's personality? Did he have a sense of humour? According to Anna, yes. 'He greatly admired *A Chameleon*; *Unter*

Prishibeev [Sergeant Prishibeev], and other stories by Chekhov. He read, stressing all those incredibly funny remarks made by Chekhov's characters. We would shriek with laughter and ask him to read more.'[28] However, he was always industrious and diligent, and, 'No matter how late he came home [he] always sat down to work after one of our tea parties or after he had had a word with Mother and Father.'[29]

Chapter 14

Stalin's Writings

Stalin was a prodigious writer, correspondent, and speechmaker. The list of his lifetime's published books, papers, telegrams, letters, reports, political speeches, wartime 'Orders of the Day', political tracts, works of literary criticism, etc runs to fifty-seven pages and amounts to in excess of 1,100 inclusions.[1] Stalin's works include: *Anarchism or Socialism* (1906–7); *Dialectical and Historical Materialism* (1938); *The Tasks of Youth* (1940); *Sochineniia* (Essays) published in thirteen volumes in Moscow (1946–1951); *Marxism and Problems of Linguistics* (1950); *Economic Problems of Socialism in the USSR* (1951).

His pamphlets include: 'Briefly about Disagreements in the Party' (1905); 'Concerning Questions of Leninism' (1926). Reports include: 'The Results of the First Five-Year Plan' (1933). Leninism was Marxism as interpreted and applied by Lenin.[2]

In January 1913, Stalin wrote a pamphlet entitled 'Marxism and the National Question'. In March 1914 he sent the pamphlet to Lenin and it was published in serial form in the Bolshevik magazine *Prosveshchenie* that same spring (March to May).

Stalin's 'The October Revolution and the Tactics of the Russian Communists' was first published in December 1924 as a preface to his book *On the Road to October*. The message was that as long as the country: 'was surrounded by a capitalist world, the danger of capitalist intervention and of the restoration of capitalism in the USSR would persist. In order to eliminate this danger, it would be necessary to destroy the capitalist encirclement and that could result only from a victorious proletarian revolution in at least several countries.

Only then could the victory of socialism in the USSR be considered complete and final.'[3] This, of course, was entirely in line with Stalin's arch enemy Trotsky's advocacy of 'Permanent Revolution'.

Marxism and the National Question, part of a collection of articles and speeches entitled *Marxism and the National and Colonial Question*, was published in 1934. The collection, said Murphy: 'was undoubtedly the product of much discussion with Lenin, but that it was wholly written by Stalin is clear enough. Every paragraph bears the imprint of his character.'

Said Stalin: 'The right of Self-Determination is an essential element in the solution of the national problem. Further: what must be our attitude towards nations which for one reason or another will prefer to remain within the general framework? The only real solution is regional autonomy, autonomy for such crystallised units as Poland, Lithuania, the Ukraine, the Caucasus, etc.'

The way forward, said Stalin, was for 'organisation on internationalist lines. The aim must be to unite the workers of all nationalities within Russia into united and integral collective bodies in the various localities and to unite those collective bodies into a single party. Thus, the principle of *international solidarity of the workers is an essential element* in the solution of the national problem.'[4]

During the Second World War, however, the countries of Eastern Europe were invaded and subsequently occupied by the Soviet Union; even though they had no desire, either 'to remain within the general framework', or to place the notion of 'the principle of *international solidarity of the workers*' above their desire to be sovereign nation states once more. As for Stalin's notion of a nation's 'right of Self-Determination', as events were to prove, this was so much 'pie in the sky'.

Many, like Stalin's daughter, Svetlana, would argue that communism in whatever form, whether Marxism, Leninism, or Stalinism, simply doesn't work. Furthermore, in the handful of countries where communism still exists, evidence points to the fact it can only exist in conjunction with a police state, thus ensuring that any opposition to it is quickly suppressed. Stalin's version of communism was surely the most catastrophic of all, in terms of human life lost and human misery: the full extent of which will be described shortly.

Intellect is defined as 'the faculty of reasoning and understanding objectively'[5] and there is no doubt that certain qualities of Stalin's intellect were, arguably, second to none. Marshal Zhukov, for example, described his 'ability to formulate an idea concisely', his 'naturally analytic mind, great erudition, and a rare memory'.[6]

Red Army Marshal Alexander M. Vasilievsky declared, 'I have never met anyone who could remember as much. He knew by name all the army and front commanders, of whom there were more than one hundred, and he even knew the names of some corps and divisional commanders. Throughout the war Stalin had the composition of the strategic reserves in his head and could name any formation at any time.'[7]

Finally, British Prime Minister Winston Churchill remarked admiringly that, 'Very few people alive could have comprehended in so few minutes the reasons which we all had so long been wrestling with for months. He saw it all in a flash.'[8]

Lenin too, recognised these qualities in Stalin, even though he clearly did not like him as a person!

However, the possession of an excellent memory and the ability to articulate the nature of a particular problem does not of itself indicate a good intellect: 'Intellect' being defined as 'the faculty of reasoning and understanding objectively'.[9] But other, far more sinister forces were at work in the mind of Lenin's protégé, as will shortly be seen!

Chapter 15

Stalin's Marriage to Nadezhda Alliluyeva (24 March 1919)

Stalin and Nadezhda Alliluyeva were married on 24 March 1919. On 21 March 1921 their son, Vasily, was born, followed on 28 February 1926 by a daughter, Svetlana.

'In spite of her mixed blood,' said Svetlana, 'my mother, of course, was Russian, a real Russian by temperament and upbringing.'[1] This was a reference to the fact that Svetlana's maternal great-grandmother, Magdalena, had originated from a 'family of German settlers'.

In 1919, shortly after her parents were married, said Svetlana, they went to Moscow, where Nadezhda 'went to work under L. A. Fotiyeva in Lenin's Secretariat'. This was Lidia Alexandrovna Fotiyeva, Private Secretary to Lenin.[2]

Svetlana described the house in which she grew up. 'Named Zubalovo,' she said, 'after the pre-revolutionary owner', it was 'not far from Usovo and less than 20 miles from the centre of Moscow. My parents made it their home from 1919 until my mother died in 1932.'

Svetlana waxed lyrical about her mother. 'The life she created shines in my memory to this day as the world of my joyous childhood.[3] Only my first six and a half years had been warmed by Mama's presence, but they remained in my memory as a childhood filled with sunshine. I remember Mama as a very beautiful, graceful woman, smelling of perfume. I was completely entrusted to the hands of my nurse and a governess, but Mama's presence expressed itself in the whole tenor of my childhood life. She considered most important our education and ethical upbringing. Honesty, labour, truth, were to her more important than anything else.'[4]

The home was 'sunny and gay, filled with the sounds of children's voices and cheerful, openhearted people. This was the house my mother created and presided over, a house that was filled with her presence. In this house my father was neither a god nor a "cult", but just the father of a family.'[5]

Nadezhda 'created the home; she was the centre of friendship and human relations; it was part of her nature to create, to give, to spread warmth. All the relatives clustered around her – the Svanidzes and Alliluyevs. My father's old Party comrades loved her; she organised an interesting life for us children. My father took all this for granted. He considered her his devoted friend, and he was sorely in need of devoted friends.'[6]

As far as she and her brother, Vasily, were concerned, said Svetlana, 'Mother was a perfectionist in everything she touched. Our education was planned and supervised seriously. Apart from the tutors at home, we went to excellent schools. Influenced by what we had been taught, my brother chose a military career and I studied History at Moscow University and followed it up with post-grad work in Russian Literature.'[7]

Of her half-brother, Yakov Dzhugashvili, Svetlana stated as follows, 'My mother was very tender and loving with my oldest brother, Yakov (my father's son by his first wife, Yekaterina [Ekaterina] Svanidze). Yakov, who was only seven years younger than she, loved and respected her greatly in return.'[8]

As for her father, during his marriage to Nadezhda, 'he was absorbed in internal party struggles, in the intricate process of seizing power, and stood remote from everything else'.[9]

Nadezhda also kept busy. 'My mother worked first on the staff of a magazine,'[10] said Svetlana. In 1931, when she was aged 'only thirty', she studied 'synthetic fibres, a new branch of chemistry at the time', in the [Moscow] Industrial Academy'.[11] Nadezhda 'was studying for a degree in engineering in the textile industry, wishing to be independent of her "high position", which oppressed her'.[12] She also found time to study music with Alexandra Pukhlyakova, and she also studied French. 'She longed to work on her own and hated being "first lady of the kingdom".'[13]

As far as politics was concerned, said Svetlana, her mother: 'was part of the younger generation of the revolution. She was one of the enthusiasts of the early Five-Year Plans, one of the dedicated builders of a new life. My mother believed in this with the full fervour of revolutionary idealism, and there were people all around her whose conduct seemed to bear out her faith. It was my father who had once seemed to her the highest embodiment of the revolutionary New Man. She was a young schoolgirl, and he was a friend of her parents and the uncompromising revolutionary just back from Siberia. He was to remain that to her for a long time, but not always.'[14]

The truth was, that there were growing tensions between Stalin and Nadezhda.

On 21 January 1924, Lenin, 'the leader and founder of the Bolshevik Party', died at Gorki, a village situated 20 miles south of Moscow.[15]

The Fourteenth Congress of the All-Union Communist Party was held in Moscow from 18 to 31 December 1925. Addressing the Congress, Stalin declared that the 'conversion' of the USSR: 'from an agrarian into an industrial country able to produce the machinery it needs by its own efforts – that is the essence, the basis of our general line'.[16]

At the Fifteenth Party Congress, held in Moscow from 2 to 19 December 1927, Stalin explained that 'the backwardness of agriculture as compared with industry … was jeopardising the national economy as a whole'. The answer, he said, was to take the course of amalgamating the small peasant holdings into large *socialist* farms, into collective farms, which would be able to use tractors and other modern machinery on an extensive scale for a rapid development of grain farming and a rapid increase in the marketable surplus of grain'. This would be achieved, 'not by pressure, but by example and persuasion', he said. The truth was, however, that a massive onslaught against the kulaks – peasants who were prosperous enough to own a farm and to hire labour – was about to begin.

The Congress also 'gave instructions for the drawing up of the first Five-Year Plan for the development of the national economy'.[17]

Chapter 16

Leon Trotsky: His Banishment (1928)

As Chairman of the Petrograd Soviet, Trotsky played a key role in the October Revolution of November 1917 that overthrew the new Provisional Government. Once in government, Trotsky initially held the post of People's Commissar for Foreign Affairs (8 November 1917–13 March 1918). He was directly involved in the 1917–18 Brest-Litovsk negotiations with Germany as Russia pulled out of the First World War (3 March 1918). From 14 March 1918 to 25 January 1925, Trotsky headed the Red Army as People's Commissar for Military and Naval Affairs. He also played a key part in the Bolshevik victory in the Russian Civil War of 1917–22. In 1919, he became one of the seven members of the first Bolshevik Politburo.[1]

However, there was a fundamental difference between Stalin's notion of socialism and that of Trotsky.

Socialism in one country 'was a theory put forth by Joseph Stalin and Nikolai Bukharin in 1924, which was eventually adopted by the Soviet Union as state policy. The theory held that given the defeat of all the communist revolutions in Europe' between 1917 and 1923', 'except for the one in Russia, the Soviet Union should begin to strengthen itself internally. This turn towards national communism was a shift from the previously held position by classical Marxism that socialism must be established globally'.[2]

This suited Stalin on two counts. Firstly, he could concentrate his energies on eliminating all his opponents within the Soviet Union: a territory that occupied no less than a sixth of the Earth's land surface; and secondly, he could marginalise Trotsky, who took a different view. In 1930 Trotsky wrote, 'The completion of the socialist revolution within national limits is unthinkable. One of the basic reasons for the crisis in bourgeois society is the fact that the productive forces created by it can no longer be reconciled with the framework of the national state. From this follows on the one hand, imperialist wars and on the other, the utopia of a bourgeois United States of Europe. The socialist revolution begins on the national arena, it unfolds on the international arena, and is completed on the world arena. Thus, the socialist revolution becomes a permanent revolution in a newer and broader sense of the word; it attains completion, only in the final victory of the new society on our entire planet.'[3]

On 11 January 1928, Trotsky was sent into internal exile and after a year he was banished from the territories of the Soviet Union. He relocated first to Turkey; in 1933 to France; in 1935 to Norway; and finally, in December 1936 to Mexico.

Meanwhile, in 1930, Trotsky's autobiography, *My Life*, was published and also his *History of the Russian Revolution* in three volumes. Trotsky's literary output was extraordinary. In the decade 1930 to 1940 he had no fewer than 420 publications to his name including books, essays, pamphlets, book reviews, speeches, and letters. In August 1936 he was found guilty of treason and condemned to death in absentia.

Trotsky made a home in Mexico City with his (second) wife, Natalia Sedova. She bore him two sons, Lyova ('Lev', born 24 February 1906, Finland) and Sergei Sedov (born 21 March 1908, Vienna).

Chapter 17

Nadezhda's Disillusionment with her Husband Stalin

Said Svetlana, 'Because my mother was intelligent and endlessly honest, I believe her sensitivity and intuition made her realise finally that my father was not the New Man she had thought when she was young, and she suffered the most terrible, devastating disillusionment.'[1] As for Stalin, he 'neither understood nor sensed' that Nadezhda 'was a young thinking human being', and 'that to her, independence was absolutely necessary, and that she had her own opinions. She argued with him, made objections; she considered herself his *equal*, and this went against his purely Oriental approach to women and to a wife. It only served to irritate him.[2] He could not tolerate a personal opinion in others.'[3] Likewise, said Svetlana, 'I believe that my mother had her own way of looking at things and stuck by it to the very end. It was not in her nature to compromise.'[4]

Svetlana struggled to present her father in a good light. 'He obviously was, himself, a person of great self-control and not an emotional person. She was more of an artistic nature, more emotional, more bound to be in moods for this and that. In any case I think he somehow tried to cope with it and tried to understand her in the later years.'[5]

Just before her mother died, said Svetlana, she said repeatedly that 'everything bored her', that she was 'sick of everything', and 'nothing made her happy'.[6]

Chapter 18

The Death of Nadezhda (9 November 1932)

Nadezhda died on the night of 8 November 1932. Stalin did not attend her funeral, said Svetlana, nor did he visit her mother's grave at Moscow's Novo-Devichy Cemetery.[1]

Henceforth, said Svetlana, 'my father couldn't bear to remain' either at Zubalovo, 'or in their old apartment in the city. Those cloudless years were a fairy tale.'[2] However, subsequently 'huge photographs of her were hung in my father's office and the dining room' of the Moscow apartment.[3]

Svetlana had many reasons to be grateful to her late mother. 'Although I was only six and a half when she died, I could already read and write both Russian and German. I could draw and model in clay and make cut-outs with scissors and glue. I could read music and write down the notes as a tune was played on the piano. My brother and I were lucky, for our mother found remarkable teachers for us.'[4]

Chapter 19

Nadezhda's Death: The Truth at Last!

It was in 1942 during the Second World War when she was aged 16, and a decade after the event, said Svetlana, that she read in a magazine that her mother, Nadezhda, 'had killed herself'.[1] 'It was a cruel discovery.[2] I was in Kuibyshev [Kuybyshev] that winter with my aunt and grandmother,' she said. 'I began questioning them at once and understood that Mama had been very unhappy, that she and my father had had different points of view on everything, from politics to the upbringing of children.'

Kuybyshev was Stalin's secret bunker located in the centre of Kuybyshev (formerly Samara), 660 miles east of Moscow. It was created 'during the desperate days of World War II. German troops were only 16 kilometres from Moscow. Leningrad (Petrograd until 1924, formerly St Petersburg) was besieged. On 15 October 1941, fearing the Germans would take the Soviet capital, the State Committee for Defence took a decision to evacuate key industries to Kuybyshev and prepare the city to act as a centre of operations in the event of the Germans reaching Moscow. Kuybyshev became the "Reserve Capital" of the Soviet Union'.[3]

'I have always loved Mama,' Svetlana continued, 'though she had never spoiled me. And now I felt that my father had clearly been in the wrong and that he was to blame for her death.'[4] In Svetlana's mind, there was no doubt whatsoever as to why her mother had died. Her father, she said, 'had driven my mother to suicide by being what he was. By driving her to this extreme, he was, of course, indirectly her murderer.'[5]

Chapter 20

Nadezhda's Death: The Aftermath

From her relatives, Svetlana learnt how her father had reacted to the death of his wife. 'He was shaken', she said, 'because he couldn't understand why it had happened. What did it mean? Why had such a terrible stab in the back been dealt to him, of all people? He was too intelligent not to know that people always commit suicide in order to punish someone. He saw that, but he couldn't understand why. What was he being punished for? He asked those around him whether it was true he'd been inconsiderate. Hadn't he loved and respected her as a wife and human being?'

'The first few days he was in a state of shock. He said he didn't want to go on living either. I was told this by my Uncle Pavel's widow [Yevgenia Alliluyev], who, together with Aunt Anna, stayed with us day and night. My father was in such a state that they were afraid to leave him alone. He had sporadic fits of rage. The reason is that my mother had left him a letter. Apparently, she wrote it the night she died.'

Although Svetlana never saw the letter, 'people who actually saw it told me of its existence', she said. 'It was a terrible letter, full of reproaches and accusations. It wasn't purely personal; it was partly political as well. After reading it, it would have been possible for my father to think that my mother had been on his side only outwardly, but that in her heart she had been on the side of those who were in political opposition to him. He was shocked and incensed. At the civil leave-taking ceremony, he went up to the coffin for a moment. Suddenly, he pushed it away from him, turned on his heel and left. He didn't even go to the funeral.

'It was a long time before my father regained his equilibrium. He never went to visit her grave at Novo-Devichy. Not even once. He couldn't. He thought my mother had left him as his personal enemy.

'It was only in his last years, not long before he died, that he suddenly started talking to me about it, nearly driving me out of my mind. I saw that he was desperately looking for the reason – looking, and not finding it. Suddenly he would start denouncing the "vile book" which my mother had read not long before she died. It was *The Green Hat* by Michael Arlen, which was very much in vogue at the time. He thought it had an important effect on her.'

Arlen, an Armenian–British novelist, published his novel in 1924. A sentimental romance, set in London and Paris, it reflects the post-war atmosphere of the 1920s and the spirit of rebellion of the 'Bright Young Things' of Mayfair.

'Then he started blaming Polina Molotov, Aunt Anna and Pavel, who had bought her a pistol so tiny it looked like a toy.' Molotov (née Zhemchuzhina) was a Soviet politician and the wife of Foreign Minister Vyachslav Molotov.

'He was trying to discover "who was guilty" and "who put her up to it".'[1]

Did Stalin feel any personal responsibility for his wife's suicide? 'I don't think he ever thought that way,' said Svetlana.

In Stalin's official biography, which was published in 1949, Svetlana said her mother was finally mentioned as '"wife and close friend", which was quite a step forward because she was just not mentioned at all.'[2]

However, if this was a reference by Svetlana to *Joseph Stalin: A Short Biography*, prepared by the Marx-Engels-Lenin Institute in Moscow in 1947, compiled by G. F. Alexandrov and colleagues, and published by the Foreign Language Publishing House, Moscow in 1949, in this volume there is no mention of Nadezhda whatsoever!

Stalin, she said, 'had finally "forgiven" her and her memory', and 'apparently, he had somewhat softened towards her'.[3]

Instead of making Stalin more understanding and more compassionate, the death of his wife had the opposite effect. When he 'realised at last the full extent of her independence, her protest, her challenge,' said Svetlana, 'it only served to harden him. He wanted no equals. Equals argued, got in the way, objected, while he wanted blind devotion and absolute submission to his will.[4] He could not tolerate a personal opinion in others.'[5]

'I believe that my mother's death, which he had taken as a personal betrayal, deprived his soul of the last vestiges of human warmth. He was now free of her moderating and, by the same token, impending presence. His sceptical, harsh judgement of men only hardened; this came naturally to his unsentimental nature.'[6]

Chapter 21

Stalin's Early Kindness to his Daughter, Svetlana

Was Stalin capable of tenderness? Undoubtedly! This, he demonstrated towards his first wife, Ekaterina, who, as already mentioned, 'died in his arms'.

Svetlana, who was born on 28 February 1926, said of her father that he 'petted and spoiled me'.[1] At Zubalovo, said Svetlana, she used to take her father currants, violets, and lilies of the valley. 'I would go trotting off and be rewarded, no matter what I brought, by a warm, tobacco-scented kiss from my father.'[2] 'He spoiled me and loved playing games with me. I was his rest and relaxation.[3]

'What splendid children's parties we all had! All the Kremlin children would be asked, twenty or thirty of them.'

Svetlana remembered the last birthday party that she had enjoyed before the death of her mother. 'It was February 1932, and I was six years old. The Kremlin apartment was filled with children. My father was there, too. He was only watching, of course, but it amused him. Once in a while he enjoyed the sounds of children playing.'[4]

It was the custom at dinner, said Svetlana, for her father to 'ask how I'd done in school that day. Since my marks were excellent until I got to the eighth grade, he was always very proud. They [the family]'d all sing my praises and send me off to bed. My father would leave late to spend the night at Kuntsevo.'

The Kuntsevo Dacha was Stalin's personal residence near the former town of Kuntsevo, in the Moscow Oblast (district).[5]

'Sometimes before he left, he'd come to my room in his overcoat to kiss me good night as I lay sleeping. He liked kissing me while I was little, and I'll never forget how tender he was to me. It was the warm Georgian tenderness to children.'[6]

'It was in these years that my father started taking me to movies and the theatre,' said Svetlana. 'My father thought it was better for me to watch movies than to sit at home. Possibly he didn't even think whether it would be better for me or not. Maybe he just liked having me along. I amused him and diverted him and was a comfort to him besides.

'Sometimes after school was out [for the holidays] in the summer, he'd take me to Kuntsevo for three days or so. The one thing I liked was our walks in the garden and woods. He'd ask me the names of various flowers and grasses and what sort of bird was that singing?'[7]

'Sometimes,' said Svetlana, Stalin 'appeared unexpectedly at Zubalovo, which, however deserted and greatly changed, was still infinitely precious to us all. Mikoyan might come over, or Uncle Pavel would appear quickly with the children.'

Anastas Ivanovich Mikoyan was an Armenian Communist revolutionary, Old Bolshevik, and Soviet statesman.

'Then we'd all have a picnic in the woods. There'd be a table, and shashlik [skewered and grilled cubes of meat] sizzling over a fire, and everyone would have an excellent, light Georgian wine. My father used to send me to the poultry yard for guinea and pheasant eggs.'[8]

On 8 September 1934, Stalin wrote to his 'Little Housekeeper!' to say he was sending her 'a few red apples' and that 'in a few days I'll send tangerines. Eat them and enjoy yourself. I'm lonely because my Housekeeper isn't with me. All the best, then, my little Housekeeper. I give you a big kiss.'[9]

Said Svetlana of her father, 'He loved me while I was still a child, a schoolgirl – I amused him. 'Funny how much you look like my mother [Ekaterina]. She, too, was redheaded, covered with freckles!' he would say, this doubtless being the main source of his tenderness for me. In my childhood, I had been the recipient of the greatest tenderness he had ever been capable of. Later, when I developed my own taste and interests, he cooled off considerably.'[10]

In 1938, when she was aged 12, Svetlana sent Stalin a photograph of herself for his birthday. Whereupon he sent it back saying, 'You have an insolent expression on your face. Before, there used to be modesty there and that was attractive.' Said Svetlana, 'In that gay photograph of a schoolgirl with a Pioneer's red tie and a grin from ear to ear, he thought he saw a challenge, an independence.'

The Pioneer Movement was an organisation for children, operated by the Communist Party.

'He would have preferred lowered eyes, a look of obedience – what he called "modesty".'[11]

Stalin 'felt real tenderness for Yakov's daughter, Gulia', said Svetlana.[12] This was a reference to Galina, born on 19 February 1938, Yakov's daughter by Yudith ('Yulia') Meltzer.

Svetlana described how Stalin also displayed love and tenderness towards her son, Josef (by her first husband Grigory Morozov. Josef was born in 1945), 'My father melted the moment he set eyes on the child.'

One day in 1949, she said, 'my father played with Josef [for] half an hour. I was in seventh heaven. With a man of few words like my father, his "He's a good-looking boy – he's got nice eyes" was like a paean [song or hymn] of praise from anybody else. He saw Josef twice more. The last time was four months before he [Stalin] died. Josef was seven and had just started the first grade [at school]. "What thoughtful eyes," my father said again. "He's a smart boy!" and again I was overjoyed.'[13]

Svetlana kept two letters from her father. 'His letters always end: "I kiss you". My father liked to kiss me until I was grown up. And until I was about sixteen, he used to call me 'Setanka' (That was what I called myself when I was little). He also called me 'Housekeeper', because he wanted me to be his housekeeper and take an active part in running the household, like my mother. Whenever I asked him for anything, he liked to answer: "Why are you only asking? Give an order, and I'll see to it right away." That's how we started the game of "orders" which we played until I was about sixteen.'

One of Stalin's letters to Svetlana read as follows: 'To My Housekeeper, Setanka: You don't write to your little papa. I think you've forgotten him. How is your health? You're not sick, are you?

What are you up to? Have you seen Lyolka? How are your dolls? I thought I'd be getting an order from you soon, but no. Too bad. You're hurting your little papa's feelings. Never mind. I kiss you. I am waiting to hear from you.' It was signed 'Little Papa'.

'"Lyolka" was a "perfect little girl" whom Stalin had 'invented … as an example for me to follow,' said Svetlana.[14]

Chapter 22

Stalin's Unbelievable Cruelty to his Relatives

In his vindictiveness, Stalin did not discriminate between family members and outsiders, and his persecution of them amounted to a veritable vendetta.

Stalin's brother-in-law, Alexander Svanidze, and his wife, Maria (née Korona)

In late December 1937, Stalin's brother-in-law, Alexander Svanidze, and his wife, Maria were arrested. 'After their arrest and investigation, he and Aunt Maria each got ten years, but she was sent to a different place, to Dolinskoye, a woman's prison camp in Kazakhstan,' said Svetlana. Meanwhile, Alexander 'was in a prison camp outside of Ukhta [in north-west Russia], to which had been sent for an indefinite term'.[1] 'How could such a thing happen? How could my father do it? The only thing I know is that it couldn't have been his idea.'[2] Svetlana laid the principal blame at Beria's door.

Alexander Svanidze is described as 'a Georgian 'Old Bolshevik' and a historian',[3] What had he done to deserve such a fate when he was, by all accounts, a worthy citizen, and he had been Stalin's comrade-in-arms, as previously mentioned?

Educated in Germany, at Jena University, Thüringia, 'he learned German and English and engaged in historical research of ancient civilisations'.[4]

Said Svetlana, 'He knew Oriental as well as European languages, and he was an expert in history, economics, and above all, finance.'[5]

When the First World War broke out in 1914, said Svetlana, Svanidze 'was in Germany and was immediately interned. The Germans released him after the revolution, and he returned to his native Georgia. He quickly became the People's Commissar of Finance and a member of the Party's Central Committee there.'[6] However, in 1919 he was 'forced by the authorities to leave independent Georgia'.[7]

The Independent Republic of Georgia existed from May 1918 to February 1921.

Svanidze 'worked for the Soviet Foreign Office in the years 1920–1921 and then served as People's Commissar for Finances of the Georgian SSR [Soviet Socialist Republic] and Transcaucasian SFSR [Russian Soviet Federative Socialist Republic] in the years 1921–1922. In 1924 he was appointed Soviet Trade Envoy to Germany and, upon his return to the Soviet Union in 1935, he became Deputy Chairman of the Soviet State Bank. At the same time, Svanidze continued his scholarship; he founded the *Journal of Ancient History*, studied the Alarodian languages, and translated into Russian the medieval Georgian poet Shota Rustaveli.'[8]

Svetlana said of Svanidze, 'He was one of the old Marxists who were highly educated and at home in the culture of Europe.'[9]

Of Alexander's wife, Maria, Svetlana stated that she '"was from a well-to-do" family. She had been educated in St Petersburg and at the music conservatory in Tiflis and was a singer with the Tiflis opera. She was from a wealthy Jewish family, the Koronas, who were of Spanish extraction.'[10]

'Uncle Alexander held out' against his interrogators. 'He refused to "confess" or "ask forgiveness". But he paid for his courage and dignity and restraint.' Alexander was shot on 20 August 1941. 'When the sentence that had been carried out against Uncle Alexander was read to my Aunt Maria [his wife], she dropped dead of a heart attack.'[11]

Stalin's sister-in-law, Maria Svanidze

Maria Svanidze ('Mariko', to avoid confusion), was secretary to Abel S. Yenukidze, a member of the Central Committee in Moscow.

Mariko was also arrested, said Svetlana, and she 'soon died in prison [in early 1942]'.[12]

Stalin's sister-in-law, Anna Redens (née Alliluyeva), and her husband, Stanislav F. Redens

Stanislav Redens 'was a colleague of Dzerzhinsky's' said Svetlana, 'and an old experienced Checkist'.[13] Felix E. Dzerzhinsky was Director of the Cheka (1917–22), and of its successors the GPU (1922–1923), which was renamed the OGPU (1923–1934), and Redens was a key member of the secret police.

The Cheka was the secret police organisation that combatted counter-revolution and sabotage, while the OGPU (Joint State Political Directorate under the Council of People's Commissars of the USSR), was the secret police of the Soviet Union from 1923 to 1934.[14]

'Redens began to work for the newly-established Cheka in 1918,' during the Russian Civil War. 'He was energetically involved in dekulakisation in Ukraine, serving as the head of the Odessa Cheka.' Subsequently, he 'held important positions in the Crimean GPU in 1922–1923'. In 1928 he was 'made a chief of the Transcaucasian GPU'.

The GPU was the State Political Directorate, the Intelligence Service and Secret Police of the Russian Soviet Federative Socialist Republic (RSFSR) from 6 February 1922, to 29 December 1922, and the Soviet Union from 29 December 1922, until 15 November 1923.[15]

In 1931, Redens 'was appointed the OGPU head in the Belorussian SSR and then in the Ukrainian SSR. During his tenure in Ukraine, Redens gained fame for a crackdown on farmers, which contributed to the "Holodomor" [Ukrainian for famine], the starvation of millions of Ukrainians as part of a larger famine across the Soviet Union. In January 1933 he was recalled to Moscow and placed in charge of the NKVD units in the Moscow Oblast' where he 'spearheaded purges following Sergei Kirov's assassination in 1934'.[16] More will be said about Soviet politician and Bolshevik revolutionary Sergei Kirov later.

In 1937, Redens 'was elected to the Supreme Soviet of the Soviet Union' and in 1938 he was 'appointed as People's Commissar for Internal Affairs of the Kazakh Soviet Socialist Republic'.[17]

The Supreme Soviet was the governing council of the USSR and its highest legislative authority.[18]

Of Stanislav Redens, Pavel Alliluyev, and Alexander Svanidze, Svetlana declared: 'All of them were honourable men. They were all open, direct, and honest with my father. None of them tried to play on his weaknesses – they had known him too long. They didn't try to deceive him – they thought it neither necessary nor possible. And each of them was the loser for it.'[19] This was undoubtedly true of both Alliluyev and Svanidze. As for Redens, he was an integral part of the hideous Soviet state terror apparatus: a fact of which Svetlana may not have been fully aware.

Regarding their arrests, said Svetlana, 'How could such a thing happen? How could my father do it? The only thing I know is that it couldn't have been his idea. But if a skilful flatterer like Beria whispered slyly in his ear that "these people are against you", that there was "compromising material!" and "dangerous connections", such as trips abroad, my father was capable of believing it.'[20]

This was a reference to Lavrenti Beria, Chief of the NKVD, Stalin's notorious secret police.

'Mama's sister [Anna] was forbidden to visit us children. Her brother, Paul [Pavel Alliluyev] died of a heart attack, shaken by the arrests of his relations and numerous friends, for whom he had vainly pleaded with my father. His widow was forbidden to see us. The old people, my mother's parents, were to all intents and purposes deprived of the possibility of seeing my father. He wanted no questions about the fate of "disgraced relatives" whose destruction no one but he could have sanctioned.'[21]

On 22 November 1938, Stanislav Redens, Anna's husband, was arrested. Shortly afterwards, said Svetlana, 'My Aunt Anna and her children came to Moscow. Unlike the wives of others who had vanished, she was allowed to keep her apartment. But she was no longer permitted to come to our house. Being only eleven at the time, I couldn't make out what had happened. Where had everybody gone? Why was the house so empty? The vague rumours to the effect that Uncle Stanislav was a bad man didn't make any sense. I merely became more and more aware how empty and deserted the house was and that I have nothing left but school and my kind nurse.'[22] Svetlana's nurse was Alexandra Bychkova.

In December 1948, said Svetlana, 'a new wave of arrests swallowed and sent back to prison those who had already served ten-year sentences starting in 1937'. Early in that same month her Aunt, Anna Redens, widow of Slanislav, who had been executed on 21 January 1940, was also arrested.[23] 'She came back six years later in the spring of 1954. She had spent part of the time in solitary confinement, but mostly she'd been in the prison hospital. The curse of heredity – the schizophrenia that plagued my mother's family – had caught up with her.'[24]

But why had Anna been victimised? 'I knew that my father had been irritated by the *Memoirs* of Anna Sergeyevna Redens,' said Svetlana.[25]

Svetlana stated that her grandmother, Olga Alliluyeva, 'could never understand why her daughter Anna should be in prison, and she was tormented by it'.[26]

'Anna Redens died in August 1964 in a section of the Kremlin hospital located outside Moscow. After prison she had a great fear of locked doors, but despite her protests she was locked up one night in a hospital ward. The next morning, she was found dead.'[27]

Svetlana stated, in regard to the arrest of her Aunt Anna, and of her Aunt Yevgenia, wife of Pavel Alliluyev, who was also arrested and imprisoned, that 'the two elderly women had no connection at all with politics. But what the aunts knew, of course, was that Stalin was systematically having members of his own family murdered!'

Svetlana reflected bitterly on her father: 'Nothing stopped him from arresting two elderly widows, who had already suffered sufficiently and whose health was poor. There is no doubt that he remembered how close they have been to all that had happened in our family, that they knew everything about Mama's suicide and the letter she had written before her death.'[28]

Stalin's brother-in-law, Pavel Alliluyev, and his wife, Yevgenia (née Zemlyanitsyn)

Svetlana said that, in 1938, 'Uncle Pavel came to my father again and again to plead for colleagues of his in the army who'd been swallowed up in the giant wave. It never did any good.' That autumn, 'Pavel went to Sochi on vacation, and it was bad for his weak heart. When he got back, he found that every one of his colleagues had disappeared. There had been so many arrests that it was as though the place had been swept by a broom. Pavel dropped dead of a heart attack in his office.'[29] The date was 2 November 1938.

Her Uncle Pavel Alliluyev 'was a soldier who had had considerable experience in the Civil War, on the General Staff, and in the Military Academy,' said Svetlana.[30]

'Towards the end,' said Svetlana, 'Uncle Pavel [Anna's brother] tried to see my father to [get him to] intercede for other people. My Aunt Anna said later that he and my father even had a quarrel; my father wouldn't tolerate the slightest attempt to change his mind about anybody. Once he had cast out of his heart someone he had known a long time; once he had mentally relegated that someone to the ranks of his enemies, it was impossible to talk to him about that person any more. He was constitutionally incapable of the reversal that would turn a fancied enemy back into a friend. Any effort to persuade him to do so only made him furious.'[31]

'The outcome was that Yevgenia Alliluyeva got ten years of solitary confinement, from which my father's death released her [and Anna] six years later.'[32]

Why was Yevgenia victimised? She maintained, said Svetlana, 'that, as far as she was concerned, Beria could not forgive her a personal insult. Having a sharp tongue, she had once, in a large company, in my father's presence, made fun of the crude way in which he [Beria] made advances to women. Beria had felt foolish, everyone had laughed, and this he had remembered.' In other words, the aforementioned victims had evidently been victimised, not because they had offended Stalin, but because they had offended Beria![33]

Also, Stalin himself had been 'annoyed that my Uncle Paul's [Pavel's] widow Yevgenia, had remarried, soon after his death, an engineer, a Jew.' This was Nikolai Molochnikov. 'Her second husband had been arrested with her. "They knew too much. They babbled a lot. It played into the hands of our enemies," was the way my father explained the arrests to me.'[34] What they knew, of course, was that Stalin was systematically having members of his own family murdered![35]

In *Twenty Letters to a Friend*, written in July/August 1963, a decade after the death of her father, Svetlana stated as follows, 'Both my aunts, Evgenia [Yevgenia] Alliluyeva, Pavel's widow, and Anna Alliluyeva, Redens's widow and my mother's sister, are back from prison. The Svanidzes' son, who is my age, is back from exile in Kazakhstan.'

Alexander and Maria Svanidze's son's given name was 'Johnreed', in honour of the eponymous US journalist John Reed, who went to Russia in 1917 and wrote *Ten Days That Shook The World*, an eyewitness account of the October 1917 Revolution. 'When he was little,' said Svetlana, 'we all called him Johnny or Johnik, but now he's Ivan Alexandrovich.'[36]

Johnreed had denounced his father, Alexander (executed in 1941), in order to save himself, but he was sent to the Gulag anyway. He was released after the death of Stalin in 1953. Johnreed 'was lucky enough to survive and is still alive today'.[37] So wrote Svetlana in summer 1963. In summary, said Svetlana of her father, 'Once he accepted the premise that X was his enemy, the premise became axiomatic, and no matter what the facts might be, they had to be made to fit. At this point – and this is where his cruel, implacable nature showed itself – the past ceased to exist for him. Years of friendship and fighting side-by-side in the common cause might as well never have been. Difficult as it is to understand, he could wipe it all out at a stroke – and X would be doomed.'[38]

Chapter 23

Others Known to Svetlana who 'Disappeared'

Apart from family members, other people whom Svetlana knew to have disappeared included the following:

Sergei Kirov, who was head of the Communist Party in Leningrad and a member of the Politburo. Kirov 'was a great friend of the family from way back,' said Svetlana, 'probably from their early days in the Caucasus. He knew the Alliluyevs exceedingly well and was very fond of my mother. After my mother died, Kirov would come to see my father at Sochi [city of the Black Sea, where Stalin had his summer residence], and they used to take me on outings. Kirov used to *live* in our house. He was one of us, an old colleague, and a friend. My father liked him and was attached to him.'

'Kirov spent his last summer, that of 1934, with us as in previous years. Then, in December, Nikolayev shot him.' This was Leonid Nikolayev, First Secretary of the Leningrad branch of the Communist Party. But who had instigated the murder? Svetlana, who generally tried to avoid seeing the worst in her father, said, 'wouldn't it be more logical to link his killing with the name of Beria rather than with that of my father, as is done by transparent hints [i.e. insinuations] today?'[1] 'I can't imagine … that Kirov would ever have allowed Beria's election to the Central Committee,' said Svetlana, who clearly believed that this was why he was murdered.[2]

'Sergo Ordzhonikidze, another of our old friends, died in 1936 [sic],' said Svetlana. Ordzhonikidze was a doctor, revolutionary, and Soviet politician. He had committed suicide on 18 February 1937. 'I expect that this too, was a result of Beria's machinations.'[3]

In 1942, said Svetlana, 'a great many people in camps [the Gulag] were shot, [even] though they might have been sentenced only to exile, hard labour, and long prison terms'.[4]

In 1948 the following were victims of a 'new wave of arrests': Solomon Lozovsky, high-ranking official in the Soviet government (Lozovsky was executed on 12 August 1952); Lina Shtern, scientist and academician; and Polina Molotov, who was 'an old and close friend of my mother's'.[5]

In late 1948, said Svetlana, 'J. G. Morozov, the father of my first husband [Grigory], was arrested. Next there was a campaign against people who were called "cosmopolitan", and a whole new group of people were arrested. They even arrested Molotov's wife, undaunted by the thought of the terrible blow they were inflicting on Molotov himself. Lozovsky was arrested and [Solomon M.] Mikhoels [Jewish artistic director of the State Yiddish Theatre in Moscow] was killed. All of them were lumped together in a single alleged "Zionist centre".'[6] In other words, Svetlana saw Stalin's anti-Semitism as being the reason for these arrests.

Stalin 'saw enemies everywhere', said Svetlana. 'It had reached the point of being pathological, of persecution mania, and it was all a result of being lonely and desolate.'[7] In fact, the reason was Stalin's paranoia, as will be seen.

Alexei Alexandrovich Kuznetsov was First Secretary of the Leningrad Regional Party Committee. In March 1946 he was removed from his post, and in January 1949 he was arrested.[8] Kuznetsov had become caught up in the so-called 'Leningrad Affair' (February 1949 to March 1953), whereby a number of prominent politicians and others based in Leningrad were falsely accused of embezzlement, which was considered to be treason.

'Over two thousand people from the Leningrad city government and regional authorities' were arrested, together with 'many industrial managers, scientists and university professors', and exiled from their city.[9]

Moscow and Leningrad were described as 'two competing power centres in the Soviet Union. Researchers argue that the motivation behind the cases was Joseph Stalin's fear of competition from the younger and popular Leningrad leaders – who had been fêted as heroes', following the siege of Leningrad by the Nazis (8 September 1941 to 27 January 1944).

The prosecutions commenced on 30 September 1950 and the following were accused of 'embezzlement of the Soviet State budget', found guilty, and sentenced to death: Nikolai Voznesensky, Chairman of the State Planning Committee, Gosplan; Mikhail Rodionov, Chairman of the Russian Soviet Federative Socialist Republic (RSFSR) Council of Ministers; Alexei Kuznetsov (already mentioned); Pyotr Popkov, First Secretary of the Party organisation in Leningrad; Yakov F. Kapustin, Second Secretary of the Leningrad Municipal Committee of the Party; and Peter G. Lazutin, Chairman of the Leningrad City Soviet.[10]

Physician and academician Vladimir Vinogradov 'who'd looked after my father for many years, was now in jail,' said Svetlana, as her father lay on his deathbed.[11] The doctor had been arrested on 4 November the previous year, 1952.[12]

Finally, said Svetlana, 'Many people have come back, thousands and thousands who managed somehow to survive. The return of so many people from prison and exile is a great historic turning point. The scale on which the dead have come back to life is difficult to imagine.'[13]

Chapter 24

Stalin's Sons, Yakov and Vasily

Yakov Iosifovich Dzhugashvili (born 31 March 1907), Stalin's son by Ekaterina (his first wife), and Svetlana's half-brother.

Stalin, said Svetlana, 'had always treated Yakov unfairly and with a coldness he did not deserve.'[1] 'Yakov always felt like a stepchild with my father, but not with my mother, whose stepson he actually was.' As for Yakov, 'He loved her very much.'[2]

In 1925, Yakov married Zoya Gunina, daughter of an Orthodox priest. The couple had one child, a daughter, who died aged only 8 months. They were divorced within 2 years. 'His first marriage was a tragic one,' said Svetlana. 'My father didn't even want to hear about the marriage, much less help. He bullied Yakov and picked on him.'[3] Svetlana spoke of Yakov's 'character and his entire scrupulous, honourable, incorruptible approach to life'. But her father, 'had no use for him', she said.[4]

'In 1928, or it may have been 1929,' continued Svetlana, 'in despair over the attitude of my father who wouldn't have anything to do with him, Yakov went to the kitchen of our Kremlin apartment and shot himself. My mother was horrified.'[5] This event occurred 'in the kitchen next to his little room. The bullet passed right through him, but he was ill for a long time. My nurse later told me that after this my father treated him worse than before, heaping contempt on him for being a "weakling".'[6] 'Ha! He couldn't even shoot straight!' Stalin sneered.[7]

In 1935, Yakov became engaged to Olga P. Golysheva, a fellow student at the Moscow Aviation School. On 10 January 1936 she bore him a son, Yevgeny Dzhugashvili.

On 18 February 1938, Yakov married Yudith ('Yulia') Meltzer, a Jewish Ukrainian ballerina from Odessa. The fact that Yudith was Jewish, of course, infuriated Stalin. She bore him a daughter, Galina, born 19 February 1938.

On 23 June 1941, the day after the outbreak of war [i.e. the invasion of the Soviet Union by Nazi Germany and her Axis allies on 22 June], said Svetlana, 'My oldest brother, Yakov left for the front with his battery and his graduating class at the Frunze Military Academy.'[8]

The Axis Powers were Germany, Italy, and Japan. Originally called the Rome–Berlin Axis, this was a military coalition that fought against the Allies in the Second World War, having signed the 'Tripartite Pact' on 27 September 1940.

In late August 1941, Svetlana learned from her father that Yakov had been taken prisoner. 'Somehow,' she said, her father had 'gotten the idea that someone had "tricked" Yakov and betrayed him intentionally. Mightn't Yulia (Yudith) have been a party to it? So Yulia was arrested in Moscow in the fall of 1941.'[9]

After Yudith's arrest, said Svetlana, she 'started wondering about something that had never occurred to me before; namely, was my father always right after all? It was blasphemy even to think such a thing then. In the eyes of everyone around me my father's name was linked with the will to win the war, with the hope of victory and an end to the war. These were my first feeble stirrings of doubt.'[10]

Yudith 'was in prison until the spring of 1943, when it turned out she'd had nothing to do with Yakov's capture'.[11] 'Gulia [Galina] was reunited with her mother,' said Svetlana, after Yudith 'had spent two years in prison under the statute providing for punishment of relatives of those who have been taken prisoner'.[12]

'After Stalingrad, in the winter of 1943–44 my father said to me suddenly, during one of our rare meetings, "The Germans have proposed that we exchange one of their prisoners for Yasha [Yakov]. They want me to make a deal with them! I won't do it. War is war."[13] He spoke to me about Yakov again in the summer of 1945 when the war was already over. "The Germans shot Yasha," said Stalin. He had been a prisoner for four years.[14] Everyone who was taken prisoner, even if they'd been wounded as Yakov was,' said Svetlana, 'was considered to have "surrendered voluntarily to the enemy". The government thereby washed its hands of millions of its own officers and men during the war and refused to have anything to do with them.[15]

'To my father the fact that Jacob [Yakov] had become a prisoner of war was nothing but a "disgrace" before the whole world. In the USSR the news was kept under cover, both during the war and after, although the press in the rest of the world was writing about it. And when a foreign correspondent officially asked for information on the subject, my father said that "in Hitler's camps there are no Russian prisoners of war, only Russian traitors, and we shall do away with them when the war is over." About Jacob he said, "I have no son called Jacob."'[16]

On 14 April 1943, in the Sachsenhausen concentration camp in Oranienburg, Germany, Yakov committed suicide by throwing himself against an electrified barbed wire perimeter fence.

Vasily Iosifovich Stalin (born 21 March 1921), Stalin's son by Nadezhda (his second wife), and Svetlana's brother.

The odds were against Vasily from the start. Said Svetlana, Stalin 'in the fashion of the Caucasus was forever giving his children wine', and as her mother Nadezhda 'saw it, this was bound to end badly'.[17] And for Vasily, as the tragedy unfolded, his mother's words proved all too prophetic!

Vasily attended the Moscow Model School No. 5, where 'his teachers and the head of his school bombarded my father with complaints about his behaviour and his lack of progress'. In 1938, Vasily enrolled at the Kachinsky Military Aviation School, Kacha, Crimea. He completed his training in 1940 and was given the rank of air force lieutenant.

In December 1940 Vasily married Galina Bourdonskaya, an art student at Moscow University. In 1941 she bore him a son, Alexander, and in 1943 a daughter, Nadezhda. The marriage did not last.

In August 1941, Vasily was sent to the front, where he took part in twenty-nine combat missions. In spring 1942 he was sent to Moscow and 'given a role inspecting conditions of the air force'.[18]

In spring 1943, Stalin accused Vasily and Svetlana of turning Zubalovo 'into a den of iniquity. Vasily was banished' from the premises, 'as I was, for "moral depravity". In addition, Vasily was given ten days in a punishment cell by personal order of my father in his capacity as Minister of Defence.'[19]

By the end of the war in Europe in May 1945, Vasily, now aged 24, had reached the rank of lieutenant general. In 1946 he married Ekaterina, daughter of Semyon K. Timoshenko, Soviet military commander and Marshal of the Soviet Union. She bore him a daughter, Svetlana, in 1947 and a son, Vasily, in 1949. Again, the marriage did not last.

In 1947, Vasily was 'made Chief of Aviation of the Moscow Military District. Yet everyone knew he was an alcoholic. He was so ill he could no longer fly his own plane.'[20] In 1950 Vasily married Soviet swimming champion Kapitolina Vasilyeva.

In 1952, Stalin ordered that Vasily be 'removed from his post'. He had disobeyed orders and his disobedience had led to several aircraft making a crash landing during a fly-past on May Day over Red Square.[21]

Stalin died on 5 March 1953. Up until then, said Svetlana, everyone had 'spoiled and corrupted' Vasily, 'just as long as they needed him. But once my father was dead and they didn't need him anymore, they abandoned and forgot him.'[22] Vasily was 'attending the General Staff Academy at the time'. However, he was deemed to be 'no longer capable of study – he was an alcoholic. Those responsible couldn't have cared less about his strengths and weaknesses, any more than they cared what his real abilities were, their one thought was to curry favour with my father.'[23]

Vasily was now 'a retired general with nothing to do but sit at home and drink', said Svetlana. He'd thrown his third wife [Kapitolina] out and persuaded his second wife [Ekaterina] to come back. By now he was so impossible, however, that even she left. He was completely alone.'[24]

On 28 April 1953, Vasily was arrested 'after a drinking bout' with foreign diplomats. He was put on trial. 'In the pre-trial investigation the shady deals, the spending, the exploitation of power and rank beyond any reasonable limit' and the 'high-level intrigues that had resulted in the arrest of some people and the deaths of others' all 'came to light. A military collegium sentenced him to eight years in jail.' By this time, Vasily had 'lost sight of who he was or where he was. Finally, they took pity on him. He was sent to a military hospital in the winter of 1954–55' and 'then to the Barvikha Sanatorium' in the village of Barvikha near Moscow.[25] However, Vasily 'started threatening people and demanding the impossible all over again'. He was therefore detained in the Vladimir Prison in order for him to complete his sentence.[26]

In January 1960, Vasily was released.[27] Subsequently, because 'his behaviour had been unsatisfactory', he was imprisoned once more, this time in the Lefortovo Prison, Moscow. In the spring of 1961, he was released 'on grounds of ill-health'.[28]

Vasily died on 19 March 1962 at the age of 40, after 'a strenuous drinking bout with some Georgians', after which he 'never regained consciousness'.[29]

Vasily's son, Alexander, and his daughter, Nadezhda (by his first marriage to Galina), attended the funeral, 'accompanied by his third wife, Kapitolina. She was the only real friend he had,' said Svetlana.[30]

To summarise, Stalin could undoubtedly have saved the life of his first (legitimate) son, Yakov, a prisoner-of-war of the Nazis; and he was almost certainly responsible for the death of his second son, Vasily, from the effects of alcoholism.

Chapter 25

Empathy: Simon Baron-Cohen

In his book, *Zero Degrees of Empathy: A New Theory of Human Cruelty and Kindness*, published in 2011, British clinical psychologist Simon Baron-Cohen begins by redefining the traditional and outdated concept of 'evil'. Instead, he equates 'evil' to an 'erosion of empathy'.[1]

'Empathy' is defined as the ability to understand and share the feelings of another.[2] 'Empathy makes the other person feel valued,' said Baron-Cohen, 'enabling them to feel their thoughts and feelings have been heard, acknowledged, and respected.'[3]

Baron-Cohen used the bell curve (a graph of normal distribution, with a large rounded peak tapering away at each end[4]) to explain that 'we all lie somewhere on an empathy spectrum (from high to low). People said to be 'evil' or cruel are simply at one extreme of the empathy spectrum. We can all be lined up along this spectrum of individual differences, based on how much empathy we have.'[5]

Baron-Cohen went so far as to develop 'a scale with which to measure empathy across the age range', and he called this measure of empathy in an individual, his or her 'empathy quotient' (EQ).[6] 'The higher your score the better your empathy.[7] At Level 0 [zero], an individual has no empathy at all.' Fortunately, however, 'not all people at Level 0 do cruel things to others' or 'have any wish to harm others'.[8]

Can lack of empathy be explained in terms of some abnormality in the brain? Yes, said Baron-Cohen. 'There is a consensus in neuroscience' that although 'the *whole* brain' is not involved in empathy, 'at least ten interconnected brain regions *are* involved (and more may await discovery)'.[9]

For the person with a zero degree of empathy 'other people's thoughts and feelings are just off your radar. It leaves you doomed to do your own thing, in your own little bubble, not just oblivious of other people's feelings and thoughts but oblivious to the idea that there might even *be* other points of view. The consequence is that you believe 100 per cent in the rightness of your own ideas and beliefs, and judge anyone who does not hold your beliefs as wrong, or stupid.'[10]

The 'psychopath' (psychopathy is now termed 'antisocial personality disorder'), said Baron-Cohen, is an example of a person with a zero degree of empathy. 'In this case, there is a willingness to do *whatever it takes* to satisfy their desires. This might take the form of a hair-trigger violent reaction to the smallest thing that thwarts them. Or it might take the form of cold, calculated cruelty. Sometimes the mindless aggression is not triggered by a perceived threat but by the need to dominate, to get what one wants.' Such people show 'a complete detachment from another person's feelings', and possibly even derive pleasure 'at seeing someone else suffer'.[11]

Did Stalin have a shred of empathy in his body? A rare occasion on which he demonstrated such a quality was when his first wife, Ekaterina, was terminally ill with typhus. The fact that she died in his arms, as already mentioned, clearly indicates that he was aware of her suffering and anxious to comfort her, despite the risk to himself of catching this deadly disease, of which he was surely aware.

In reality, however, whatever empathy Stalin possessed was overridden by far more powerful forces within him, as will be seen.

Chapter 26

For Svetlana the World Closes in

When her mother, Nadezhda, died on 9 November 1932, said Svetlana, 'Our carefree life, so full of gaiety and useful pastimes, fell apart. Our governess, Natalia Konstantinova, whose lessons in German, drawing, and reading I'll never forget as long as I live, left right away. Whether she left voluntarily or was dismissed I don't know, but the rhythm of our studies was broken.'[1]

'Starting in 1937, someone – I don't know whether it was my father, [or Nikolai] Vlasik [head of Stalin's personal security], or some committee of the secret police – decided that a plain clothes man was to follow at my heels everywhere I went: to the country, the theatre, to and from school every day.'[2]

By 1937 or 1938, when Svetlana was aged 11 or 12, she said, 'except for my nurse, there was no one left of the people my mother had found, of the people who loved and respected her, who remembered and still tried to adhere to her ways of doing things. As the years went by all of them gradually vanished.' They included Elizaveta, the cook; Tanya, the kitchen assistant, and the housekeeper, Carolina Till.[3]

In September 1937 or 1938, a new housekeeper was appointed – Alexandra Nakashidze – who was also a 'Lieutenant of the State Security Forces.[4] Alexandra threw out the cupboard and everything in it, without stopping to realise that she was throwing out my most cherished childhood mementos. She did the same with my brother's room and took away every reminder of our comfortable old apartment where everything was my [late] mother's creation and which my mother had adapted to our needs and convenience.

'Everything vanished, and we came to realise that under the new system everything in the house was considered state property and anything old and dilapidated would be "inventoried" each year and carted off God knows where.'[5]

Soon after this, said Svetlana, 'my aunts were barred from our Kremlin apartment [and] Yakov [her half-brother] and my grandparents were the only ones still allowed to come there'.[6]

For Svetlana, the last straw was in 1939 'when I heard there was a plot afoot to get rid of my nurse', Alexandra Bychkova. 'I set up an outcry. My father couldn't stand tears,' and he relented.[7] 'After my mother's death my nurse was the only stable, unchanging thing left. She was the bulwark of home and family, of what, if it hadn't been for her, would have gone out of my life forever.'[8] Nonetheless, said Svetlana, 'No household had such an official, even quasi-military atmosphere as ours. None was so subject to the orders of the secret police.'[9]

It was in the winter of 1942–43, said Svetlana, when she was aged 16, that she met filmmaker Alexei Yakovlevich Kapler, and 'because of him my relationship with my father was ruined'.[10] 'To me, Kapler was the cleverest, kindest, most wonderful person on earth. He radiated knowledge and all its fascination. He helped me discover the world of art, which was new to me and which I was only beginning to explore.'[11] In late October 1942, said Svetlana, 'Vasily brought Kapler to Zubalovo. Vasily was advising Kapler on a projected film about pilots in the air force.'[12]

However, on 1 March 1943, just as Kapler was about to leave for Tashkent 'to make a movie on the partisans of Belorussia called *In Defence of the Fatherland*', he was detained and taken to Moscow's notorious Lubyanka Prison.[13]

Stalin had arranged for Svetlana's telephone calls from Kapler to be intercepted and he now demanded that she hand over his love letters to her. 'Your Kapler is a British spy,' he told her. 'He's under arrest.'

'"But I love him!" I protested at last, having found my tongue again.'

'"Love!" screamed my father, with a hatred of the very word [which] I can scarcely convey. And for the first time in his life he slapped me across the face, twice. Apparently, the fact that Kapler was a Jew was what bothered him most of all.' The outcome was that Kapler 'was sent to the north for five years'. In other words, to the Gulag![14]

Meanwhile, Svetlana enrolled at Moscow University to study history, social sciences, and economics.[15] Here she met Grigory Morozov, a student at the Institute of International Relations. They were married in 1944.[16]

On 9 May 1945, Svetlana heard on the radio that the war was over.[17] (The war in Europe had ended on 7 May 1945.) On 22 May her son, Josef, was born. However, her marriage to Morozov only lasted for three years.[18]

When Kapler was released in 1948, he visited Moscow, even though he had been forbidden by the authorities to do so. Whereupon, he was detained again, and 'sentenced to work in the mines in the terrible [prison] camps near Inta [north-western Russia]'.

Svetlana graduated in 1949 and in that same year she married Russian chemist Yuri Andreyevich Zhdanov.[19] On 5 May 1950 she gave birth to a daughter, Yekaterina ('Katya').[20] In 1952, Svetlana and Zhdanov divorced.

Svetlana proceeded to take a Master's degree in Russian Literature. From 1953 to 1965, she taught Soviet Literature and English Language at the university before joining Moscow's Progress publishing house (specialising in English-language books on Marxism-Leninism). Here she translated Russian literature into English. However, even though she possessed the qualifications to become a teacher, she 'never took that road, forever dreaming of becoming a writer, instead'.[21]

In 1952 the Party was renamed the Communist Party of the Soviet Union. That winter, Nikita Khrushchev (who was appointed First Secretary of the Party of the Soviet Union in September 1953), witnessed, at first hand, Stalin's maltreatment of his daughter, Svetlana: 'It happened in the last year of his life. Stalin had invited us all to the Nearby Dacha [at Kuntsevo] to celebrate the New Year with him. I would say that the general mood of the Party was good. Then Svetlanka [affectionate form of 'Svetlana'] appeared. I don't know if she'd been summoned or if she came on her own. She found herself in the middle of a flock of people older than she, to put it mildly. As soon as this sober young woman arrived, Stalin made her dance. I could see she was tired.'

'She hardly moved while dancing. She danced for a short time and tried to stop, but her father still insisted. She went over and stood next to the record player, leaning her shoulder against the wall. Stalin came over to her, and I joined them. We stood there together. Stalin was lurching about. He said, "Well, go on Svetlanka, dance! You're the hostess, so dance!" She said, "I've already danced, Papa. I'm tired." With that, Stalin grabbed her by the forelock of her hair with his fist and pulled. I could see her face turning red and tears welling up in her eyes. I felt so sorry for Svetlanka. He pulled harder and dragged her back onto the dance floor.'[22]

Continued Khrushchev, 'It was as though the devil himself held a string attached to Stalin's main nerve, and no one knew when the devil would give the string a jerk, sending Stalin into one of his fits of rage.'[23]

In July 1953, Kapler was set free, Stalin having died four months previously on 5 March. In 1954 'at the Second Congress of Soviet Writers in the Kremlin, I ran into Kapler in the glitter of St George's Hall', said Svetlana. 'It was eleven years since we had seen one another.'[24]

Writing in 1963, Svetlana stated that, 'Alexei Kapler is all right now and is living in Moscow. He's writing film scripts, giving seminars, and teaching at the Institute of Cinematography.' This was 'after ten years of exile and prison camps'.[25]

Chapter 27

For Svetlana the Light Dawns

Looking back, said Svetlana, 'For twenty-seven years I was witness to the spiritual deterioration of my own father: watching day after day how everything human in him left him and how gradually, he turned into a grim monument to his own self.' However, she confessed that she had been brainwashed. 'But my generation was trained to think that this monument was the embodiment of all that was most beautiful in the ideals of communism, it's living personification.'[1]

Svetlana's mother, Nadezhda, died on 9 November 1932. 'For me the ten years after my mother's death,' she said, 'passed in monotonous isolation. I lived in the Kremlin as in a fortress, in which the only kind being [person] near me was my nurse. I was unable then to grasp what was going on in the country, but the cruel tragedies of those years didn't spare our family.'[2]

Svetlana spoke of, 'Kremlin walls all around me, secret police in the house, in the kitchen, at school. And over it all a wasted, obdurate man, fenced in from his former colleagues, his old friends, from all those who had been close to him, in fact from the entire world, who with his accomplices had turned the country into a prison, in which everyone with a breath of spirit and mind was being extinguished; a man who aroused fear and hatred in millions of men – this was my father.'[3]

Referring to Sergei Kirov (murdered on 1 December 1934); Sergo Ordzhonikidze (committed suicide on 18 February 1937); and Nikolai Bukharin (executed on 15 March 1938), Svetlana declared, 'The deaths of such close friends of my mother's … were seen at the time as the destruction of everything that had to do with her. This is how it appeared to the family and the members of the household.'[4]

Said Svetlana, her father 'always killed people "indirectly": all those millions whom he had sent to their death at the hands of his agents. He himself would turn away and forget about them, never giving a thought as to how they had perished.'[5] Svetlana was right. Stalin always left his henchmen to do his dirty work for him.

'It was impossible for a schoolgirl of twelve and thirteen to grasp all that was happening. At the same time, it was inconceivable to think of "Uncle Alyosha" [Alexander Svanidze], "Aunt Marusya" [Maria, Alexander's wife], and "Uncle Stakh" [Stanislav Redens] as "enemies of the people", which is what even schoolchildren were repeatedly told by the official propaganda of the time. I could only assume that they must have become the victims of some frightful mix-up, which even Father himself could not disentangle. Many years had to go by before everything that had taken place, not only in our family but all over the country, could range itself in my consciousness with my father's name, before I could realise that all of it had been done by him. In those years I just couldn't conceive of his being capable of condemning to death people whose innocence and decency were well known to him. Only later, as a young adult, did several discoveries convince me of this.[6]

'After the war Father hardly ever stayed in the Kremlin apartment, preferring his dacha, and we seldom saw one another. I was no longer the beloved daughter, while my filial love and respect for him had vanished like smoke.'[7]

Had her mother, Nadezhda, lived, said Svetlana, 'I often wonder what sort of life she'd have had. It couldn't have been good. Sooner or later, she'd have sided with the opposition to my father. She couldn't have looked on in silence as all the best of her good old friends perished – Bukharin, Yenukidze, Redens, and both the Svanidzes. She could never have survived it.'[8]

On 19 December 1966, Svetlana left Russia to begin a new life in the USA. 'I was forty years old,' she said. 'Twenty-seven of those years I had lived under a heavy weight; the next thirteen had been spent gradually liberating myself from it. In the USSR those twenty-seven years (1926–53) have been named by historians the "Period of Stalinism" – a time of single-handed despotism, bloody terror, economic hardships, the cruellest of wars, and an ideological reaction.[9]

'To me, in my earlier years, communism was an unshakable stronghold. Unshakable remained my father's authority and the belief that he was right in everything without exception. But later I began to doubt that he was always right. I became more and more convinced of his senseless cruelty. The theories and dogmas of Marxism-Leninism began to wither away and fade in front of my eyes. The Party lost its heroic halo of righteousness.[10]

'Little by little, it became more than obvious not only that my father had been a despot and had brought about a bloody terror, destroying millions of innocent people, but that the whole system *which had made it possible* was profoundly corrupt; that all its participants could not escape responsibility, no matter how hard they tried. And it was then that the whole edifice, whose foundation rested on a lie, crumbled from top to bottom.

'When you have, once again, sight, it is impossible to feign blindness. To me, this process came neither easily nor quickly. It is still evolving. My generation was far too ignorant of its country's history in general, of the history of the revolution, of the Party. Truth had been concealed from us for too long.'[11]

Despite her new-found loathing of her father, Svetlana's love of her homeland was undiminished. 'I continue to love the beautiful land I was born in, and I bend my knees before the great Russian culture in which I was brought up: that magnificent culture that seventy years of oppression has been unable to destroy permanently.'[12]

Svetlana's manuscript, 'The Faraway Music: 1983–1986: England-USA' begins with the following quotation from US poet, Henry D. Thoreau:

> 'If the man does not keep pace
> With his companions
> Perhaps it is because he hears
> A different drummer.
> Let him step to the music he hears
> However measured or far away.'

Here she was thinking, not of her father, but of herself, for she continued, 'I have always managed to hear a different drummer.'[13] This is Svetlana saying, 'I am not a clone of my father, I am not a robot, I have my own inner store of knowledge and experiences and my own sense of morality, and I will make my own mind up on where I stand in matters of life and politics.'

In regard to socialism and Marxism, Svetlana was scathing, 'Socialism ALWAYS means for me a loss of individuality, whether it is Soviet Russian "developed" socialism, or any other brand of socialism in the world, Marxism, non-Marxism, Trotskyist, Leninist, or whatever, European or Asian.[14]

'The truth is not in the extremes, but in the moderate democratic process, which does not permit ANY dictatorship – Marxist or military of any kind – to usurp the rights of the people, to usurp peace on earth.'[15] Svetlana concluded: 'Marxism today can be installed only with the help of Soviet armaments, army, ammunitions, money, and false promises, given freely to the most poor, most desolate peoples of Asia, Africa, South America – wherever people are less educated, and full of hatred for America, only BECAUSE it is a rich country where these people cannot live. Hatred and envy breed the so-called "anti-Americanism" all over the world, and yet the young ones all over the world are reaching out towards America and her values.'[16]

Chapter 28

Professor Vladimir Bekhterev and Stalin's Paranoia

A shocking example of Stalin's cloak and dagger tactics is illustrated by his treatment of a distinguished member of the Russian medical profession.

Russian neurophysiologist and psychiatrist Vladimir Mikhailovich Bekhterev was Professor of Psychiatric Diseases at Kazan University in south-west Russia. In 1907 he founded the Bekhterev Psychoneurological Research Institute at St Petersburg.

In 1989, Russian writer Oleg Moroz gave an account of the doctor's death and of the mysterious circumstances that surrounded it.

In December 1927, Bekhterev was due to travel from Leningrad 'to Moscow to participate in the First All-Russian Congress of Neurologists and Psychiatry', of which he was a co-founder.

In the autumn of 1971, said Moroz, a conversation took place between Soviet psychiatrist Mikhail I. Buyanov and Soviet psychologist Vladimir N. Myasishchev who, in 1939, became the Director of Bekhterev's Leningrad Institute, which he 'headed for about thirty years'. Myasishchev recollected that, 'Just before leaving for Moscow,' Bekhterev 'received a telegram from the Kremlin Medical Department telling him to telephone immediately on his arrival in Moscow. Bekhterev did telephone, and then went to the Kremlin.' The date was 23 December 1927.

'Bekhterev was very late for the session of the Congress,' at which he was appointed Honorary President, 'and one of the delegates asked what had delayed him. Bekhterev replied irritably (in the presence of several people), "I was examining a paranoiac with a withered arm."'[1]

Bekhterev was correct on both counts: yes, Stalin was paranoid, and yes, he did have a withered arm: the explanation for which is as follows. According to Radzinsky, Stalin told his second wife, Nadezhda 'that a phaeton, a horse and cart [actually a light, open, four-wheeled horse-drawn carriage[2]], had run into him when he was a child and that because there was no money for a doctor his arm had not mended properly. The contusion had turned septic and as a result the arm had become crooked.' This, said Radzinsky, 'coincides with the version (dictation by him [Stalin]) which I found in his "Medical History": "Atrophy of the shoulder and elbow joints of the left arm. Result of a contusion at the age of six, followed by prolonged septic condition in the region of the elbow joint."'[3] This may well have been a case of osteomyelitis, from which Stalin was fortunate to survive in the days before antibiotics.

'After the session, Bekhterev, together with other delegates, went to the Bolshoi Theatre; there he was approached by some men who were not among the delegates and who were not known to anybody. They took him to the buffet, where he ate some sandwiches. Then his companions vanished, and no one ever saw them again.'

According to the journal *Vestnik Znaniya* ('Herald of Knowledge'), after his visit to the theatre, Bekhterev 'felt indisposed. On the morning of 24 December' he 'was visited by Professor D. A. Burmin [neuropathologist], who diagnosed a gastric disorder.'[4]

Somewhat later, when Bekhterev's condition deteriorated (according to newspapers), Burmin was joined by 'Professor Shirvinsky, Dr Konstantinovsky and others'. This time they diagnosed 'an acute gastrointestinal disorder'. Bekhterev died that evening. 'Previously,' said Buyanov, 'he had been 'physically very fit and had no complaints whatever regarding his health. His sudden death shocked everybody, and many suspected foul play.'

After Bekhterev's death 'there was a meeting of prominent medical specialists, such as Professors Rossolimo, Minor, Kramer, Gilyarovsky, Shirvinsky, Burmin, and Abrikosov, representatives of the Commissariat for Public Health, and others'. Whereupon, it was decreed that the brain of the deceased should be removed and given to the Brain Institute for research purposes, while the body 'should be cremated',[5] allegedly according to the will of the deceased.[6]

'One cannot help concluding,' said Moroz, 'that the very purpose of cremation without an autopsy was precisely to prevent clarity.' Moroz also pointed to the 'blatant absurdity of the situation', whereby 'a person dies of an "acute gastrointestinal disorder", and a post-mortem examination is performed on his brain rather than his body!'.[7]

Finally, it is significant that after Bekhterev's death, Stalin had the professor's 'name and all of his works removed from Soviet textbooks'.[8]

There can be little doubt that both the murder of Bekhterev and its subsequent cover-up were attributable to Stalin. The famous Russian neuropathologist had told the truth, and as a consequence, paid for it with his life.

Chapter 29

Suppression of the Kulaks (1929–32)

'Dekulakization' was the Soviet campaign of political repression, including arrests, deportations, or executions of millions of kulaks and their families during the 1929–32 period of the first Five-Year Plan.[1]

Stalin distinguished between the peasants – poor smallholders or agricultural labourers – on the one hand, and the kulaks – farm owners and employers of labour – on the other. 'The transition to collectivisation,' he said: 'could not be expected to take place as a simple and peaceful influx of the peasants into the collective farms, but would be accompanied by a struggle of the peasant masses against the kulaks. The kulaks would have to be defeated in open battle in full view of the peasantry, so that the peasants might see for themselves how weak the capitalist elements were. Hence, solid collectivisation inevitably entailed the elimination of the kulaks as a class.'[2]

On 27 January 1929, Stalin gave a speech on 'The Agrarian Question' to a conference of Marxist students. The intention was, he said, 'to *replace* the capitalist production of the kulaks by the socialist production of the collective farms and state farms. To this end, we, as a Party, as the Soviet power:

a) have developed an offensive along the whole front against the capitalist elements in the countryside.
b) this offensive, as you know, has yielded and continues to yield very appreciable, positive results.'

Stalin continued: 'Until recently the Party adhered to the policy of *restricting* the exploiting tendencies of the kulaks. Now, however, it was necessary 'to launch an offensive against the kulaks', which 'means that we must smash the kulaks, eliminate them as a class. To launch an offensive against the kulaks means that we must prepare for it and then strike at the kulaks, strike so hard as to prevent them from rising to their feet again.' And as he repeated the word 'kulaks' four times, one can almost sense the venom in Stalin's voice!

To Stalin, the question as to 'whether the kulaks should be permitted to join the collective farms' seemed 'ridiculous'. His answer was, 'Of course not, for they are sworn enemies of the collective-farm movement.'

The speech was full of menace. There was no question of giving the kulaks the opportunity to integrate peacefully into the collectivisation movement. Instead, they would be murdered, exiled, or left to starve.[3]

Said Svetlana, 'My father could never agree to a gradual rapprochement of socialism and the peasantry. He chose what was closer to his nature: a sharp break, with the aid of violence, the liquidation of a whole social group of the well-to-do peasantry – the so-called kulaks – virulent castigation, suppression.'[4]

As to the outcome, it was disastrous! For example, when in 1932 'the word got around that famine had broken out in the Ukraine,' said Khrushchev, 'I couldn't believe it. I'd left the Ukraine in 1929, only three years before, when the Ukraine had pulled itself up to pre-war living standards. Food having been plentiful and cheap. Yet now, we were told people were starving. It was incredible.'

But why choose to eliminate the kulaks? Why not simply integrate them into the Collective system? After all, they had valuable expertise in the field of agriculture, which could have been harnessed for the greater good. But no. For Stalin the kulaks had 'exploiting tendencies'. They were therefore a threat, and as such had become the object of his anger. They must therefore be eliminated.

An estimate of the number of kulaks who were sent to the Gulag and the number who lost their lives will be given shortly.

Chapter 30

A Purge of Politicians (1936–38)

The 'Great Purge' or 'Great Terror' was Stalin's campaign of political repression that occurred in the Soviet Union from 1936 to 1938. It included repression of the Communist Party, government officials, and the Red Army.

The purge of politicians was an attempt by Stalin to eliminate potential opposition from the left of the Party, led by Leon Trotsky, and from the right of the Party, led by Nikolai Bukharin. However, 'During that period,' said Khrushchev, 'the Party started to lose its authority and to be subservient to the NKVD.'[1]

Nikolai I. Yezhov was head of the NKVD (from September 1936 to 25 November 1938). He is described by Montefiore as 'sly, able, perceptive, and without moral boundaries'.[2] However, said Khrushchev, when Beria succeeded Yezhov in late 1938, he then proceeded to 'purge the purgers'![3]

Said Khrushchev, 'You could put together a whole book consisting of nothing but the names of the important military, Party, administrative, and diplomatic leaders – all men of the Leninist school – who were Stalin's first victims. Honest, loyal Leninists, devoted to the cause of the revolution – they were the first to go when Stalin imposed his arbitrary rule on the Party'.[4]

Soviet political and Bolshevik revolutionary Sergei Kirov, Leningrad Party Chief, Member of the Politburo, and Secretary of the Central Committee, was shot in his Leningrad office on 1 December 1934. This was allegedly on the orders of Stalin, as a pretext for a purge of politicians. It was soon after the murder, said Khrushchev, that the 'political terror started.[5] The flower of the Party was stamped out in the savage violence which erupted shortly after that scene.[6] I was personally acquainted with many victims of the political terror. They included not only politicians, but also industrialists [who were also Party members].

'I knew Treivas [not identified]. His name had been widely known in the twenties as a prominent figure in the Lenin League of Communist Youth. He was an intelligent, capable, decent man. He didn't escape the meat-mincer when the butchery began in 1937.

'Take Ivan Tarasovich Kirilkin, for instance. He was manager of the Ruchenkov mines in 1925–26 and later was made director of the Makeyev metal works, which he ran very competently. Then there was Vasily Bazulin. He did a pretty good job supervising a factory near Yuzovka. Both men perished in 1937. They disappeared off the face of the earth, without leaving so much as a trace. Nobody would tell me what had happened to either of them.'

Georgy I. Lomov 'was put in charge of coal output in the Ukraine and I used to see him frequently at his office in Kharkov. He was much respected in the Party as a man with a Party record going back to the days of the pre-revolutionary underground. But you still want to know, where is this Lomov now? The answer is – shot! No more Lomov.'

'Even the people closest to Stalin were swept up in the frenzy of the hunt. Take [Sergo] Ordzhonikidze's fate. "Comrade Sergo", as we always called him, was a popular figure. He enjoyed well-deserved respect throughout the Party. Sergo was a man of chivalrous character: much respected for his accessibility, his humanity, and his sense of justice. Sergo by no means approved of the butchery that was going on in the Party. At the beginning of 1937 he shot himself. He said it was impossible to tolerate what Stalin was doing to the Party, and he didn't have the strength to fight it any more.'[7]

Khrushchev wondered how he himself had managed to stay alive. 'I've often asked myself, how was I spared?' he said. 'I think part of the answer is that [Stalin's second wife] Nadya's [presumably favourable] reports helped determine Stalin's attitude towards me. I call it my lottery ticket. Nadezhda Sergeyeneva and I were fellow students at the Academy [Industrial Academy, Moscow]. She studied chemistry in the textile faculty, specialising in artificial fibres. She was a Party group organiser, and I used to meet with her regularly in my capacity as Secretary to the Party organisation.'[8]

But why vilify and eliminate the Leninists, when Stalin himself had been a great admirer of Lenin and his policies? And in any case, given the fact that Stalin presided over a police state with its vast network of prisons, informers, 'judicial' murderers and torturers, his political opponents were hardly likely to be a threat.

An estimate of the total death toll of politicians from Stalin's Great Terror will be given shortly.

Chapter 31

Alexander Solzhenitsyn: The Inhumanity of the Gulag System

In 1976, Russian novelist and former political prisoner Alexander Solzhenitsyn was interviewed by French author and translator of Russian descent Nikita Struve. Solzhenitsyn described how he became 'the accredited chronicler of labour camp life, one to whom people brought the whole truth'.[1] In other words, former internees of the Gulag sent Solzhenitsyn their personal recollections of life in the camps to add to his own.[2] (As already mentioned, the Gulag is not to be confused with 'Special Settlements', to which political prisoners such as Stalin were exiled.)

'Alexander Solzhenitsyn was born into a middle-class family at Rostov-on-Don [southern Russia] in 1918. After graduating at Rostov University, he began his military service and gradually worked his way up to the rank of captain. Early in 1945, Solzhenitsyn was arrested and charged with making insulting remarks about Stalin. The punishment for this crime was eight years' confinement in forced labour camps – first with common criminals in the Arctic, and later in special camps for long-term prisoners, including the camp at Karaganda [in Kazakhstan]', which inspired him to write the semi-autobiographical novel, *One Day in the Life of Ivan Denisovich*, first published in 1962. After Stalin's death in 1953, Solzhenitsyn was eventually released.[3]

In *One Day in the Life of Ivan Denisovich*, Solzhenitsyn recreates life in the camps, with all its attendant brutality and inhumanity, based on his first-hand experience. The protagonist is prisoner, Ivan Denisovich Shukhov. The novel begins: 'At 5.00 a.m., as usual, reveille was sounded – a hammer banged against a rail just by the staff barracks. The intermittent ringing came faintly through the windowpanes, two fingers thick with frost.'[4]

The prisoners 'walked past the high wooden fence around the stone-built prison block within the camp; past the barbed wire which guarded the camp bakery from the inmates; past the corner of the staff barracks where the frost-covered rail (used to sound reveille) was fixed to a post by thick wire; past another post where – in a sheltered place to prevent it falling too low – hung the thermometer, coated over with frost. Shukhov cast a hopeful sideways glance at the milk-white tube: if it is showing −41 [degrees], they should not be sent out to work. But today it wasn't even approaching −40.[5]

'Shukhov ate his bread almost to the end, keeping back, however, a little bare crust – a semicircular bit from the top of the loaf. You could not clean out the porridge from your bowl as effectively with any spoon as you could with a piece of bread. This small crust he wrapped up again in the white cloth in preparation for his dinner, shoved the cloth into the inside pocket of his jacket, buttoned himself up against the cold and began to get ready for work.'[6]

Finally, at the end of the day, 'Shukhov went off to sleep, and he was completely content. Fate had been kind to him in many ways that day: he hadn't been put in the cells; the gang [work detail] had not been sent to the Socialist Community Centre; he'd fiddled himself an extra bowl of porridge for dinner; the gang leader had fixed a good percentage [presumably a good rate for the work to be done]; he'd been happy building that wall; he'd slipped through the church with that bit of blade; he'd earned himself something from the Tsesar [a well-to-do prisoner with special privileges] in the evening; he bought his tobacco. And he hadn't fallen ill – had overcome his feelings of illness in the morning.

'The day had gone by without a single cloud – almost a happy day. There were three thousand six hundred and fifty-three days like that in his sentence, from reveille to lights out. The three extra days were because of the leap years …'[7]

The creation of the Gulag system of hard labour camps is attributed to Lenin and Trotsky as a place to exile anyone who disagreed with the

Soviet Government. In fact, the Gulag was simply a continuation of the prison system created by Tsar Alexis of Russia in the seventeenth century. It also provided a source of labour for the exploitation of the country's natural resources such as coal and timber. The Gulag was expanded enthusiastically by Stalin.

An estimate of the number of people sent to the Gulag, and of the number who died in the camps, will be given shortly. However, such statistics tell only part of the story. The human suffering was incalculable: the pain of being separated from loved ones; the burning sense of injustice on the part of people who were for the most part innocent of any crime; the resultant psychological damage; the broken and diseased bodies and shattered minds that would never be the same again.

Chapter 32

Stalin and his Mother Ekaterina: His 'Rock'

In the Stalin Museum in Gori (eastern Georgia), said Svetlana, she saw a 'unique photograph taken during the last visit of Stalin to his mother, Ekaterina, who died on 4 June 1937. 'Both were sitting at a table in her room: she is holding her arm around his shoulder – looking very pleased: he looks so happy and so relaxed that I gasped involuntarily. I have never seen my father in such an elated, in such an enlightened state.'[1]

His mother 'eternally occupied a pre-eminent place in his heart. She was his eternal, positive, loving force, the only one he knew.'[2] In fact, Ekaterina was a rare example of someone who could criticise Stalin, i.e. by telling him that he ought to have become a priest, without fear of reprisals!

As for Ekaterina, from the time that Stalin had been imprisoned in the Metekhi Prison in Tiflis in the year 1900, she said of Stalin: 'My dear son, whenever a misfortune fell on me – whenever he was arrested or exiled to Siberia – he always informed me of what had happened to him through someone. But now I'm through with misfortunes. The entire world knows of my son "who has been in prison". He is in good health, which makes me glad. I am happy that he has achieved his goal and become a benefactor and patron of all oppressed people. I wish Beso [her late husband Besarion] had also lived to see him become the pride of our country.'[3] Besarion had died in 1910.

When Ekaterina wrote this in 1935, Stalin had been General Secretary of the Communist Party of the Soviet Union (USSR: Union of Soviet Socialist Republics) for thirteen years. She died in 1937, by which time Stalin had demonstrated that he had, in fact, become the very opposite of what his mother had hoped for: namely an oppressor of the most brutal kind, rather than a benefactor and force for good.

Chapter 33

Elections to the Supreme Soviet (December 1937)

On 12 December 1937 elections took place for the Supreme Soviet of the USSR. They were the first to be held under the new Soviet Constitution of 1936. 'On the eve of the election,' said Alexandrov: 'Stalin addressed the voters of the district in which he had been nominated for election, the Stalin district in Moscow. In the speech, he pointed to the fundamental difference between elections in the USSR which are free and democratic, in every sense of the word, and elections in capitalist countries, where the people are under the pressure of the exploiting classes. In the USSR the exploiting classes had been eliminated; Socialism had become a part of everyday life, and this was the basis on which the elections were taking place. Further, Stalin described the type of political figure the people should elect to the Supreme Soviet. The people must demand that they should be political figures of the Lenin type.'

The result of the election was as follows: 'Of a total of 94,000,000 voters, over 91,000,000, or 96.8 per cent, went to the polls; 90,000,000 people voted for the Communist and non-Party bloc, a fervent testimony to the victory of Socialism.'[1]

In fact, as Stalin had hinted at, the elections were a complete farce.

'The elections were originally announced as being multi-candidate; however, by halfway through the year the announcement was reversed.' Nevertheless, 'a number of individuals attempted to hold the government to the multi-candidate promise, including members of the Russian Orthodox Church who attempted to field religious candidates as a result of Article 134 of the new constitution, which promised freedom of religion. Many of the early individuals attempting to run as alternate candidates were arrested after the decision for multiple candidates was reversed. Additionally, the NKVD conducted mass arrests shortly before the elections.'[2]

Chapter 34

Stalin's Purges of the Red Army (1937–39 and 1940–42)

1937–39

'The whole Red Army development programme was nearly wrecked in the 1937–39 period when Stalin's paranoiac purge of Tukhachevsky and some 35,000 other high-ranking officers in the Red Army brought the whole military machine to the verge of chaos.'[1]

Mikhail N. Tukhachevsky was Marshal of the Soviet Union and former Commander-in-Chief of the Red Army. He was executed on 12 June 1937.

The scale of the purge 'was staggering', said US historian John W. Osborn Jr. It included the murder of: '13 of 15 army commanders; 50 of 57 corps commanders; 154 of 186 divisional commanders; 220 of 406 brigade commanders; all 11 vice-commanders of defence; 98 of 108 members of the Supreme Military Soviets; all army political commissars, 25 of 28 corps commissars; 58 of 64 divisional commissars. Even the lower ranks were not spared: almost half the colonels and 7,403 captains fell victim to the purge.

'This is worse than when artillery fires on its own troops,' commented General Konstantin Rokossovsky. 'More Soviet generals and colonels were killed by Stalin than were to fall in World War II.'[2]

To Khrushchev, Stalin's motive for condoning these murders, if not initiating them, was incomprehensible. Tukhachevsky, for example, 'was our brilliant Deputy People's Commissar of Defence. At the age of 26 he had commanded the Western Front in the Civil War. He had a deep understanding of military innovations and a high regard for them.

I'm convinced that if he hadn't been executed, our army would have been much better trained and better equipped when Hitler attacked.

'[Jan] Garmarnik was Chief of the Red Army Political Directorate, so he was an important political figure as well as a good soldier. He had played a significant part in the creation of the Red Army. Gamarnik wasn't executed. He shot himself. He foresaw that he would be arrested, and when they came pounding on his door, he put a pistol to his head and pulled the trigger.[3]

'Other victims were [Alexander] Yegorov – one of our greatest military leaders, our commander on the Southern Front in the Civil War. General [Jonah] Yakir was a relatively young fellow. His career began during the Civil War when he joined a newly formed detachment. He and his troops were cut off from the Red Army in the south, but he managed to break out of the encirclement and lead his division right through the White-Guardist lines to rejoin our main forces.

'After the Civil War, Yakir commanded troops in the Ukraine and the Crimea. Suddenly, he was arrested and executed. So was [Robert] Eideman, a poet as well as a soldier and one of our outstanding military leaders.

'Blücher [Vasily Blyukher] was a self-made military man. He got his first experience in World War I, and then commanded entire formations in the Civil War. He also commanded the troops of the Far Eastern Military District. We trusted him, both as a military leader and as a political figure. He was arrested and shot as an enemy of the people.'[4]

Of Yepivan Kovtyukh, Khrushchev said, 'This was the man who displayed such brilliance, skill, and courage when he broke an encirclement by the Whites and led the Taman army through enemy lines.'

The Taman Army was an armed group within the Red Army, operating in the south of Russia during the Russian Civil War.[5]

'Everyone who saw this general in action has nothing but praise for him.' He was 'rounded up with the enemies of the people and shot'.[6]

Khrushchev added, 'I was personally very close to Ivan Naumovich Dubovoy. When the Civil War broke out he was made deputy commander of a division commanded by [Nikolay] Shchors. Dubovoy commanded the Kiev Military District. I was very pleased that we had commanders like him in the Red Army – men devoted body and soul to the revolution, to Soviet Power, and to socialism.'[7] Dubovoy was executed on 29 July 1938.

1940–42

'Between October 1940 and February 1942, in spite of the ongoing German attack on the Soviet Union in June 1941, the Red Army, in particular the Soviet Air Force, as well as Soviet military-related industries, were subjected to purges by Stalin.' About 300 military commanders were executed on 16 October 1941. Forty-six more high-ranking military officers and the People's Commissar of Ammunition, Ivan Sergeyev, were executed on the Day of the Red Army, 23 February 1942.[8]

The Red Army was created on 28 January 1918, but the official 'Red Army Day' was 23 February.

In respect of the 1937–39 purge the Red Army, Khrushchev posed the question, 'Why did Stalin commit these crimes? Was he deceived? If he was deceived, then by whom?[9]

In respect of the 1940–42 army purge, given Stalin's paranoia the question arises, who or what put the idea into his head that the Red Army was a threat? The answer is Vyacheslav M. Molotov.

In early 1937 at the 10th Plenary Session of the Central Committee (23 February to 5 March), Voroshilov stated as follows, 'Happily, we have not as yet discovered many enemies in the army. I say happily in the hope that they are not very many enemies in the Red Army. That is how it should be. For the Party sends its best cadres [groups of activists] into the army.'

Vyacheslav M. Molotov, Chairman of the Council of People's Commissars, however, took a different view, 'If we have wreckers in every branch of the economy, can we imagine that in one place alone, the War Department, there are none? It would be absurd to do so. The War Department is a very large affair, and its work will be checked not now but a little later. And it will be examined very rigorously.'[10]

Molotov's ominous words indicated that a purge of the Red Army was imminent. Said Radinsky, 'Extermination of the former commanders' – i.e. who had been imprisoned – 'had, of course, to begin with the most dangerous of them, [Mikhail] Tukhachevsky.

And it was 'V. [Vitaly M.] Primakov, second in command of the Leningrad military district, and V. [Vitovt K.] Putna, Soviet military attaché in the United Kingdom', who had both been 'arrested in autumn 1936', who 'provided the necessary evidence against Tukhachevsky, who was now labelled a "German spy"'.[11]

August Kork, head of the Frunze Military Academy, Moscow, 'was arrested first in May 1937. Tukhachevsky himself was arrested on 27 May. By the 29th, as his case record shows, the hero had confessed to all the false charges brought against him. There are reddish-brown marks on some pages of his deposition. Forensic examination has shown that they are bloodstains.'[12]

'The Army Council met in the People's Commissariat of War from June 1 to 4. Stalin arrived with the Politburo. More than a hundred military chiefs had been called in from the provinces because the ranks of the Military Council itself had by then been thinned out catastrophically: a quarter of its members had been arrested as conspirators.'

By now, 'Their comrades of yesterday, the army's idols – Tukhachevsky, Kork, [Ieronim] Uborevich, [Iona] Yakir, and the rest of them – had confessed that they were spies for Hitler's intelligence service.'

'A summary trial took place on June 11. The sentence of course was death.'[13]

Chapter 35

Lavrenti Beria

Khrushchev, in a speech delivered on 25 February 1956 at the Twentieth Party Congress of the Communist Party of the Soviet Union, stated as follows: 'In organising the various dirty and shameful cases, a very base role was played by the rabid enemy of our Party, an agent of a foreign intelligence service – Beriya [Beria], who had stolen into Stalin's confidence.'

It is unlikely, of course, that Beria *was* an agent of a foreign power, but this suited Khrushchev's narrative!

'In what way could this provocateur gain such a position in the Party and in the State,' Khrushchev enquired, 'so as to become the First Deputy Chairman of the Council of Ministers of the Soviet Union and a member of the Central Committee Political Bureau? It has now been established that this villain had climbed up the government ladder over an untold number of corpses. The practical means for achieving Stalin's goals were all in Beria's hands.'[1]

Not only that, said Khrushchev, Stalin was also aware that his own fate too was in Beria's hands: 'Stalin realised that if Beria could eliminate anyone at whom Stalin pointed his finger, then Beria could also eliminate someone of his own choosing, on his own initiative. Stalin feared that he would be the first person Beria might choose. Naturally, Stalin never told anyone about this, but I could sense it, nonetheless. I first began to realise the intensity of Stalin's fear one day after the war, when I was at Stalin's for dinner.' Beria even controlled Stalin's entourage, said Khrushchev, 'including his Chekist bodyguard'.[2] A Chekist was an agent of the Cheka.

Svetlana had her own opinion of Beria, 'I do not have any personal hatred or feelings of vengeance towards any personalities in the ruling

Soviet top leadership. Beria, though, holds a unique position in my thoughts. He managed to destroy half of my family. But the matter is not [entirely] with him. I consider them all equally bad, one no better nor worse than another, for they all continue to oppress the grand, the talented Russian people and the other peoples of Russia: an oppression that, seventy years ago, the Bolshevik Party initiated.'[3]

Khrushchev, in his speech, had therefore lent weight to Svetlana's assertion that it was Beria, and not her father, who was pulling the proverbial strings. 'My father was astonishingly helpless before Beria's machinations,' she said. 'All Beria had to do was to bring him the record of the interrogation' in which the accused person 'confessed'.[4] What my father didn't want to realise was that in the cellars of the secret police, X, Y and Z could be made to testify to anything.'[5]

'I speak advisedly' of Beria's 'influence on my father,' said Svetlana, 'and not the other way around. Beria was more treacherous, more practised in perfidy and cunning, more insolent and single-minded than my father. In a word, he was a stronger character. My father had his weaker sides. He was capable of self-doubt. He was cruder and more direct than Beria and not so suspicious. He was simpler and could be led up the garden path by someone with Beria's craftiness.

'Beria's role was a terrible one for all our family. How my mother feared and hated him! And it was her friends – Alexander Svanidze, his wife Maria, his sister, Mariko who was Yenukidze's secretary, to say nothing of Yenukidze himself – who were the first to fall: the moment Beria was able to convince my father that they were hostile to him.'[6]

Her aunts, Anna Alliluyeva and Yevgenia Alliluyeva, said Svetlana, were also 'inclined to blame Beria for the arrests which had fallen upon our family'. The aunts 'stuck to this opinion, basing it on the fact that Beria had had encounters and scores to settle with Svanidze, Redens, [and] with all the old Georgian Bolsheviks who, in the days when they were still in Georgia, had stood in the way of his obtaining the post of First Secretary of the Central Committee of Georgia'.[7]

The sequence of events, therefore, appears to be that as often as not, it was Beria who selected those who were to be the victimised.

He then fabricated a case against them; obtained evidence by threats and torture, and feeding on Stalin's paranoia, presented his case. Whereupon, Stalin concurred, and the fate of Beria's chosen victims was sealed. 'But, of course, no one but my father could have sanctioned the execution of Redens and Svanidze [and] the arrest of other relatives,' said Svetlana. 'Such power Beria did not possess.'[8]

Chapter 36

The Second World War: Stalin as a Wartime Leader

On 22 June 1941 in Operation Barbarossa, and in violation of the Molotov–Ribbentrop Non-Aggression Pact, the Germans invaded Russia. Y. E. Chadaev, Administrator of Affairs of the Council of People's Commissars, described a meeting that occurred two days later, on 24 June, between Stalin and Soviet statesman and People's Commissar for Tank Production Vyacheslav Malyshev. 'As Malyshev was giving his report, Stalin interrupted: "You're a long time getting a move on," he said, and started asking concrete questions about ways to expand arms production, and how best to organise production of armour plating. It was decided to create a new base for tank production in the Urals and Siberia.'

'If worst came to worst,' said Radzinsky, 'if the Germans occupied the whole of European Russia, then the limitless expanse of Siberia, and the Urals with their great mineral wealth, would still be left. The war could be carried on from there.'[1]

'To ensure the rapid mobilization of all the forces of the country and to repulse the enemy, the Presidium of the Supreme Soviet of the USSR, the Central Committee of the CPSU(B) [Bolshevik], and the Council of People's Commissars of the USSR decided on June 30, 1941, to set up a State Committee of Defence in whose hands all power in the state was concentrated. Joseph Stalin was appointed Chairman of the Committee.'[2]

On 12 July 1941, 'Great Britain concluded with the USSR an Agreement for Joint Action in the War Against Germany. In June 1942 the USA signed with the USSR an Agreement on the Principles

Applicable to Mutual Aid in the Prosecution of the War Against Aggression. An Anglo–Soviet–American coalition was formed for the purpose of destroying the Italo–German coalition.'[3]

On 19 July 1941 the Presidium of the Supreme Soviet 'appointed Stalin People's Commissar of Defence'.[4]

In a speech delivered at the Twentieth Party Congress of the Communist Party of the Soviet Union on 25 February 1956, Khrushchev challenged the notion that victory in the Second World War was 'completely due to the strategic genius of Stalin'.

Khrushchev pointed to the immense damage caused by Stalin's purge of the Red Army in 1937, 'Very grievous consequences, especially in reference to the beginning of the war, followed Stalin's annihilation of many military commanders and political workers during 1937–41 because of his suspiciousness and through slanderous accusations. During these years repressions were instituted against certain parts of military cadres beginning, literally, at the company and battalion-commander level and extending to the higher military centres; during this time the cadre of leaders who had gained military experience in Spain and in the Far East was almost completely liquidated.'[5]

Also, said Khrushchev, when there were early indications of an imminent German attack, Stalin chose to ignore them. Said he, 'Stalin put forward the thesis that the tragedy which our nation experienced in the first part of the war was the result of the unexpected attack of the Germans against the Soviet Union. But, comrades, this is completely untrue. As soon as Hitler came to power in Germany [in March 1933], he assigned to himself the task of liquidating communism. The Fascists were saying this openly; they did not hide their plans. In order to attain this aggressive end, all sorts of pacts and blocs were created, such as the famous Berlin-Rome-Tokyo Axis [military coalition]. Many facts from the pre-war period clearly showed that Hitler was going all out to begin a war against the Soviet state and that he had concentrated large armed units, together with armoured units, near the Soviet borders.'

'Information of this sort concerning the threat of German armed invasion of Soviet territory', said Khrushchev, was 'coming in also from our own military and diplomatic sources. However, because

Vissarion (Besarion) Dzhugashvili, Stalin's father. (Official Photographer of Gori)

Ekaterina Dzhugashvili, Stalin's mother, 1892.

Gori Church School, Russian Empire (today Georgia): students and teachers, 1892. Back row, centre: Ioseb Dzhugashvili (Joseph Stalin) aged 13. (Georgian MIA Academy Archive)

Stalin in 1893.

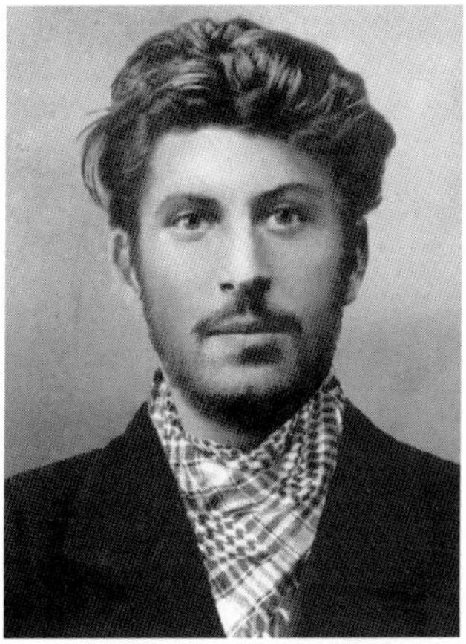

Stalin, 1902. From the book *Josef Wissarionowitsch Stalin.*

Police record, 1 April 1902. Stalin is 23 years old.

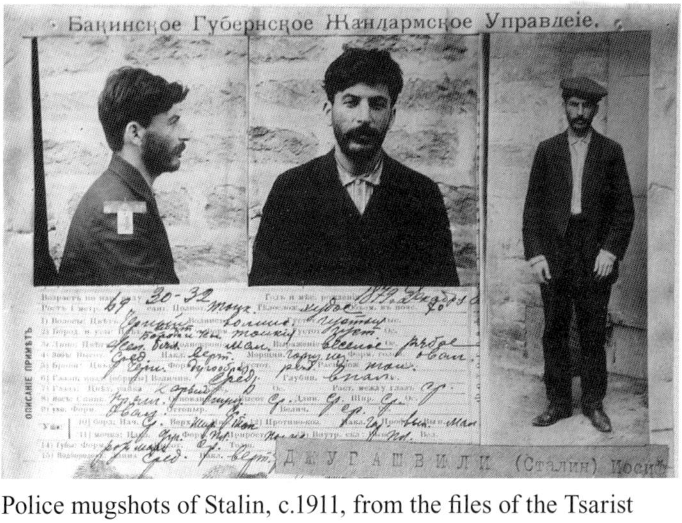

Police mugshots of Stalin, c.1911, from the files of the Tsarist Secret Police in St Petersburg. (Tsarist police document)

Ekaterina Svanidze, Stalin's first wife, 1904.

Funeral of Ekaterina ('Kato') Svanidze, first wife of Joseph Stalin (right), 8 December 1907.

Group of exiled Bolsheviks in Siberia, gathered to discuss the trial of the Bolshevik Duma deputies, in the summer of 1915, in the village of Monastyrskoye (now Turukhansk). Back row, left to right: Suren Spandarian (2nd); Joseph Stalin (4th); Lev Kamenev (6th);, Alexsei Badayev (7th). Front row left to right: Jacob Sverdlov (4th).

Vladimir Ilyich Lenin, 1 October 1918. From the Fourth Edition of the *Collected Works of V.I. Lenin*. First page.

Lenin and Stalin at Gorki, district of Moscow, 1 September 1922. Photographed by Maria Ilyinichna Ulyanova, Lenin's sister.

Stalin's second wife, Nadezhda Alliluyeva. (Sovieteca)

Stalin in 1920. From the journal *Kommunist*.

Delegates to the 12th Congress of the Russian Communist Party (Bolsheviks), Moscow, 17–25 April 1923: Middle row, left to right: (3rd) Nikolai Ivanovich Bukharin; (4th) Alexei Ivanovich Rykov; (4th) Joseph Vissarionovich Stalin. Front row, centre: Sergo Konstantinovich Ordzhonikidze.

Leon Trotsky in Brest Litovsk, 1918. (Rijksmuseum Amsterdam)

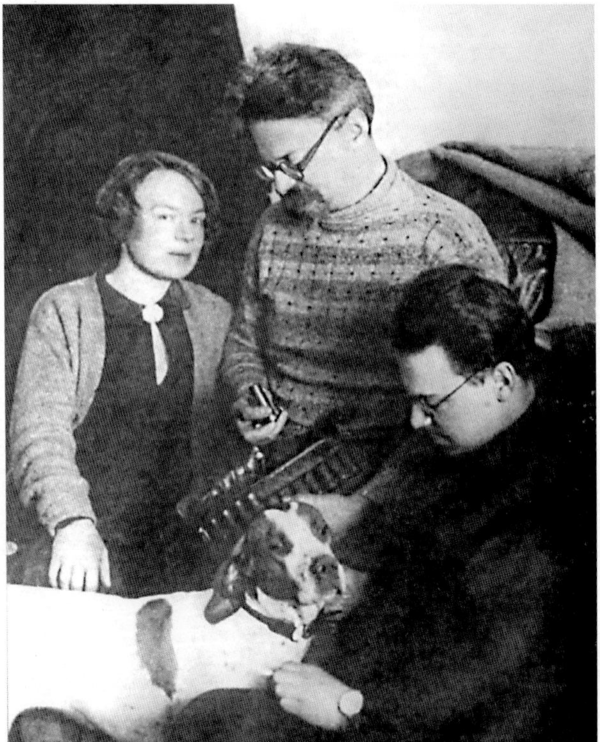

Leon Trotsky, his wife Natalia and their son Leon in exile in Alma-Ata, Kazakhstan, 1928. (State Museum of Political History of Russia)

Yakov Dzhugashvili, Stalin's son, 1941.

Joseph Stalin, General Secretary of the Soviet Union, 1930. (Workers Library Publishers)

Stanislav Franzevich Redens, 1931.

Stalin and Nikita Khrushchev at the May Day demonstration in Moscow, 1932.

Alexander Isayevich Solzhenitsyn, 14 February 1974. (Dutch National Archives, The Hague)

Joseph Stalin with daughter Svetlana, 1935. (*Pravda*, Moscow, 1940)

Lavrenti Beria with Stalin and daughter, 25 September 1931.

Soviet Foreign Minister Vyacheslav Molotov signs the German–Soviet Treaty of Friendship in Moscow, 28 September 1939; behind him are Richard Schulze-Kossens (Ribbentrop's adjutant), Boris Shaposhnikov (Chief of Staff of the Red Army), Joachim von Ribbentrop (German Minister of Foreign Affairs), Joseph Stalin, Vladimir Pavlov (Soviet translator). Alexei Shkvarzev (Soviet ambassador in Berlin), stands next to Molotov. (National Archives & Records Administration, USA)

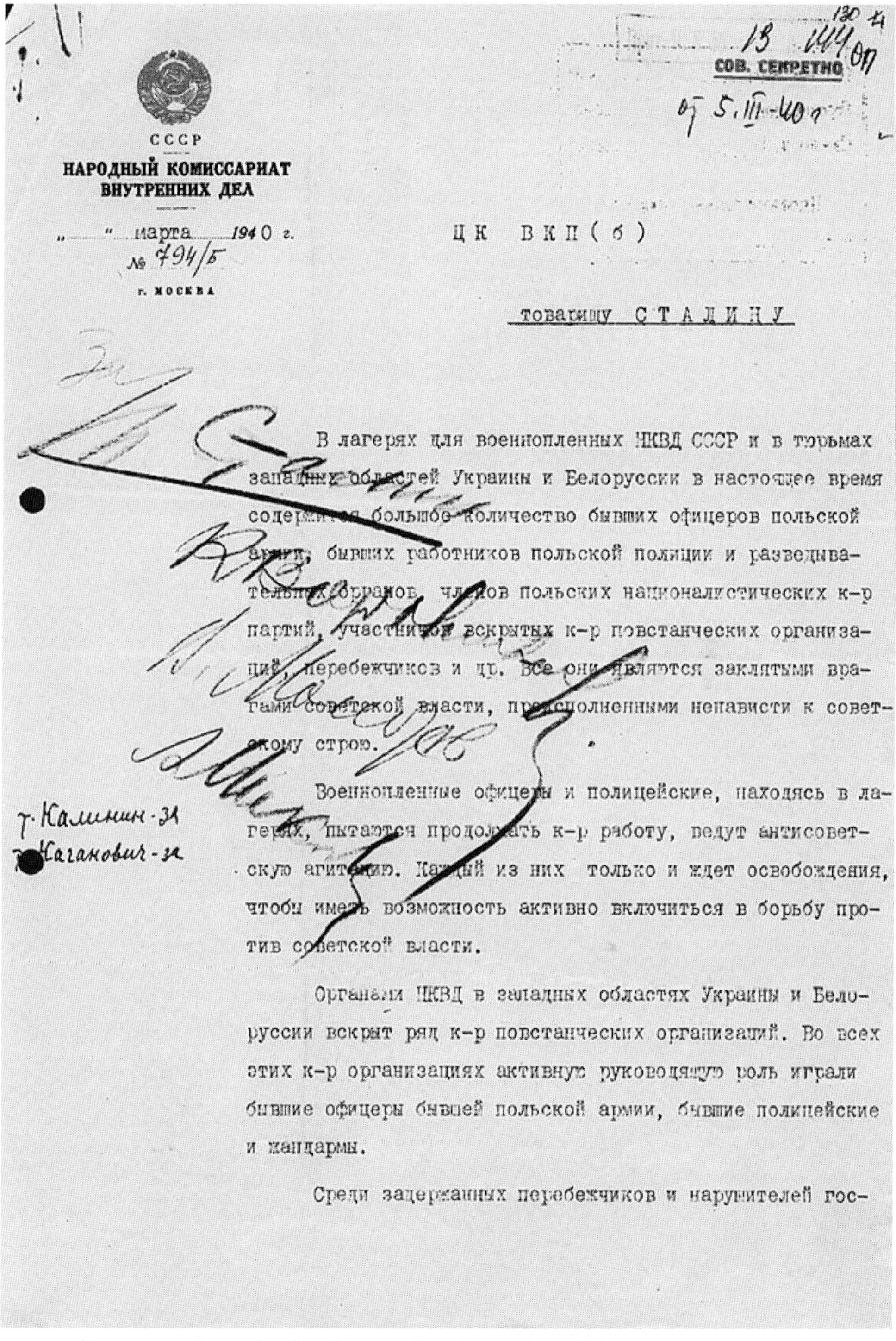
СОВ. СЕКРЕТНО

13 144/оп

от 5.III-40 г.

СССР
НАРОДНЫЙ КОМИССАРИАТ ВНУТРЕННИХ ДЕЛ

„......" марта 1940 г.
№ 794/Б
г. МОСКВА

ЦК ВКП(б)

товарищу СТАЛИНУ

В лагерях для военнопленных НКВД СССР и в тюрьмах западных областей Украины и Белоруссии в настоящее время содержится большое количество бывших офицеров польской армии, бывших работников польской полиции и разведывательных органов, членов польских националистических к-р партий, участников вскрытых к-р повстанческих организаций, перебежчиков и др. Все они являются заклятыми врагами советской власти, преисполненными ненависти к советскому строю.

Военнопленные офицеры и полицейские, находясь в лагерях, пытаются продолжать к-р работу, ведут антисоветскую агитацию. Каждый из них только и ждет освобождения, чтобы иметь возможность активно включиться в борьбу против советской власти.

Органами НКВД в западных областях Украины и Белоруссии вскрыт ряд к-р повстанческих организаций. Во всех этих к-р организациях активную руководящую роль играли бывшие офицеры бывшей польской армии, бывшие полицейские и жандармы.

Среди задержанных перебежчиков и нарушителей гос-

т. Калинин – за
т. Каганович – за

Proposal by Lavrentiy Beria, dated 5 March 1940, to the Politburo of the Communist Party, that 25,700 Polish military and political prisoners be executed. The proposal was approved of and signed by Stalin, Voroshilov, Molotov, and Mikoyan.

Georgy Konstantinovich Zhukov, Soviet commander, Marshal of the Soviet Union.

Stalin's daughter, Svetlana Alliluyeva, New York City, 1967.

Alexei Navalny meeting voters in the 2013 Moscow mayoral elections.

JOSEPH STALIN
RELEVANT FAMILY TREE

Besarion Dzhugashvili 1850-1910 = Ekaterina Geladze 1858-1937

Josef Stalin (given name Dzhugashvili)
18 Dec 1878-5 Mar 1953

M(1) = Ekaterina Svanidze
2 Apr 1885-22 Nov 1907

Yakov Dzhugashvili
1907-1943

M(1) = Zoya Gunina

M(2) = Yudith Meltzer

M(2) = Nadezhda Alliluyeva
22 Sep 1901 – 9 Nov 1932

Vasily Stalin
1921-1962

M(1) = Galina Bourdonskaya

M(2) = Ekaterina Timoshenko

M(3) = Kapolitana Vasilyeva

Svetlana Alliluyeva
1926-2011

M(1) = Grigory Morozov

Josef Morozov

M(2) = Yuri Zhdanov

Yekaterina Zhdanova

M(3) = William Peters

Olga Peters

Stalin's family tree.

STALIN'S FIRST WIFE EKATERINA (NÉE SVANIDZE) AND HER SIBLINGS

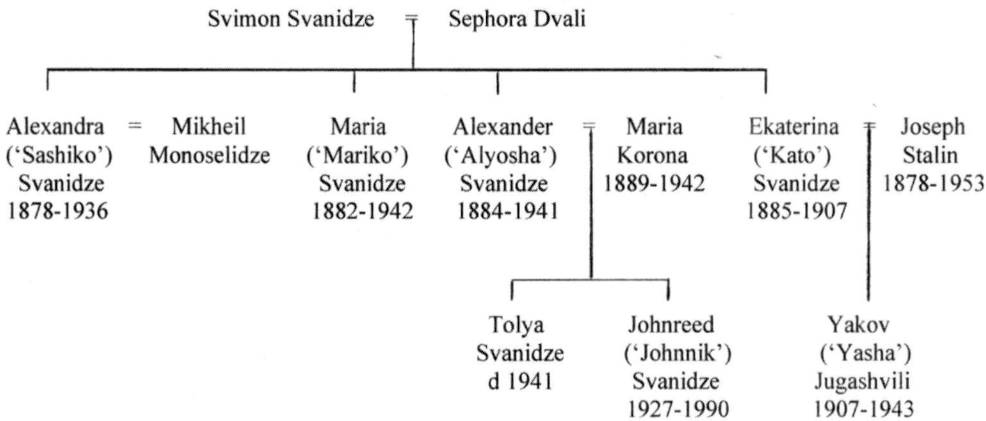

STALIN'S SECOND WIFE NADEZHDA (NÉE ALLILUYEVA) AND HER SIBLINGS

The family tree of two wives.

the leadership was conditioned against such information, such data was dispatched with fear and assessed with reservation. Despite these particularly grave warnings, the necessary steps were not taken to prepare the country properly for defence and to prevent it from being caught unaware. Did we have time and the capabilities for such preparations? Yes; we had the time and capabilities. Our industry was already so developed that it was capable of supplying fully the Soviet Army with everything that it needed. Had our industry been mobilised properly and in time to supply the army with the necessary material, our wartime losses would have been decidedly smaller. Such mobilisation had not been, however, started in time. And already in the first days of the war it became evident that our Army was badly armed; that we did not have enough artillery, tanks, and planes to throw the enemy back.'

Stalin, however, must be given credit for his resilience. For example, when the German Army was approaching Moscow in the autumn of 1941, said Svetlana: 'There was a plan of moving the government to Kuybyshev [in south-west Russia] and residences were prepared. I saw those, and bomb shelters were prepared there too, but then my father changed his mind and stayed.' Why? Because of the fortitude of one of his female servants whose task it was to carry trays of food from the kitchen in the main house to 'the little cottage' in the grounds where her father 'used to stay':

Shells from Soviet anti-aircraft guns were 'dropping down and she was running under that, because the anti-aircraft artillery was shooting all the time. So, she came in with the tray of food and he asked her, "Are you afraid to be there?" And she said, "No, Comrade Stalin, we are not afraid." And he said, "Well, but they're shooting there!" "Well," she said, "It's all right, sort of." And they were all prepared to move, all the kitchen and everything was packed, and the household was packed, actually the train was on the rails, all ready to pack it all in and move, and within half an hour he called his chief bodyguard and said, "We're not going, we're staying." Not only that, a decision was made, presumably by Stalin, to hold a parade in Moscow's Red Square.'

This, said Svetlana, 'had a great impact on the troops. I know people who were on the Red Square, and there was very good poetry from some wartime poets; and then there was the usual gathering in the bomb shelter with speeches and so on, and then the counter-offensive was started.'

The parade was held on 7 November 1941. The day before, 'The traditional meeting of the Moscow Soviet of Working People's Deputies and representatives of the Moscow Party and public organisations was held in the city to celebrate the anniversary, the 24th, of the Great October Socialist Revolution. The meeting was addressed by Stalin.'

Of the German invaders, he declared, 'These men, destitute of conscience and honour, these men with the morals of beasts, have the insolence to call for the extermination of the great Russian nation, the nation of Plekhanov and Lenin, Belinsky and Chernyshevsky, Pushkin and Tolstoy, Glinka and [T]Chaikovsky, Gorky and Chekhov, Sechenkov and Pavlov, Repin and Surikov, Suvorov and Kutuzov.'

And then, said Stalin ominously, 'The German invaders want a war of extermination against the peoples of the USSR. Well, if the Germans want a war of extermination, they will get it. Ours is a just cause – victory will be ours!'[6]

The following day, Stalin addressed the parade, 'Let the heroic images of our great forebears – Alexander Nevsky, Dmitri Donskoi, Kuzma Minin, Dmitri Pozharsky, Alexander Suvorov, and Mikhail Kutuzov – inspire you in this war! May you be inspired by the victorious banner of the great Lenin!'[7]

Stalin showed further grit and determination when Stalingrad was being besieged by the Germans. The Battle of Stalingrad lasted from 17 July 1942 to 2 February 1943, he having ordered that the city 'must not be surrendered to the enemy'.[8]

In this, Stalin had clearly shown both courage and leadership. 'Obviously,' said Svetlana, 'it was a crucial moment' because if the government had left the capital, Moscow 'things could be [i.e. have been] different.'[9] Furthermore, in naming the aforementioned writers, poets, musical composers, Marxist theoretician, painters, physiologists, and past military commanders and defenders of the nation, he had displayed his knowledge of Soviet history and culture.

Without industrialisation, of course, the Soviet Union could have offered only limited resistance to the invading German forces, and Stalin had been justified when he pointed out, in a speech delivered at an election meeting in Moscow on 9 February 1946, that the 'historic transformation' of the Soviet Union 'from an agrarian into an industrial country … was brought about in the course of three Five-Year Plans'.[10] The nationwide, centralised Five-Year Plans for industrialisation had come about as a consequence of the New Economic Policy proposed by Lenin in 1921, and enthusiastically promoted by Stalin thereafter. The first Five-Year Plan was announced by Stalin as Soviet leader on 1 October 1928. 'However, because the first Five-Year Plan was carried out in four years, and the third Five-Year Plan was interrupted by the war, the transformation took only about thirteen years.'

Said Alexandrov, 'The second Five-Year plan was fulfilled by April 1937, ahead of schedule in four years and three months. With the completion of the reconstruction of industry and agriculture, the national economy of the Soviet Union found itself equipped with the most advanced technique [i.e. technology] in the world. Industry had received a vast quantity of machines, machine tools, and other implements of production. Agriculture had received first-class Soviet tractors, harvester combines, and other complex agricultural machines. The transport system had received first-class motor vehicles, locomotives, ships, and aeroplanes. The Armed Forces had received excellent equipment – artillery, tanks, aircraft, and warships.'[11]

Svetlana stated that her father had received only a 'poor education'. However, from his writings and speeches it is clear that Stalin was self-taught and knowledgeable to a high degree. ('Educated' would be too strong a word, in regard to Stalin, an educated person being deemed to have embraced intellectual, moral, and social guidance.)

'In the field of technical knowledge', she said, 'everything concerning industrialisation, armament, interested him – he considered it of importance. He knew the essentials about tractors, tanks, airplanes, cannon, automobiles; he amazed high government officials, builders, and foreign generals with his questions and knowledge.'

'During the last three years of the war,' said Stalin, 'our tank industry produced annually an average of over 30,000 tanks, self-propelled guns and armoured cars. It is well known, further, that in the same period our aircraft industry produced annually up to 40,000 aeroplanes. It is also well known that our artillery industry in the same period produced annually up to 120,000 guns of all calibres, up to 450,000 light and heavy machine guns, over 3 million rifles, and about 2 million automatic rifles. Lastly, it is well known that our mortar industry in the period of 1942–44 produced annually an average of up to 100,000 mortars. It goes without saying that simultaneously, we produced corresponding quantities of artillery shells, mines of various kinds, air bombs, and rifle and machine gun cartridges. It is well known, for example, that in 1944 alone, we produced over 240 million shells, bombs and mines and 7 million, 400,000 cartridges.'[12]

Credit must be given to Stalin for the fact that, in order to prevent them from being overrun by the Germans, 'Entire factories were moved east to Nizhny Tagil, Omsk, and Sverdlovsk. And existing factories switched production. For example, the Chelyabinsk Tractor Works now manufactured tanks, and by 1944, employed 60,000 or so people, so that Chelyabinsk became known as "Tank City".'

On Tuesday 8 May 1945 – Victory in Europe (VE) Day – the Allies formally accepted the unconditional surrender of Germany's armed forces. This marked the end of the Second World War in Europe.

On 9 August 1945 the Soviet Union declared war on Japan.

On 15 August 1945 – Victory over Japan (VJ) Day – Japan surrendered to the Allies. This marked the end of the Second World War.

Chapter 37

The Katyn Atrocity

In April and May 1940 during the Second World War, a large-scale massacre of Polish soldiers and civilians took place, the truth about which was covered up for five decades. This episode in Soviet history is important as it sheds further light on Stalin's character.

The background to relations between Poland, the Soviet Union, Great Britain, and France is as follows. A Franco–Polish military alliance had existed since 1921 (it was formalised in 1923). On 25 July 1932 a three-year-non-aggression pact was signed between Poland and the Soviet Union. On 26 January 1934 came the Polish–German agreement of non-aggression. On 31 March 1939, Britain and France guaranteed their support should Polish independence be threatened. On 6 April 1939, Britain formalised the agreement with Poland as an Anglo–Polish military alliance. On 23 August 1939 the Molotov–Ribbentrop Non-Aggression Pact (named after Soviet and German Foreign Ministers Vyacheslav Molotov and Joachim von Ribbentrop respectively) was signed between the Soviet Union and Nazi Germany. On 25 August 1939 the Anglo–Polish Military Alliance was formalised.

On 1 September 1939 the Germans invaded Poland from the west. Whereupon, under the Anglo–Polish and Franco–Polish treaties of alliance, Britain and France declared war on Germany.

On 17 September 1939 the Soviet Union invaded Poland from the east in accordance with a secret clause contained in the Molotov–Ribbentrop Pact, whereby the country was to be partitioned. The Soviet Red Army met with little resistance as the Polish forces facing them were under orders not to resist.

From 17 to 30 September 1939 some 250,000 to 450,000 Polish military personnel and civilians were apprehended in the Soviet-occupied territory and detained in 100 or more 'transition camps' in the Soviet Union. They were run by the NKVD.

From September to November 1939 the NKVD segregated 14,400 or so Polish military officers and others, including professors, doctors, judges, lawyers, engineers, teachers, police and intelligence officials, prison guards, border guards, landowners, factory owners, and those whom the Soviets labelled 'Polish nationalists and counter-revolutionaries [i.e. those opposed to the Russian Revolution]'. They were transported by rail to the western Soviet Union and interned at three camps: two in Russia viz. Kozelsk (Optina Monastery) and Ostashkov (Stolobny Island on Lake Seliger near Ostashkov); and one in Ukraine, namely Starobielsk. The greater number of high-ranking officers were interned at Starobielsk, including eight Polish generals.[1]

In June 1941 the Nazis occupied the remainder of Poland when Nazi Germany invaded the Soviet Union on 22 June in Operation Barbarossa.

On 13 April 1943 it was announced by Reichssender Berlin radio 'that German military forces in the Katyn Forest near Smolensk in western Russia had uncovered a ditch that was '28 metres long and 16 metres wide [92 ft by 52 ft] in which the bodies of 3,000 Polish officers were piled up in 12 layers'. The exhumations were carried out by the German Army's Medical Corps under the supervision of anthropologist Professor Gerhardt Butz of Braslau University, Wroclaw, Poland. Furthermore, the Soviet NKVD was accused of carrying out this massacre.[2] Two days later the Soviets denied that they had committed the crime and stated that the Poles had been executed by the Germans. Stalin also broke off diplomatic relations with the Polish government, which was in exile in London.

In 1943 the Red Army conducted a summer–autumn campaign, in the course of which Smolensk was liberated on 25 September. A Soviet medical commission subsequently investigated the Katyn massacre and a cover-up operation now began. A cemetery that the Germans had permitted the Polish Red Cross to build was removed and instead a memorial cross was erected by the Soviets bearing the inscription: 'Polish prisoners of war executed by Hitler's troops in 1941. Rest in Peace'. Also, local witnesses were told that their testimonies must accord with the official line, under pain of arrest and a charge of collaborating with the Nazis.[3] Finally, false documents were planted on the dead by the Soviet secret police to make it appear that the massacre had occurred during the period of German occupation.

From 11–14 April 1990, half a century after the Katyn atrocity, Polish President Wojciech Jaruzelski made an official visit to Moscow. During the visit, Soviet President Mikhail Gorbachev finally acknowledged his country's responsibility for the so-called 'Katyn massacre', and presented Jaruzelski with documents containing the names of the murdered victims. Gorbachev also revealed that two other mass graves had been discovered: at Mednoye near Tver, in Russia; and at Piatykhatky, Kharkiv, in Ukraine.

In October 1992, Russian President Boris Yeltsin ordered that further documents be released to the new Polish president, Lech Walesa. They showed that the extrajudicial execution of the Poles had been carried out by order of the Soviet leadership. Among the documents was a memorandum from Lavrenti Beria, Head of the NKVD to 'Comrade Stalin'. Marked 'Top Secret', it contained a proposal by Beria, dated 5 March 1940, to execute 25,700 Poles from the Kozelsk, Ostashkov and Starobielsk camps, and from certain prisons in Western Ukraine and Belarus. It read as follows, 'In prisoner-of-war camps run by the USSR NKVD, and in prisons in western Ukraine and Belorussia there are currently a large number of former Polish army officers, former officials of the Polish police and intelligence services, members of Polish nationalist counter-revolutionary parties, members of unmasked rebel counter-revolutionary organisations, defectors and others. They are all sworn enemies of Soviet power, filled with hatred towards the Soviet system.

'The POW officers and police in the camps are trying to continue counter-revolutionary work and are engaged in anti-Soviet agitation. Each of them is just waiting for liberation so as to actively join the struggle against Soviet power.

'In total in the prisoner-of-war camps (not counting soldiers and non-commissioned officers) there are 14,736 former officers, government officials, landowners, policemen, military police, jailers, settlers and spies. More than 97% are of Polish nationality.

'In total the prisons of western Ukraine and Belorussia contain 18,632 detainees (of whom 10,685 are Poles).

'Based on the fact that all of them are steadfast incorrigible enemies of Soviet power, the USSR NKVD deems it essential:

I. To propose that the USSR NKVD give special consideration to:
   1) the cases of 14,700 people remaining in the prisoner-of-war camps – former Polish army officers, government officials, landowners, policemen, intelligence agents, military policemen, settlers and jailers …
   2) and also the cases of those arrested and remaining in prisons in the western districts of Ukraine and Belorussia, totalling 11,000 (members of various counter-revolutionary spy and sabotage organisations, former landowners, factory owners, former Polish army officers, government officials and defectors).

   Imposing on them the sentence of capital punishment – execution by shooting.
II. The cases are to be handled without the convicts being summoned and without revealing the charges; with no statements concerning the conclusion of the investigation and the bills of indictment given to them.'

The letter is signed 'L. Beria' in blue pencil, under the title 'USSR People's Commissar for Internal Affairs'.

In other words, this was to be an entirely underhand and secretive operation.

'The first page of the letter bears the word Za – "In Favour" – scrawled in blue pencil with the signatures of the then Soviet leader Joseph Stalin and of Politburo members K. Voroshilov and

A. Mikoyan, along with V. Molotov in ordinary pencil. In the margin are the names Kalinin and Kaganovich – also aides to Stalin – added in blue ink and also with the word "Za".'[4]

Clearly Beria, playing on Stalin's paranoia yet again, had managed to persuade him that the Polish prisoners, both civilian and military, were a serious threat. The nature of Beria's influence on Stalin, which is of great significance as far as this narrative is concerned, will be discussed in detail shortly. Meanwhile, what was the total death toll? According to Radzinsky, Anatoly Krayushkin: 'head of one of the directorates of the Federal Security Service (as the former KGB is now called), at a press conference in Smolensk in April 1995, informed the Russian and Polish journalists present that the number of Polish prisoners killed in various camps was 21,857. The documents concerning those shot were destroyed, with Khrushchev's consent, in 1959. What remains is a letter from A. [Alexander N.] Shelepin, then head of the KGB, informing Khrushchev that 'in all, 21,857 people were shot on orders from the KGB, including 4,421 in the Katyn Forest; 6,311 in the Ostashkovo [Ostashkov] camp; and 3,820 in the Starobel [Starobielsk] camp near Kharkov.'[5] The total number of murders from Katyn, Ostashkovo, and Starobel therefore adds up to 14,552.

In addition, said Polish historian, Andrew (Andrzej) Kawczak, 'it is now generally accepted that the shooting of 7,305 [Polish] arrestees held in prisons in Belarus and Ukraine should be considered an integral part of the 1940 massacre'.[6] This accounts for the final total being 21,857, as stated above.

To reiterate, here was Beria, dripping proverbial poison into the ear of the paranoic Stalin with tragic consequences for tens of thousands of innocent people.

Chapter 38

Stalin's Unashamedly Violent Tendencies

Stalin perpetrated violence vicariously. This violence was organised by his henchmen and effected by, for example, the torturers and murderers in Moscow's Lubyanka prison, or by the guards in the Gulag, who murdered, or allowed their prisoners to perish through cold or starvation.

During his meetings with Winston Churchill in 1942 (12–15 August), the British Prime Minister asked him, 'What did you do with all the rich kulaks?' 'We killed them,' replied Stalin.

On 28 June 1942 the Germans launched an offensive code-named, Operation Blue. Army Group 'B' headed towards Stalingrad on the River Volga; Army Group 'A' advanced south-east towards the oil fields of the Caucasus. Shortly after the German offensive was launched, Nikolai Baibakov, Soviet Deputy Minister for Oil, was summoned to an urgent meeting with Stalin.

'Everything must be done to prevent the oil falling into German hands,' said Stalin. 'Bear in mind that if you leave the Germans even one ton of oil, we will shoot you, but if you destroy the oil installations prematurely, and the Germans don't grab them, we will also shoot you.'

'Stalin made a very big impression on me,' said Baibakov. I don't know if I was afraid or not, but I had a great respect for him. I would have said the same thing if I was in his place,' remarked Baibakov. 'The ends justify the means!'[1]

A speech by Stalin that he delivered at an election meeting in Moscow on 9 February 1946 reveals just how two-faced he was. In regard to the outbreak of the Second World War, the Soviet leader, as one who presided over the most repressive and murderous regime in history in terms of sheer scale, stated as follows: 'It must be borne in mind that before attacking the Allied countries, the major fascist states – Germany, Japan and Italy – destroyed the last vestiges of bourgeois-democratic liberties at home and established there a cruel, terroristic regime, and trampled upon the principle of sovereignty and free development.'[2]

Stalin not only perpetrated violence vicariously, he also threatened and perpetrated it personally, viz. his treatment of Svetlana, his daughter.

Chapter 39

From Battered Child to Angry and Violent Adult

Evidence previously presented indicates that Stalin, as a child, was physically and verbally abused to a severe degree by his father, Besarion (who was frequently drunk and had come to believe that his wife had been unfaithful to him and that Joseph was not his child) and physically abused by his mother, Ekaterina. Nonetheless, Stalin was always loved by his mother, and he always loved her, and initially he was loved by his father. But when Besarion degenerated into drunkenness he began rejecting his infant son in the most violent manner.

During his time at the Tiflis Seminary, Stalin experienced further abuse, for example by being denied access to any literature other than what was prescribed, be it political or non-political, and being punished by solitary confinement for what were deemed to be his misdemeanours. Therefore, throughout his entire childhood, Stalin was abused in one way or another.

Suppressed anger in the child

According to German sociologist Theodor W. Adorno, 'Rigid and punitive child rearing fosters anger towards parents.' However, such anger 'can be neither expressed nor acknowledged for fear of parental reprisals'.[1] Said US psychology professors Michael Milburn and Sheree D. Conrad, 'children react to punishment and abuse with rage. In a family system based on denial, however, they are prohibited from expressing their anger or are trained to deny their feelings, to believe that they have nothing to be legitimately angry about.' However, 'This unexpressed anger does not go away.'[2]

Anger as a consequence of the invasion of personal space

'Victims of trauma experience severe violations of personal boundaries. Consequently, persistent anger and anger management problems are common characteristics of individuals who have experienced traumatic events.'[3]

Blatant anger and rage in the adult

Said Baron-Cohen, 'One reason why parental rejection might be linked to a child developing aggression in adulthood is that inside – emotionally – the child is quietly *raging* against the parental rejection and is developing high levels of hate. Such extreme, negative emotions are hard to regulate. The child has to vent their rage somewhere and, if as a child they were unable to express it towards the rejecting parent, it may build up, like steam in a pressure cooker, just waiting to be vented in adolescence and adulthood. The result can be explosive violence.'[4]

A failure to thrive emotionally

Being let down by abusive parents leaves the child unable to develop emotionally as a normal human being.

'Physical, emotional, or sexual abuse in childhood can interrupt the normal development of skills needed for healthy emotional management and relationship building. Consequently, abused children may need to learn age-appropriate interpersonal boundaries, assertiveness, and coping strategies for strong emotion since they learn the emotional management skills modelled by the abusive adults in their lives.'[5]

The greater the Adverse Childhood Experiences (ACEs), the greater the anger produced

Said US psychologist Bernard Golden, 'Numerous studies have found a correlation between ACEs and anger. One reviewed the records of 22,575 delinquent youths and found that every additional adverse childhood experience that the child had increased the risk of their becoming a serious, violent, and chronic juvenile offender.[6] A more recent study concluded that greater childhood trauma was associated with trait anger expression as an adult.'[7] Trait anger is a predisposition for anger arousal and hostility.

Finally, a study by Chinese psychologist Wenfeng Zhu and colleagues in 2020 'concluded that hostile attribution', defined as 'the tendency to ascribe harmful or adverse intent to the ambiguous behaviour of others', 'and anger rumination' – mediated the link between child maltreatment and aggressive behaviours.[8]

Anger rumination is a tendency to dwell on frustrating experiences and recall past anger experiences.[9] Mediate is where A causes B, and B causes C.

To judge by the results, Stalin was angry with the kulaks, the Jews, his so-called friends and colleagues, members of the military, politicians, political dissidents (of who he himself had once been), members of his own family even. In fact, as many have testified, whenever anyone opposed him, he tended to fly into a violent rage.

The use of anger to manipulate and problem solve

'Angry, aggressive, and abusive adults,' such as Stalin's father, Besarion 'demonstrate disregard of the emotional, psychological, and physical boundaries of others. Children exposed to such behaviour learn that anger and aggression can be used in relationships to communicate, establish dominance, exert control, solve problems, and resolve conflict.' Put simply, the child learns from its abusive parents that anger and violence are the norm, and a normal way of dealing with problems.[10]

This became Stalin's trademark. No one learnt this lesson better than he!

Feelings of betrayal

'Another significant source of anger for adults who were abused as children is the deep sense of betrayal and abandonment experienced during childhood abuse.'

Surely, Stalin would have felt extremely let down by his father Besarion, who, with his mother, were the two people in the world who he ought to have been able to rely on for love and support.

'Children look to significant adults in their lives for protective nurturance. Frustration is a normal response to having unmet dependency needs. Chronic frustration, as in situations of prolonged or frequent abuse, will typically develop into chronic anger.'[11]

Fantasizing about 'getting even'

'Additionally, revenge fantasies often fuel chronic anger-management problems for victims of childhood abuse. Revenge fantasies also play a significant role in anger problems related to abuse situations in later life.'[12]

It is quite likely that the young Stalin dreamed of getting his revenge, at a later date.

Chapter 40

Stalin's Anti-Semitism

'I've tried to give to Stalin his due and to acknowledge his merits,' said Khrushchev, 'but there was no excuse for what, to my mind, was a major defect in his character – his hostile attitude toward the Jewish people.' However, 'as a leader and a theoretician he took care never to hint at his anti-Semitism in his written works or in his speeches'.[1]

Referring to a time (date not specified) when 'a group of Jews' at the Stalin Automobile Factory in Moscow were put on trial, Khrushchev declared, 'Stalin was looking for [i.e. suspecting] schemes of American imperialism operating through Zionists. It was all pure nonsense of course.'[2] In addition to his anti-Semitism, here is yet another example of Stalin's paranoia!

Yakov's first wife, Yudith ('Yulia') 'was Jewish', said Svetlana, 'and that displeased my father. He never liked Jews, though he wasn't as blatant about expressing his hatred for them in those days as he was after the war.'[3]

Referring to Svetlana's first husband, Grigory Morozov, whom she married in 1944, Stalin declared, 'That first husband of yours was thrown your way by the Zionists. The entire older generation is contaminated with Zionism.'[4]

One day, Svetlana bore witness personally to an anti-Semitic act in which her father was complicit when she overheard Stalin speaking on the telephone. 'Something was being reported to him and he was listening.' In fact, Stalin was listening to an account of the death of Soviet–Jewish actor and artistic director of the Moscow State Jewish Theatre, Solomon Mikhoels on 12 January 1948.

'Then, as a summary of the conversation, he said, "Well, it's an automobile accident." I remember so well the way he said it: not a question but an answer, an assertion. He wasn't asking. He was suggesting "an automobile accident". When he got through [i.e. finished], he greeted me, and a little later he said: "Mikhoels was killed in an automobile accident."

'But when next day I came to my classes in the university a girl student, whose father had worked for a long time in the Jewish Theatre, told me, weeping, how brutally Mikhoels had been murdered while travelling through Belorussia in a car. The newspapers of course, reported the event as an "automobile accident".'[5]

Chapter 41

Trotsky's Criticisms of Stalin

If Trotsky was bitter about being exiled from his native land, this is understandable. However, his criticisms of Stalin, the person who had exiled him, were based on facts and reasoned argument.

Stalin as opportunistic and authoritarian

For example in 1932, Trotsky wrote in respect of: 'some of the landmarks of Stalin's political biography. They give a sufficiently complete picture in which energy, will and determination are combined with empiricism, near-sightedness, organic inclination to opportunist decisions in big questions, personal rudeness, disloyalty and a readiness to abuse power for the suppression of the party.'[1]

Empiricism is the theory that all knowledge is based on experiences derived from the senses, rather than from theorising or from the application of logic.[2]

Trotsky was quick to see Hitler as a danger, whereas Stalin's head was buried in the proverbial sand

In March 1933, Trotsky wrote, 'Allowing for all diversion, the foreign policy of Fascist Germany is essentially directed against the Soviet Union.'[3]

Stalin: a megalomaniac at the head of an insane regime

In July 1937, Trotsky stated as follows, 'The political goal was – to create an automatic guillotine for every opponent of the ruling clique: whoever is not for Stalin is a hired agent of imperialism.'

'This rude schema, reinforced by personal vindictiveness, is wholly in the spirit of Stalin. Apparently, he did not for a moment doubt that the "voluntary confessions" of his victims would succeed in convincing the whole world of the authenticity of the accusations and thus, solve once and for all, the problem of the inviolability of the totalitarian regime.'

Totalitarian relates to a system of government that is centralised, dictatorial, and requires complete subservience to the state.[4]

'Out of the latest "purge" the regime has emerged so covered with infamy that the organs of the world press have begun to speculate seriously whether Stalin has not lost his senses. Too simple a solution for this problem! First it was deemed that Stalin had emerged victorious owing to the exceptional qualities of his intellect. But when the reflexes of the bureaucracy become epileptic in character, those who worshipped the 'leader' yesterday begin asking themselves whether he had not gone mad?'

Bureaucracy is a system of government in which most of the important decisions are taken by state officials rather than by elected representatives.

'Both appraisals are false. Stalin is no "genius". In the proper sense of the term, he is not even intelligent, that is, if by intelligence is meant the ability to view events in their connection and development. But neither is Stalin a madman. He was carried to the top by the wave of Thermidor. He came to believe that the source of his power lay in himself. But the caste of parvenus, who had proclaimed him genius, disintegrated and corroded within a short space of time. The land of the October Revolution is in urgent need of a different political regime. The position of the ruling clique leaves no more room for any rational politics. "Insanity" is located not in Stalin but in the regime which has completely drained itself. This explanation, however, does not contain even a hint of any moral justification of Stalin. He will depart from the scene as the most tarnished figure in mankind's history.'[5]

The Kremlin as a lie factory presided over by the chief liar

In 1940, Trotsky declared that: 'Our epoch is above all an epoch of lies. I do not think that in all of human history anything could be found even remotely resembling the gigantic factory of lies which was organised by the Kremlin under the leadership of Stalin.'[6]

Stalin as a cruel anachronism

In 1940, Trotsky wrote of Stalin, 'This throw-back to the most cruel Machiavellianism seems incomprehensible to one who, until yesterday, abided in the comforting confidence that human history moves along a rising line of material and cultural progress.'[7]

Machiavelli, Niccolò di Bernardo dei was an Italian statesman and philosopher who, in *The Prince* (published in 1532), advised rulers that the acquisition and effective use of power may necessitate unethical methods.[8]

Stalin as a shallow propagandist

In 1940, Trotsky wrote scathingly about Stalin's lack of intellect, 'He came to power not as an orator, but above all as a writer, as an instructor of the propagandists who had trained his cadres including, also, the cadres of orators.' Stalin, he said, 'represents a phenomenon utterly exceptional. He is neither a thinker, a writer nor an orator.'[9]

Chapter 42

Stalin's Persecution of Trotsky

Trotsky made several 'mistakes' in his life as far as Stalin was concerned. Firstly, he was born a Jew. Secondly, his masterful direction of the Red Army during the Civil War made him a hero in the eyes of the Communist Party and throughout the land as saviour of the revolution. Thirdly, he differed from Stalin in his views as to how quickly world revolution was to be achieved. Lastly, in his writings, he was highly critical of Stalin.

When Trotsky was exiled in 1928, his son, Lev Sedov, accompanied him. Just prior to Adolf Hitler's coming to power (in March 1933), Lev relocated to Paris from Berlin, where he had been studying. Lev became a qualified engineer. In Paris he 'went to work' as a labourer 'and became an important activist in the Trotskyist movement'. However, 'He was frequently followed by agents of the Soviet NKVD.'

In 1936, Lev's *The Red Book on the Moscow Trials*, an exposé of the first Moscow Trial, was published. The 'Moscow Trials' were a series of show trials conducted between 1936 and 1938 against Trotskyists and right-wing critics of the Communist Party.

'After an acute attack of appendicitis in February 1938, Mark Zborowski, an NKVD agent who had posed as Sedov's comrade and friend, arranged to take him to a private clinic instead of a Paris hospital. At the same time, Zborowski notified the NKVD that Sedov had been transported under an assumed name to the Clinique Mirabeau, which was operated by a White Russian with connections to Soviet intelligence, who performed an appendicectomy. Complications set in after the operation, but Sedov apparently received no further treatment. He was later taken to a Paris hospital, where he died.'[1] Lev died on 16 February 1938.

'As I write these lines,' said Trotsky, 'with Leon [Lev] Sedov's mother [Natalia] by my side, telegrams of condolence keep coming from different countries. Each telegram is a new token of his death, but we are unable to believe it as yet. And this, not only because he was our son: truthful, devoted, loving, but above all because he had, as no one else on earth, become part of our life, entwined in all its roots, our co-thinker, our co-worker, our guard, our counsellor, our friend.'

Lev's 'studies in the Superior Technical Academy progressed very favourably,' said Trotsky, 'but they took up only a part of his working day. Most of his time, strength, and spirit were devoted to the cause of the revolution. For him, the revolution was not an abstraction. Oh, no! It seeped into his very pores.

'Whence then this malignant disease, and lightning death? In twelve days? For us, the question is shrouded in deep mystery. Will it ever be cleared up? The first and natural supposition is that he was poisoned. It presented no serious difficulty for the agents of Stalin to gain access to Leon, his clothing, his food.

'Before they killed him, they did everything in their power to slander and blacken our son in the eyes of contemporaries and of posterity. Cain [Biblical figure who murdered his brother Abel] Dzhugashvili [i.e. Stalin] and his henchmen tried to depict Leon as an agent of fascism; a secret partisan of capitalist restoration in the USSR; the organiser of railway wrecks and murders of workers. The efforts of the scoundrels are in vain. Leon was a thoroughly clean, honest, pure human being.'[2]

In May 1940, Trotsky revealed the extent of the murderous activities of Stalin's Secret Police (which he referred to by it's former name, the GPU): 'During the last few years, Stalin has shot hundreds of real or supposed friends of mine. He actually exterminated my entire family, except me, my wife and one of my grandchildren. Through his agents abroad he assassinated one of the old leaders of the GPU, Ignace Reiss, who had publicly declared himself a partisan of mine. This fact has been established by the French police and the Swiss judiciary. The same GPU agents who killed Reiss trailed my son in Paris. On the night of November 7, 1936, GPU agents broke into the Scientific Institute of Paris and stole part of my archives. Two of my secretaries, Erwin Wolff and Rudolf Klement, were assassinated by the GPU: the first in Spain; the second in Paris.'

Ignace Reiss was a Soviet spy who broke with the Soviet Union in 1937. Rudolf Klement was a German linguist. Klement's body 'was found in the Seine with the head, hands and legs cut off,' said Trotsky.

'All the theatrical Moscow trials during 1936–1937 had as their aim, to get me into the hands of the GPU.'[3]

In an article written by Trotsky on 8 June 1940, entitled 'Stalin Seeks My Death' he described, in detail an attempt on his life: Early on the morning of 24 May 1940, he and his (second) wife, Natalia (née Sedova), were asleep at their home in Viena Street, Coyoacán borough, Mexico City. Natalia was the daughter of a Russian merchant and revolutionary. By her, Trotsky had two sons: Lyova (aka Lev or Leon) Sedov (born 24 February 1906, Finland); and Sergei Sedov (born 21 March 1908, Vienna).

Also present in the house was Trotsky's grandson, Vsevolod (aka 'Seva' or 'Esteban') and Volkov, son of Zinaida, Trotsky's daughter by his first wife, Alexandra Sokolovskaya.

'The attack came at dawn, about 4 a.m. I was fast asleep, having taken a sleeping drug after a hard day's work. Awakened by the rattle of gunfire but feeling very hazy, I first imagined that a national holiday was being celebrated with fireworks outside our walls. But the explosions were too close, right here within the room, next to me and overhead. The odour of gunpowder became more acrid, more penetrating. Clearly, what we had always expected was now happening: we were under attack. Where were the police stationed outside the walls? Where were the guards inside? Trussed up? Kidnapped? Killed?

'My wife had already jumped from her bed. The shooting continued incessantly. My wife later told me that she helped me to the floor, pushing me into the space between the bed and the wall. This was quite true. She had remained hovering over me, beside the wall, as if to shield me with her body. But by means of whispers and gestures I convinced her to lie flat on the floor. The shots came from all sides, it was difficult to tell just from where. At a certain time my wife, as she later told me, was able clearly to distinguish spurts of fire from a gun. Consequently, the shooting was being done right here in the room although we could not see anybody. My impression is that altogether some two hundred shots were fired, of which about one hundred fell right here, near us. Splinters of glass from windowpanes and chips from walls flew in all directions. A little later I felt that my right leg, had been slightly wounded in two places.

'As the shooting died down, we heard our grandson in the neighbouring room cry out: "Grandfather!" The voice of the child in the darkness under the gunfire remains the most tragic recollection of that night. The boy (after the first shot had cut his bed diagonally as evidenced by marks left on the door and wall) threw himself under the bed. One of the assailants, apparently in a panic, fired into the bed, the bullet passed through the mattress, struck our grandson in the big toe and imbedded itself in the floor. The assailants threw two incendiary bombs and left our grandson's bedroom. Crying, "Grandfather!" he ran after them into the patio, leaving a trail of blood behind him and, under gunfire, rushed into the room of one of the guards.

'At the outcry of our grandson, my wife made her way into his already empty room. Inside, the floor, the door and a small cabinet were burning. "They have kidnapped Seva," I said to her. This was the most painful moment of all. Shots continued to ring out but already away from our bedroom, somewhere in the patio or immediately outside the walls. The terrorists were apparently covering their retreat. My wife hastened to smother the incendiary flames with a rug. For a week afterward she had to treat her burns.' Seva survived the ordeal and grew up to become a chemist in Mexico City.

'I am informed that Stalin has several times admitted that my exile abroad was a "major mistake",' Trotsky continued. 'No other way remained of rectifying the mistake except through a terrorist act.'

Trotsky went on to describe how, 'In recent years [the GPU (Soviet Secret Police)] 'has destroyed many hundreds of my friends, including members of my family in the USSR. In Spain they killed my former secretary, Erwin Wolfe and a number of my political co-thinkers. In Paris they killed my son, Leon Sedov whom Stalin's professional murderers hunted for two years. In Lausanne the GPU killed Ignace Reiss, who had left the GPU and joined the Fourth International.'

As for the present, Trotsky affirmed that he had, 'received many letters from my friends, chiefly in New York and Paris, concerning agents of the GPU who were being sent into Mexico from France and the United States. The names and photographs of some of these gentlemen were transmitted by me in time to the Mexican police. The outbreak of the war aggravated the situation still further because of my irreconcilable struggle against the foreign and domestic policy of the Kremlin. My declarations and articles in the world press on the dismemberment of Poland, the invasion of Finland, the weakness of the Red Army beheaded by Stalin, etc. were reproduced in all countries of the world in tens of millions of copies.'

For these reasons, declared Trotsky, 'Stalin could not have failed to issue orders to his agents to finish me as quickly as possible.' Furthermore, 'for Stalin it would have been most profitable to have organised the murder in such a way as to represent it before the world's working class as a sudden and spontaneous chastisement of an "enemy of the people" by Mexican workers.'

Trotsky was certain, however, that this was not the end of the matter, and that he was not long for this world, 'The accidental failure of the assault, so carefully and so ably prepared, is a serious blow to Stalin. The GPU must rehabilitate itself with Stalin. Stalin must demonstrate his power. A repetition of the attempt is inevitable.' The question was in what form would a future attempt on his life be made?

'To justify their persecution of me, and to cover up the assaults of the GPU, the agents of the Kremlin talk about my "counter-revolutionary" tendency. It all depends on what one understands as revolution and counter-revolution. The most powerful force of the counter-revolution in our epoch is imperialism, both in its fascist form as well as in its quasi-democratic cover. Not one of the imperialist countries wishes to permit me inside its territories.'

Nevertheless, 'Mexico extended hospitality to me because Mexico is not an imperialist country. For this reason, it's government proved to be, as a rare exception, sufficiently independent of external pressure to guide itself in accordance with its own principles.'[4] Mexico had become independent from Spain on 24 August 1821.

On 20 August 1940 the inevitable happened, when Spanish communist and NKVD agent Jaime Ramón Mercader del Río 'ingratiated himself into the household of Trotsky' and stabbed him with an ice pick. Trotsky died the following day.[5] Mercader was apprehended and served a total of nineteen years and eight months in Mexican prisons for the murder.

At the time of his death Trotsky was working on his book, *Stalin: An Appraisal of the Man and His Influence.* The incomplete manuscript was edited and translated by US writer Charles Malamuth and published in 1946.

Chapter 43

Stalin Versus Trotsky

Trotsky defined his notion of the 'Permanent Revolution' as: 'a revolution which welds together the oppressed masses of town and country around the proletariat organised in soviets; as a national revolution that raises the proletariat to power and thereby opens up the possibility of a democratic revolution growing over into the socialist revolution.

'The permanent revolution is no isolated leap of the proletariat; rather it is the rebuilding of the whole nation under the leadership of the proletariat. That is how I conceived and interpreted the prospect of the permanent revolution, beginning with [in] 1905.'[1]

Trotsky also believed that the permanent revolution should be exported to the entire world!

Stalin, on the other hand, believed in 'Socialism in one country', as already mentioned. He was far too preoccupied with seeking out new enemies at home, vilifying them, often prescribing the appropriate torture necessary to persuade them to confess to their alleged 'crimes' and signing their death warrants, instead of concerning himself with what was going on abroad.

As regards motivation, Trotsky always remained focused on the goal of achieving world socialism. Stalin, on the other hand, was primarily concerned with wreaking a paranoic vengeance on those who, in the main, were mistakenly believed by him to be his opponents.

Did Stalin believe in democracy? Surely a superfluous question! Stalin was first and last a dictator, whose overriding ambition was to crush all opposition, whether real, imagined, or conjured up by the likes of Beria, and impose 'Stalinism' on the Russian people.

Stalinism was the ideologies and policies adopted by Stalin, based on centralisation, totalitarianism, and the pursuit of communism.[2]

As for Trotsky, he declared, 'As Marxists, we have never been idol-worshipers of formal democracy. In a society of classes, democratic institutions not only do not eliminate class struggle, but also give to class interests an utterly imperfect expression.

'If, in the final analysis, it is to the advantage of the proletariat to introduce its class struggle and even its dictatorship, through the channels of democratic institutions, it does not at all follow that history always affords it the opportunity for attaining this happy consummation. There is nothing in the Marxian theory to warrant the deduction that history always creates such conditions as are most "favourable" to the proletariat.'[3]

In other words, a dictatorship by the proletariat might be preferable to democracy.

Both men were ruthless. Stalin, in a bizarre manner, directed his venom at mostly innocent targets on an industrial scale. Trotsky stated that, 'An army cannot be built without reprisals. Masses of men cannot be led to death unless the army command has the death penalty in its arsenal. So long as those malicious tailless apes that are so proud of their technical achievements – the animals that we call men – will build armies and wage wars, the command will always be obliged to place the soldiers between the possible death in the front and the inevitable one in the rear.'

'And yet,' Trotsky continued, 'armies are not built on fear.' For soldiers to fight, they needed to be inspired by a compelling ideology and good leadership. 'The strongest cement in the new army,' he said, 'was the ideas of the October Revolution.'[4]

But unlike Stalin's violence, Trotsky's violence was not gratuitous (perpetrated without good reason).

Would Trotsky have condoned violence abroad in an attempt to achieve 'Permanent Revolution'? Of course! His support of the Bolsheviks in the October Revolution, during which he oversaw Soviet military operations in Petrograd, the then Russian capital; and his position as Soviet Commissar for Military Affairs between March 1918 and January 1925, fully attests to that.

Trotsky's mantra was, 'A means can be justified only by its end. But the end, in its turn, needs to be justified.'[5]

'Intelligence' is defined as the ability to acquire knowledge and skills. 'Intellect' is the faculty of reasoning and understanding objectively.[6] Trotsky certainly possessed both of these qualities in abundance. If Stalin possessed either of these qualities, it was not apparent, corralled as he was in the prison of his paranoia!

What of the end result? What had the revolution achieved? In his book, *The Revolution Betrayed*, published in 1936, Trotsky stated that in Stalin's Soviet Union there was a conflict between the Communist Party of revolutionists and the bureaucratic state, in which bureaucracy was the victor.

'From the first days of the Soviet regime the counterweight to bureaucratism was the Party. If bureaucracy managed the state, still the Party controlled the bureaucracy. Keenly vigilant lest inequality transcend the limits of what was necessary, the Party was always in a state of open or disguised struggle with bureaucracy. The historic role of Stalin's faction was to destroy this duplication, subjecting the Party to its own officialdom and merging the latter in the officialdom of the state. Thus, was created the present totalitarian regime. It was his doing the bureaucracy this not unimportant service, that guaranteed Stalin's victory.' In other words, Stalin had created not social democracy, but a dictatorship with himself at the helm.

'In their persecution of revolutionists, the Thermidorians [counter-revolutionaries] pour out all their hatred upon those who remind them of the past and make them dread the future. The prisons; the remote corners of Siberia and Central Asia; the fast-multiplying concentration camps, contain the flower of the Bolshevik Party, the most sturdy and true. Even in the solitary confinement prisons of Siberia the Oppositionists are still persecuted with searches, postal blockades and hunger. In exile, wives are forcibly separated from their husbands with one sole purpose: to break their resistance and extract a recantation. But even those who recant are not saved. At the first suspicion or hint from some informer against them, they are subjected to redoubled punishment.'[7]

Chapter 44

Did Stalin Ever Show Remorse or Insight into his Condition?

Did Stalin ever acknowledge his guilt, or show remorse for his terrible misdeeds? George VI of Georgia was Catholicos (Chief Bishop and spiritual leader) of the Armenian Apostolic Church from 1945 to 1954. Svetlana stated that 'Katolikos [Catholicos] spoke of a time during the Second World War when her father was visited by a delegation from the Church of Georgia. The delegation was headed by Callistrat' – a reference to Callistratus of Georgia, Catholicus-Patriarch of all Georgia. 'How great was their astonishment when Stalin greeted them with his arms open; invited them to the table, and began by asking, "What does the Church need? Tell us. We shall give you everything." Callistrat returned home astounded, because he was sure that he had seen almost repentance in Stalin's behaviour, or at least, some admission of guilt.'[1]

Finally, did Stalin realise that he was a paranoiac and admit to the fact? The nearest he came to doing so was when he told Zhukov, 'I'm a most unfortunate person. I'm afraid of my own shadow.'[2]

Chapter 45

Stalin and his Paranoia

Did Stalin exhibit the signs of paranoia? According to *DSM-5* (the *Diagnostic and Statistical Manual of Mental Disorders*), Paranoid Personality Disorder (PPD) is defined as 'a pervasive distrust and suspiciousness of others such that their motives are interpreted as malevolent, beginning by early adulthood'.

For a diagnosis of PPD to be made, at least four of the following features are required to be present. The person:

1. Suspects, without sufficient basis, that others are exploiting, harming, or deceiving him or her.
2. Is preoccupied with unjustified doubts about the loyalty or trustworthiness of friends or associates.
3. Is reluctant to confide in others because of unwarranted fear that the information will be used maliciously, against him or her.
4. Reads hidden, demeaning, or threatening meanings into benign remarks or events.
5. Persistently bears grudges (i.e. is unforgiving of insults, injuries, or slights).
6. Perceives attacks on his or her character or reputation that are not apparent to others and is quick to react angrily or to counterattack.
7. Has recurrent suspicions, without justification, regarding fidelity of spouse or sexual partner.

Furthermore: 'individuals with this disorder assume that other people will exploit, harm, or deceive them, even if no evidence exists to support this expectation'. Also, 'they are so amazed when a friend or associate shows loyalty, that they cannot trust or believe it'.

'They are constantly vigilant to the harmful intentions of others. They very often feel that their character or reputation has been attacked or that they have been slighted in some other way. They are quick to counter-attack and react with anger to perceived insults. Individuals with this disorder may be pathologically jealous, often suspecting, without any adequate justification, that their spouse or sexual partner is unfaithful to them. They may gather trivial and circumstantial "evidence" to support their jealous beliefs.'

'They want to maintain complete control of intimate relationships to avoid being betrayed.' Finally, 'they tend to develop negative stereotypes of others, particularly those from population groups distinct from their own'.

Here, it should be mentioned that PPD may occur during the course of schizophrenia or other psychiatric disorders, some medical disorders, or certain drug-induced disorders.[1] However, Stalin's thought processes and behaviour do not entirely accord with the required profile for him to be diagnosed as a schizophrenic.

As has been amply demonstrated, Stalin displayed the symptoms of paranoia, to use a modern phrase, 'in spades'. In fact, he demonstrated almost all, if not all of the above features of PPD to an excessive degree!

Those whom Stalin targeted as a result of his paranoia were those people or organisations who or which he believed had betrayed him, or were likely to do so. The truth was, however, that it was *he* who was an existential threat to the citizens of the Soviet Union, and it was *he* who had betrayed *them*, 'in deepest consequence', to quote the words of Banquo in William Shakespeare's play, *Macbeth*.[2]

Chapter 46

Stalin's Jealousy: Georgy Zhukov

'Early on,' said US historian, Paul R. Gregory, Soviet politician Nikolai I. Bukharin 'understood the intensity of Stalin's jealousy. When a Politburo member objected to Lenin's 1919 decision to award Stalin the Order of the Red Banner [Soviet military decoration] alongside Trotsky, Bukharin explained to him, "Can't you understand? Stalin can't live unless he has what someone else has."'[1]

As previously mentioned, jealousy is a feature of paranoia, and nowhere was Stalin's jealousy more graphically demonstrated than in his treatment of Marshal Georgy Zhukov, Commander-in-Chief of the Soviet Army.

On 24 June 1945 a huge victory parade was held in Moscow's Red Square with military bands, march pasts, water fountains playing, and red banners (including one huge one bearing a gold hammer-and-sickle motif topped by a gold-edged red star). Said Simon S. Montefiore, 'Stalin decided to take the review on horseback. He could not ride but his hunger for glory still burned, and he started secretly training to ride a white Arab stallion, chosen by [cavalryman Semyon] Budyonny. Around 15 June, a week before the parade, a spurred and booted Stalin in jodhpurs, apparently accompanied by his son, Vasily, mounted the steed. He jerked his spurs. The horse reared. Stalin grabbed the mane and tried to stay in the saddle but was thrown, bruising his shoulder. Pulling himself to his feet, he spat: "Let Zhukov take the parade. He's a cavalryman."'[2]

British writer Edward Crankshaw summed up Zhukov as follows: 'Marshal Zhukov was Stalin's most outstanding commander in the USSR's painful triumph over Germany.' During the Second World

War he 'directed the first major Soviet success in the defence of Moscow; turned the German tide at the Battle of Stalingrad; lifted the siege of Leningrad, and led the Russian advance from Warsaw to Berlin'.[3]

Said Svetlana Kazakova, Communications Officer at Zhukov's headquarters: 'The victory parade was a brilliant event in the life of the Soviet Union, and I can still see it in my mind's eye. It was a summer's day. The Red Square was decorated with red banners. People were wearing medals and orders, which were shining so much that the light reflected on the whole of the square. As the hands of the clock moved closer to 10, everyone stood to attention. Then came the chimes of the Kremlin clocks, and at that moment Georgy Zhukov, three times Hero of the Soviet Union rode into the square on a white horse. He sat on the horse so elegantly, as if he were a junior lieutenant.'[4]

Zhukov, Inspector of the Parade, rode the same white charger that had thrown Stalin. Behind him rode Marshal Konstantin Rokossovsky, commanding officer of the Parade, on Budyonny's own black charger. 'As the chimes rang out,' said Montefiore, 'the bands played "*Slavsya*" ["Glory, Glory to You Holy Russia", the final song from Russian composer Mikhail Glinka's opera *A Life for the Tsars* [lyrics by Vasily Zhukovsky and Egor Rozen] and tanks and Katyushas [rockets on their launchers] rumbled over the cobblestones. Silence fell on Red Square. "Then a menacing staccato beat of hundreds of drums could be heard,' wrote [Soviet aeronautical engineer Alexander S.] Yakovlev."'[5]

Continued Svetlana Kazakova, 'I think that when Stalin himself saw those two army commanders on their horses he felt jealous, because of course he should have inspected or commanded the parade. But he couldn't do it. I think that's how Stalin's jealousy of Zhukov started.'[6]

On 22 April 1946, Air Marshal Alexander A. Novikov was 'arrested and tortured in Lefortovo Prison. Novikov was forced by Beria into a "confession" which implicated Zhukov in a conspiracy.'[7]

In March 1946, Minister for State Security Viktor S. Abakumov made a search of Zhukov's various houses, where a treasure trove of booty looted from the Nazis was discovered.[8] Beria stated that looted items discovered to be in Zhukov's possession included: '17 golden rings, three gemstones, the faces [presumably pendants] of 15 golden necklaces, more than four kilometres (2.5 miles) of cloth, 323 pieces of fur, 44 carpets taken from German palaces, 55 paintings and 20 guns.'[9]

On 1 June 1946, Zhukov was summoned to a meeting of the Supreme Military Council. 'Stalin strode in "as gloomy as a black cloud." Without a word, he tossed a note to [Soviet general Sergei] Shtemenko. "Read it," he snapped. Shtemenko read out Novikov's testimony that Zhukov had claimed credit for the Soviet victory, criticised Stalin, and created his own clique. "This was 'intolerable," declared Stalin, turning to the generals. Zhukov, however, defended himself but admitted to having inflated his importance.'

'"What shall we do with Zhukov?" asked Stalin who, typically, had expressed no opinion.' When Zhukov was accused of 'planning a Bonapartist [i.e. dictatorial] revolutionary coup', Stalin for once, sided with the accused. 'I don't trust anyone who says Zhukov could do this,' he said. 'I know him very well. He's a straightforward, sharp person, able to speak plainly to anyone but he'll never go against the CC [Central Committee].'[10]

Nonetheless, retribution for Zhukov's alleged crimes followed on 9 June 1946 with an 'ORDER OF THE MINISTER OF THE ARMED FORCES OF THE UNION SSR' (marked 'Top Secret'):

'Council of Ministers of the USSR by decree of 3 June approved the proposal of the Supreme Military Council of June 1 for the release of Marshal of the Soviet Union, Zhukov from the post of Commander-in-Chief of the Ground Forces and by the same resolution freed Marshal Zhukov from his duties as Deputy Minister of the Armed Forces.'

Zhukov, it was alleged, had been guilty of 'untrustworthy and harmful behaviour … toward the government and Supreme Council', and also of 'arrogance'. He had 'made serious mistakes', and 'expressed dissatisfaction with the decisions of government'.

Zhukov was now 'assigned command of the Odessa Military District, far from Moscow and lacking in strategic significance and troops'.[11] The distance from Moscow to Odessa in Ukraine is 825 miles.

It is significant that Zhukov was neither tortured nor murdered, which was invariably the fate of anyone unfortunate to be targeted by

Stalin. Why? Perhaps because Stalin realised that to have condemned to death the man who had masterminded the Soviet Union's war-winning strategy was a step too far. So, for once in his life, Stalin had managed to overcome his homicidal tendencies, driven by his paranoia, and Zhukov had survived.

Zhukov arrived in Odessa on 13 June 1946. In January 1948, he suffered a heart attack and spent a month in hospital. 'In February 1948 he was given another secondary posting: this time, command of the Urals Military District.'[12]

In February 1953, Stalin relieved Zhukov of his post and recalled him to Moscow. However, on 5 March 1953 at 9.50 a.m., Stalin died of a stroke. But for Stalin's timely death, Zhukov may well have been executed. Said Svetlana Kazakova, 'We were very hurt on behalf of Zhukov. In our hearts we were very upset. We all kept silent. Our feelings couldn't change anything. Stalin didn't want Zhukov to overshadow his glory. It's easy to explain why it happened: out of jealousy.'[13]

Chapter 47

A Purge of Doctors

Between 1951 and Stalin's death in March 1953, and doubtless at his instigation or certainly with his consent, 'a group of predominantly Jewish doctors from Moscow were accused of a conspiracy to assassinate Soviet leaders. This was later accompanied by publications of anti-Semitic character in the media, which talked about the threats of Zionism and condemned people with Jewish surnames.' Subsequently, 'many doctors, both Jews and non-Jews, were dismissed from their jobs, arrested, and tortured to produce admissions'.[1]

This plot against the doctors had its origins in a letter written by Lydia Timashuk, 'head of the Kremlin Hospital Cardiographic Unit' to Nikolai Vlasik, head of the Kremlin Guards and 'dated 29 August 1948'. This concerned Andrei Alexandrovich Zhdanov, Second Secretary to the Communist Party (from 31 March 1919).

Zhdanov had been Chairman of the Leningrad Communist Party during the siege of that city by the Nazis (1941–44). In 1947 he had overseen the founding of the Cominform (international Soviet propaganda arm).

At Szklarska Poręba in south-west Poland on 25 September 1947, Zhdanov gave what became known as his 'two camps speech', describing how the post-war world was becoming divided into the imperialist and anti-democratic camp on the one hand, and the anti-imperialist and democratic camp on the other. Shortly afterwards, he suffered a heart attack.

In June 1947, Zhdanov 'suffered another cardiac crisis and a minor stroke'. On 1 July, Stalin replaced him as Second Secretary with Georgy Malenkov, Deputy Chairman of the Council of Ministers. 'Stalin sent his own doctors to supervise Zhdanov, who was moved to a sanatorium' at Valday Novgorod Oblast, 250 miles north-west of Moscow. On 23 July, Zhdanov suffered a heart attack (myocardial infarction). Whereupon, 'Stalin sent his deputy, [Nikolai] Voznesensky and his own physician, [Vladimir] Vinogradov to visit the patient.' Having been prescribed 'exercises and harmful massages', said Montefiore, Zhdanov suffered another heart attack on 29 August. 'Once again, Stalin sent Vinogradov and ordered Voznesensky and Kuznetsov to check the treatment.'

'Before the politicians arrived, a row broke out over the patient. Dr Lydia Timashuk, the cardiographer, diagnosed a "myocardial infarction". However, the distinguished professors made her rewrite her report to specify a much vaguer "dysfunction due to arteriosclerosis [thickening and hardening of the walls of the arteries] and hypertension [high blood pressure]". The doctors pooh-poohed her grave diagnosis and prescribed walking in the park. Hence, Zhdanov suffered another heart attack.

'Timashuk denounced her superiors and had Zhdanov's chief bodyguard deliver the [aforementioned] letter to General Vlasik to give personally to Stalin. When nothing happened, Timashuk, an MGB agent, wrote to the secret police.'

The MGB was the Ministry of State Security, successor to the NKGB, People's Commissariat for State Security.

'Abakumov forwarded the letter to Stalin that same day. Stalin signed it, wrote "Into the archive", but did nothing.' On 31 August 1947, Zhdanov 'got out of bed to visit the lavatory and died of a massive coronary'. (A coronary thrombosis is a blockage of the flow of blood to the heart, caused by a blood clot in a coronary artery.)[2]

Bearing in mind Stalin's murderous nature, the question must be asked, was it at his instigation that Timashuk composed her letter, and if Zhdanov was murdered, did Stalin have a hand in that murder? On both counts, probably not. The fact that Stalin did not commence the major purge of Soviet doctors for another two years suggests that Timashuk's letter took him by surprise. However, the letter would provide him with useful ammunition to be used against the doctors when the time came! As far as Zhdanov was concerned, Khrushchev stated that he 'had been in poor health for some time. One of his ailments was that he had lost his willpower and wasn't able to control himself when it came to drinking.' The drink 'certainly hastened Zhdanov's death to a considerable degree'.[3]

Responsibility for treating Zhdanov rested with the doctors and not with Timashuk, the cardiographer, who was there simply to present, explain, and provide a diagnosis according to what Zhdanov's electrocardiogram demonstrated. However, the fact that prior to his last two heart attacks, Zhdanov's doctors had prescribed exercise and a walk in the park, when after a heart attack, bed rest is mandatory, supports the notion that Timashuk's diagnosis was correct.

Perhaps it was exasperation at what she regarded as a misdiagnosis on the part of the doctors that prompted Timashuk to write her letter, together with indignation that her expertise had been ignored.

Another possibility is that the doctors were well aware of Zhdanov's heart attacks but were anxious not to prolong his life. After all, there was no love lost between Zhdanov and Malenkov: 'The pragmatist faction of Georgy Malenkov … stressed the universal values of science and engineering, and proposed to promote the technological experts to the highest positions in the Soviet administrative elite. Zhdanov's faction said proper ideology trumped science and called for prioritising political education and ideological purity.'[4]

And had Zhdanov recovered, Malenkov might well have had to renounce his new-found position as Second Secretary (and natural successor to Stalin) in Zhdanov's favour. In writing her letter, Timashuk may therefore have feared that she herself would be implicated in this mismanagement – not to say crime!

Stalin subsequently claimed that Timashuk's letter had been withheld from him by Abakumov. This was a lie on Stalin's part because he had, in fact, received the letter 'one day after it was sent', i.e. on 30 August 1948, 'and filed it in his personal archive. He signed the document and wrote "archive" across the bottom.'[5]

Of the Kremlin physicians who had treated Zhdanov, said Khrushchev, 'These doctors could only have been the best and most trusted of their profession. Only men well-known and much respected in the Soviet medical world have been enlisted to work in the Kremlin Hospital. But they were arrested and thrown in jail like common criminals.'[6]

Svetlana provided evidence to corroborate this view. Stalin's housekeeper, Valentina ('Valechka') Istomina, was 'waiting at table' when she heard Stalin discussing the 'case of the Kremlin doctors' who had treated Zhdanov. 'My father remarked that he didn't believe the doctors were "dishonest"' and he stated, "that the only evidence against them, after all", were "the 'reports' of Dr Timashuk".'[7]

The first victim of Stalin's notorious purge of the doctors was Professor Yakov Gilyarievich Etinger, physician and cardiologist, who was arrested on 8 November 1950. Given Stalin's anti-Semitic nature, it was surely no coincidence that Etinger was of Jewish heritage. Etinger died 'under mysterious circumstances in prison' on 8 March 1951', said US writer, Jonathan Brent: 'In July 1951, without any evidence, a "Secret Letter" composed by the Central Committee at Stalin's behest, alleged that Etinger had confessed to the medical murder in 1945, of Central Committee secretary, Alexander Shcherbakov; that this assassination was the work not of Etinger alone, but of a "conspiratorial group" of doctors; and that Abakumov was implicated in the affair.' Abakumov was arrested in July 1951.

Stalin's net spread further when Lev L. Shvartzman, 'the Jewish Deputy Head of the Investigative Unit for Especially Important Cases, an investigative arm of the MGB [Ministry of State Security]' and 'and other Jewish MGB officers were made to confess their complicity in this conspiracy'.

Then, between 1951 and January 1953, a 'core group of 37 doctors', which included seventeen Jews 'and their wives were arrested', one of whom was Miron Vovsi, 'Chief Internist of the Red Army from 1941 to 1950. Many others were added between January and March 1953.' Meanwhile, in December 1952, Stalin also accused Viktor Abakumov and Nikolai Vlasik of 'having participated in Zhdanov's murder'.

Shvartzman was executed on 13 May 1955 for using torture to extract false confessions from prisoners. Abakumov was executed on 19 December 1954 for fabricating the 'Leningrad Affair'. Vlasik survived, but in 1955 he was charged with abuse of power and embezzlement. He served a period of five years in exile. It was not until the year 2000, thirty-three years after his death on 18 June 1967, that he was completely exonerated.

'The interrogations of the doctors, which were accompanied by torture, sought to establish links within a widespread conspiracy involving Jewish nationalists, the American government; the security organs, and Party leaders, including Central Committee Secretary, Alexei Kuznetsov, a former boss of the Leningrad Party and protégé of Zhdanov. Ultimately, it was alleged [the so-called conspirators] would have made an attempt on the life of Stalin himself.'[8]

'On 13 January 1953, nine eminent doctors in Moscow were accused of taking part in a vast plot to poison members of the top Soviet political and military leadership. *Pravda* reported the accusations under the headline "Vicious Spies and Killers under the Mask of Academic Physicians", "Today the TASS [Russian] news agency reported the arrest of a group of saboteur-doctors. This terrorist group, uncovered some time ago by organs of state security, had, as their goal, shortening the lives of leaders of the Soviet Union by means of medical sabotage. Covering themselves with the noble and merciful calling of physicians, men of science, these fiends, and killers dishonoured the holy banner of science. Having taken the path of monstrous crimes, they defiled the honour of scientists.

"Among the victims of this band of inhuman beasts were [the aforementioned] Comrades A. A. Zhdanov and A. [Alexander] S. Shcherbakov [Head of the Political Directorate of the Red Army and Director of the Soviet Information Bureau].

"The criminals confessed that, taking advantage of the illness of Comrade Zhdanov, they intentionally concealed a myocardial infarction [heart attack]; prescribed inadvisable treatments for this serious illness and thus killed Comrade Zhdanov. Killer doctors, by incorrect use of very powerful medicines and prescription of harmful regimens, shortened the life of Comrade Shcherbakov, leading to his death [on 10 May 1945].""[9]

In a speech delivered on 25 February 1956 at the Twentieth Party Congress of the Communist Party of the Soviet Union, Khrushchev stated that, 'Such a letter was sufficient for Stalin to reach an immediate conclusion that there are doctor plotters in the Soviet Union. He issued orders to arrest a group of eminent Soviet medical specialists. He personally issued advice on the conduct of the investigation and the method of interrogation of the arrested persons. He said that the academician [Professor Vladimir N.] Vinogradov should be put in chains; another one should be beaten.'

'Present at this Congress, as a delegate, is the former Minister of State Security, Comrade [Semyon D.] Ignatiev. Stalin told him curtly, "If you do not obtain confessions from the doctors, we will shorten you by a head."'[10]

Khrushchev described Ignatiev as 'mild, considerate, and well liked. Stalin used to berate him viciously over the phone in our presence. Stalin was crazy with rage, yelling at Ignatiev and threatening him; demanding that he throw the doctors in chains, beat them to a pulp, and grind them into powder. It was no surprise when almost all the doctors confessed to their crimes.'[11] Fits of rage were a characteristic feature of Stalin's make-up.

Although Vinogradov 'had once treated Stalin,' said Khrushchev, Stalin 'had him arrested and beaten. They also arrested V. [Vladimir] K. Vasilenko, a reputable physician and professor. Vasilenko was in China when the arrests started. He was called home, and the minute he stepped across the Soviet border he was thrown in chains.'[12]

After the arrests, said Khrushchev, 'Stalin circulated and published copies of Timashuk's letter with his own postscript, in which he invoked the anger of the masses against the doctors who had "committed such villainy" by doing away with Zhdanov.'[13]

Khrushchev stated that one of the doctors who was 'purged' in this way was known to him personally, though he chose not to name that doctor in his book, *Khrushchev Remembers* (published 1970). Prior to the Nineteenth Party Congress (5–14 October 1952), he said, 'I fell ill, and I had to stay in bed for a few days. An elderly doctor came to examine me. While he was listening to my heart, he put his ear against my chest. I was touched by his thoughtfulness and his care. I felt terrible at that moment, but not because I was sick. I was tormented because I had already read the testimony against this old doctor whose concern for my health I found so touching, and I knew that no matter what I said, Stalin wouldn't spare him.'[14]

Said Khrushchev, 'The arrest of the Kremlin doctors in January 1953 on charges of poisoning Andrei Zhdanov and other Soviet luminaries was a preliminary move in what was to have been Stalin's last purge: one designed to get rid of some of his closest colleagues; Beria above all, but probably Molotov and Mikoyan too.'[15] In the event, both Vyacheslav Molotov and Anastas Mikoyan survived.

After Stalin's death on 5 March 1953, 'the new leadership quickly dismissed all charges related to the plot; the doctors were exonerated in a March 31 decree', issued ironically enough 'by the newly-appointed Minister of Internal Affairs, Lavrenti Beria, and on 6 April, this was communicated to the public in *Pravda*. Chief MGB investigator and Deputy Minister for State Security, Mikhail Ryumin was accused of fabricating the plot, arrested, and later executed [on 22 July 1954].'[16]

After Stalin's death Beria became First Deputy Chairman of the Council of Ministers and head of the Ministry of Internal Affairs. But his tenure was to be short-lived. On 26 June 1953, Beria was arrested. He was tried and found guilty of treason and terrorism and executed on 23 December 1953.

Finally, Khrushchev, in his speech delivered on 25 February 1956, referred to 'the affair of the doctor plotters': 'Actually, there was no affair outside of the declaration of the woman doctor [cardiologist], Timashuk, who was probably influenced or ordered by someone (after all, she was an unofficial collaborator of the organs of state security) to write Stalin a letter in which she declared that doctors were applying supposedly improper methods of medical treatment.'[17]

What was the role of Lydia Timashuk in all this? The likelihood is that she was simply doing her best, in the best interests of the patient, Zhdanov. However, when the letter to Vlasik came to the attention of Stalin, this fed into his paranoid mind and he had it archived in order to make use of it at an appropriate time. And, of course, the origins of Stalin's paranoia, as far as the medical profession was concerned, probably had its roots in the affirmation two decades previously in 1927 by Vladimir M. Bekhterev, Professor of Psychiatric Diseases, that he was a 'paranoic'.

Was Zhdanov suffering from heart failure, where the heart is unable to pump sufficient blood around the body; angina, where narrowing of the arteries supplying the heart reduces its blood supply; or a heart attack, whereby the blood supply to the heart is suddenly blocked, usually by a blood clot? An ECG can show evidence of a previous heart attack, or of one that is in progress. An ECG can also show whether chest pain is due to reduced blood flow to the heart muscle.

In the 1940s, all that could be done in the case of a heart attack or severe angina was to prescribe rest, amyl nitrite (which relaxes the blood vessels and thus increases blood supply to the heart), and morphine (a strong analgesic that also creates a sense of well-being). In cases of heart failure, with breathlessness, swelling of the ankles and legs, bed rest, restricted fluids, and a salt-free diet was prescribed. Whereas the ECG would have been helpful, the doctors treating Zhdanov would probably have been able to make the diagnosis on clinical grounds alone, based on their experience.

Chapter 48

Stalin is Rewarded

On 20 December 1939, to mark his 60th birthday which had occurred two days previously, Stalin, 'by decision of the Presidium of the Supreme Soviet of the USSR, was granted the title of Hero of Socialist Labour in recognition of his outstanding services in the organisation of the Bolshevik Party, the creation of the Soviet state, the building of Socialist society in the USSR, and in strengthening the ties of mutual friendship between the Soviet peoples'![1]

On 22 December 1939, 'Stalin was elected an honorary member the Academy of Sciences of the USSR.'[2]

On 6 March 1943, the Soviet Government demonstrated its 'high appreciation of the outstanding services of the Supreme Commander-in-Chief of the Armed Forces' when the Presidium of the Supreme Soviet conferred on Stalin, the title of Marshal of the Soviet Union'.[3]

On 27 June 1945, 'Stalin was invested with the supreme military title – Generalissimo of the Soviet Union.'[4]

Chapter 49

Stalin's Final Years

During the last years of Stalin's life, said Svetlana, 'he was unusually cold, even with me, closed up like a shell, sunken into some kind of darkness. Only with my son [Josef Morozov] and daughter [Yekaterina Zhdanova], then aged seven and two, did he warm up like a normal grandpa. He would treat them to fruit and the fine foods on his table.'[1]

Chapter 50

Stalin's Death (5 March 1953): Aftermath

Within days of Stalin's death 'millions of prisoners were released' from the Gulag. Stalin's successor, Nikita Khrushchev, was a staunch critic of the camps, the purges, and most of Stalin's policies'. However, 'the camps did not disappear completely. Some were restructured to serve as prisons for criminals, democratic activists, and anti-Soviet nationalists during the 1970s and 1980s.'

'It wasn't until about 1987 that Soviet leader, Mikhail Gorbachev, the grandson of Gulag victims, officially began the process of completely eliminating the camps.'[1]

By contrast, and on a personal note, Svetlana said of her father, 'I shall never forget his affection, his love and tenderness to me as a child. He was rarely as tender to anyone as he was to me. At one time he must have loved my mother very much. And he also loved and respected his own mother.'[2]

After her father's death on 5 March 1953, Svetlana said of Stalin: 'Yet he was, after all, my father. A father who had done his best to love me and to whom I owed good things as well as bad.'[3] Even though 'I had been a bad daughter', and her father 'had been a bad father', she said, 'he had loved me all the same, as I loved him.'[4]

However, in September 1957, said Svetlana, 'I changed my name from "Stalina" to "Alliluyeva" – under Soviet law children could bear either their father's or their mother's name. I could no longer tolerate the name of Stalin: its sharp metallic sound lacerated my ears, my eyes, my heart.'[5]

Chapter 51

February 1956: Khrushchev Acknowledges Stalin's Crimes

On 25 February 1956, Khrushchev delivered a speech at the Twentieth Party Congress of the Communist Party of the Soviet Union entitled 'On the Cult of Personality and Its Consequences'. In it, he described what he saw as a fundamental problem with Stalin, that he promoted himself above the Party, 'Comrades, the cult of the individual acquired such monstrous size, chiefly because Stalin himself, using all conceivable methods, supported the glorification of his own person.

'Allow me first of all to remind you how severely the classics [i.e. tenets] of Marxism-Leninism denounced every manifestation of the cult of the individual. Engels and I first joined the secret society of communists on the condition that everything making for superstitious worship of authority would be deleted from its statute. The great modesty of the genius of the revolution, Vladimir Ilyich Lenin, is known. Lenin had always stressed the role of the people as the creator of history; the directing and organisational role of the Party as a living and creative organism; and also the role of the Central Committee.'

'Marxism,' said Khrushchev, 'does not negate the role of the leaders of the workers' class in directing the revolutionary liberation movement.' However, 'While ascribing great importance to the role of the leaders and organisers of the masses, Lenin at the same time, mercilessly stigmatised every manifestation of the cult of the individual.'

To Lenin, such words as 'hero' were 'foreign-to-Marxism,' said Khrushchev. Instead, he 'taught that the Party's strength depends on its indissoluble unity with the masses; on the fact that, behind the Party follow the people – workers, peasants and intelligentsia. During

Lenin's life the Central Committee of the Party was a real expression of collective leadership of the Party and of the Nation'. Furthermore, Lenin had issued a *specific warning* about Stalin, saying, 'Comrade Stalin, having become General Secretary, has concentrated enormous power in his hands; and I am not sure that he always knows how to use that power with sufficient caution. Stalin is too rude and this fault, entirely supportable in relations among us communists, becomes insupportable in the office of General Secretary. Therefore, I propose to the comrades to find a way to remove Stalin from that position and appoint to it another man who, in all respects, differs from Stalin in one superiority: namely, that he be more tolerant, more loyal, more polite, and more considerate to comrades, less capricious, etc.'[1]

'As later events have proven,' said Khrushchev, 'Lenin's anxiety was justified. The negative characteristics of Stalin, which, in Lenin's time, were only incipient, transformed themselves during the last years into a grave abuse of power.' This 'caused untold harm to our Party. Stalin acted not through persuasion, explanation, and patient co-operation with people, but by imposing his concepts and demanding absolute submission to his opinion. Whoever opposed this concept or tried to prove his viewpoint and the correctness of his position, was doomed to removal from the leading collective and to subsequent moral and physical annihilation.

'Stalin's wilfulness vis-a-vis the Party and its Central Committee, became fully evident after the Seventeenth Party Congress which took place in 1934. It was determined that of the 139 members and candidates of the Party's Central Committee who were elected at the 17th congress, 98 persons, that is, 70 percent, were arrested and shot (mostly in 1937–38). The same fate met not only the Central Committee members, but also the majority of the delegates to the Seventeenth Party Congress. Of 1,966 delegates with either voting or advisory rights, 1,108 persons were arrested on charges of anti-revolutionary crimes, i.e., decidedly more than a majority.

'After the criminal murder of S. M. Kirov [on 1 December 1934], mass repressions and brutal acts of violation of Socialist legality began. On the evening of 1 December 1934, on Stalin's initiative (without the approval of the Political Bureau – which was passed two days later, casually) the Secretary of the Presidium of the Central Executive Committee, Yenukidze, signed the following directive:

I. Investigative agencies are directed to speed up the cases of those accused of the preparation or execution of acts of terror.

II. Judicial organs are directed not to hold up the execution of death sentences pertaining to crimes of this category in order to consider the possibility of pardon, because the Presidium of the Central Executive Committee, USSR, does not consider as possible the receiving of petitions of this sort.'

In other words, once sentence had been passed, there was to be no possibility of appeal.

III. 'The organs of the Commissariat of Internal Affairs are directed to execute the death sentences against criminals of the above-mentioned category immediately after the passage of sentences.'

Said Khrushchev, 'This directive became the basis for mass acts of abuse against Socialist legality. During many of the fabricated court cases the accused were charged with "the preparation" of terroristic acts; this deprived them of any possibility that their cases might be re-examined, even when they stated before the court that their confessions were secured by force, and when, in a convincing manner, they disproved the accusations against them.

'Now when the cases of [i.e. against] some of these so-called spies and saboteurs were examined,' said Khrushchev, 'it was found that all their cases were fabricated. Confessions of guilt of many arrested and charged with enemy activity were gained with the help of cruel and inhuman tortures.'

After the war, said Khrushchev, 'Stalin became even more capricious, irritable, and brutal; in particular his suspicion grew. His persecution mania reached unbelievable dimensions. Many workers were becoming enemies before his very eyes. After the war Stalin separated himself from the collective [leadership] even more. Everything was decided by him alone, without any consideration for anyone or anything.'

'Comrades, in order not to repeat errors of the past,' said Khrushchev, 'the Central Committee has declared itself resolutely against the cult of the individual. Comrades, we must abolish the cult of the individual decisively, once and for all.'[2]

'Cult' in this context is defined as a misplaced or excessive admiration.

Chapter 52

Excess Mortality in the Soviet Union under Joseph Stalin

Following the dissolution of the Soviet Union on 31 December 1991, certain records from the Soviet archives were declassified. These records indicate how Soviet citizens and others met their deaths between the years 1921 and 1953.

Some have argued that the records are incomplete and unreliable. However, the opposite may be true, and those who kept the records may have been diligent and meticulous in order to please their master, Stalin, who was known to be a stickler for detail and liable to deal harshly with anyone who fell short in this regard.

Forced settlements in the Soviet Union: 1920–50

Between 1920 and 1952 in excess of 5 million persons were deported to forced settlements.[1] NB. The author, Russian historian Pavel M. Polonian, does not distinguish between Forced and Special Settlements and the figure given presumably represents the sum total of both.

'Data from the Soviet archives lists 309,521 deaths in the Special Settlements' between 1941 and 1948, and 73,454 between 1949 and 1950.[2] NB. Figures from 1951 to 1953 are not given.

Judicial executions: 1929–53

'According to official figures,' between 1929 and 1953 'there were 777,975 judicial executions' of those charged with political offences.

The vast majority of these, 681,692, occurred in 1937 and 1938, the years of Stalin's 'Great Purge'.[3]

The Gulag: 1930–53

The 'tentative historical consensus' is that 18 million people 'passed through the Gulag system' between 1930 and 1953, and that 'between 1.5 and 1.7 million died as a result of their incarceration'.[4]

Population transfers by the Soviet Union: Deportation of kulaks: 1930–40

Data from the Soviet archives indicates that '2.4 million kulaks were deported' between 1930 and 1934.[5] Furthermore, 'the reported number of kulaks and their relatives' who 'died in labour colonies' between 1932 and 1940 was 389,521.[6]

Purge of the Red Army: 1937–39

During this purge, some 35,000 'high-ranking officers in the Red Army' were executed, as already mentioned.

Also, 'most of the 1,836,000 surviving Red Army prisoners of war liberated from the Axis powers at the end of World War II were sent to the Gulag as "traitors to the motherland"'.[7]

Purge of the Red Army: 1940–42

During this purge, as already mentioned, about 300 military commanders were executed, together with forty-six more high-ranking military officers and others connected with the military.[8]

The Katyn massacre: April–May 1940

'The number of victims is estimated at about 22,000.'[9]

Summary

The total official 'excess death toll', over and above what would normally be expected and based on the above figures, is as follows:

Forced settlements in the Soviet Union of 1939–53	382,975
Judicial executions/The Great Purge	777,975
The Gulag	1,600,000
Population transfer by the Soviet Union: deportation of kulaks	389,521
Purge of the Red Army: 1937–39	35,000
Purge of the Red Army: 1940–42	346
The Katyn massacre	21,857
Total	3,207,674

The question is, should famine-related deaths also be included? During this period there were two great Soviet famines: one in the 1930s and another in the 1940s:

The Soviet famine of 1932–33

The death toll was between '5.5 and 6.5 million'.[10] In April 2019, Professor Viktor Kondrashin, Doctor of Historical Sciences at Penza University, Penza, Western Russia, pointed out that this famine 'was a tragedy that afflicted the entire Soviet countryside, particularly in Ukraine and Russia'. The famine: 'was the result of the Stalinist regime's anti-peasant policy during the first Five-Year Plan, its miscalculations, and the antihuman, criminal measures that were instituted against the peasantry, which led to the collapse of agriculture throughout the country and to famine.'[11]

In other words, the 1932–33 famine was the result of a lethal combination of ideological bigotry, criminality, and incompetence on the part of the Stalinist regime.

The Soviet famine of 1946–47

Economist Michael Ellman claimed, 'that the famine resulted in an estimated 1 to 1.5 million lives lost'. Ellman also declared that 'the state could have fed all those who died of starvation. He argued that had the policies of the Soviet regime been different, there might have been no famine at all, or a much smaller one.'[12]

Said US political scientist Rudolph J. Rummel, 'It is not by chance that the greatest famines have occurred within the Soviet Union (about 5,000,000 dead during 1921–23 and 7,000,000 from 1932–33) and communist China (about 27,000,000 dead from 1959–61).'[13] I.e. under communist regimes.

The consensus is, therefore, that the deaths from both these famines were preventable, and their numbers should therefore be added to the grand total of excess deaths: the vast majority of which occurred under Stalin's leadership (1924–53). The final total is therefore:

3,207,674 + 6,000,000 + 1,500,000 =
10,707,674 lives lost.

Other sources give a considerably higher figure. For example:

	Million lives
Roy Alexandrovich Medvedev (Georgian historian):	20
Alexander Solzhenitsyn (Russian novelist and former political prisoner)	60
Iosef G. Dyadkin (Russian geophysicist)	34–49
Norman Davies (British historian)	50
Alexander Nikolaevich Yakovlev (Soviet politician and historian)	35
Robert Conquest (British historian)	20–30[14]
Average estimate	41.5 million

Chapter 53

Was Stalin the Twentieth Century's Bloodiest Dictator?

In his book, *Death by Government* (published in 1994), R. J. Rummel stated that 'for about eight years', he had 'been sifting through thousands of sources trying to determine the extent of democide in this century'. He defined 'democide' as 'the premeditated killing of a person in cold blood or causing the death of a person through reckless and wanton disregard for their life'.

However: 'Judicial executions for crimes that internationally would be considered capital offences, such as for murder or treason (as long as it is clear that these are not fabricated for the purpose of executing the accused, as in communist show trials), are not democide. Nor is democide the killing of enemy soldiers in combat or of armed rebels, nor of non-combatants as a result of military action against military targets.'[1]

In the twentieth century the country in which the greatest number of state-sponsored murders occurred – of 61,000,000 people – was the Soviet Union, and, 'Stalin himself is responsible for almost 43,000,000 of these.'[2]

Of all the men 'most notorious and singularly responsible for the mega-murders of this century,' said Rummel, 'Stalin, by far, leads the list,' and he gave the following statistic:

Joseph Stalin 1929–53: Murdered 42,672,000.

This figure is greatly in excess of that principally derived from released Soviet archives, as previously quoted.

Rummel also concluded that of all the 'episodes and institutions' for which twentieth-century mass murderers were responsible, 'far and above' was the Gulag, created by Lenin and Trotsky in 1918 and massively expanded by Stalin which 'in some 70 years', accounted for the deaths of some 40,000,000 people.

But Rummel issued a caveat: 'All the totals and figures in this book,' he said, 'should 'be viewed as rough approximations, as suggestive of an order of magnitude.'[3]

As for the other twentieth-century mass murderers, their grim tally was, according to Rummel (in millions):

Mao Tse-tung	37.828
Adolf Hitler	20.946
Chiang Kai-shek	10.214
Vladimir Ilyich Lenin (1917–24)	4.017[4]

Chapter 54

Was Communism a Greater or Lesser Evil than Tsarism?

An article entitled, 'Comparison of Tsar and Communist Rule', published in 2018, draws comparisons between life under the tsarist regimes and life under the Soviet regimes:

Government: similarities and differences

'While the ideologies on which Imperial and Soviet Russia were founded lay at opposite ends of the political spectrum, the machinery of government operated in much the same way in both cases. It is difficult to assess which form of government was more autocratic.

'There were certainly huge differences in the ultimate aims and objectives of the two forms of government. While Imperial Russia strove to secure the succession of the Romanov dynasty through maintaining the hereditary monarchy, Soviet Russia sought to achieve world revolution in pursuit of the Communist ideal.

'While the concentration of government dominance appeared greater under communism, especially during the Stalinist era, the state in both cases, to all intents and purposes, retained almost full control over agriculture, industry, the military, education, and the judiciary.'[1]

Imprisonment in the Gulag

British historian Daniel Beer estimates that between 1801 and 1917, more than one million subjects of the Russian Tsars were banished to Siberia.[2]

By comparison, estimates of the total numbers imprisoned in the Gulag between 1929 and 1953 vary between 25 million (British historian Orlando Figes) and 40–50 million (Alexander Solzhenitsyn).

State-sponsored deaths under Tsar Nicholas II

The Secret Police of Imperial Russia – the Okhrana – was created following the assassination of Tsar Alexander II (grandfather of Tsar Nicholas II) in 1881. Examination of official files after the 1917 Russian Revolution suggests that the Okhrana had previously been responsible for in excess of 26,000 extra-judicial killings. However, because the Okhrana 'did not have the resources to combat mass opposition', the military was drafted in 'on 1,500 occasions from 1883 to 1903 to curb large-scale public disturbances'.[3]

Said Rummel of Tsar Nicholas II, who ruled Russia from 1900 until he was deposed in 1917, 'He was an absolute nationalist, an autocrat and anti-Semitic. Under him Jewish pogroms were encouraged, opposition repressed, dissident minorities bloodily subjugated, and in particular, during the First World War, German and other prisoners of war were treated atrociously, many dying as a result. Taking into account all the democide under the Tsar, possibly near 900,000 to almost 1,500,000 Russians, subjects of the Russian empire, and foreigners were killed; perhaps around 1,000,000. But this figure is very uncertain. There are too few sources for the largest democides that earn the Tsar's regime full status as a mega-murderer, but still there is sufficient evidence to at least issue an indictment.'[4]

State-sponsored deaths under Soviet leader Vladimir Lenin

The Cheka (Russian Extraordinary Commission for Combating Counter-Revolution and Sabotage) 'was the first of a succession of Soviet state security organisations. It was created by decree on 20 December 1917 by Vladimir Lenin. After 1922, the Cheka underwent a series of reorganisations and had numerous successors until the creation of the KGB [state security police of the former USSR] in 1954.

From its founding, the Cheka was an important military and security arm of the Bolshevik communist government.'

The Cheka was primarily concerned with punishing and executing political opponents of Bolshevism. However, because when 'anarchists and other political dissidents' were executed they were recorded as 'criminals, armed bandits, or armed gangsters', estimating the number [of political dissidents] killed is problematical. 'Several scholars put the number of executions at about 250,000.'[5]

Although the killing of any one human being is a tragedy, these numbers are dwarfed by the total number murdered on Stalin's watch.

Democracy

Was there ever democracy in Russia/the Soviet Union, either under the Tsars or under communism? The answer is no. The Russian Constituent Assembly of 1918 'was Russia's first-ever, genuinely representative, constitution-making body. One reason behind the February Revolution (1917) was Tsar Nicholas II's autocratic government. What emerged was the Russian Provisional Government, which was to hold power until a more democratic system could be decided upon by a representative constituent assembly. This was elected (November 1917) on the basis of proportional representation. The Socialist Revolutionary Party gained over half the seats (380 out of 703); the Bolsheviks less than a quarter (168). Lenin still let the Assembly meet in January 1918 in the half-hearted hope that it would legitimise his new government. When it refused on the first day, he dissolved it on the second, thus ending all democratic experimentation for the next 70 years.'[6]

This was a reference to the first multiparty elections held in March 1990, when Boris Yeltsin emerged as leader of Russia. This was shortly before the dissolution of the Soviet Union on 31 December 1991, and the adopting of the new Constitution of the Russian Federation on 12 December 1993. This 'declared Russia a democratic, federative, law-based state with a republican form of government. The right to a multiparty political system is upheld.'[7]

What is Lenin's legacy? Firstly, he inspired the people to depose the autocratic Tsar Nicholas II, who had failed to recognise and respond to their needs quickly enough. Secondly, he destroyed Russia's fledgling democracy, using the Gulag to incarcerate his opponents and imposed a dictatorship, not of the proletariat but of himself! Thirdly, by these actions, he made civil war inevitable.

Chapter 55

The Fate of Svetlana

'It never crossed my mind,' said Svetlana, that 19 December 1966 'was to be my last day in Moscow and in Russia.' She would now begin a new life in the USA.[1]

'The official Decree of the Supreme Soviet of USSR stripped me "of the honour" of being a Soviet subject – to my great joy. I had already applied through the Soviet Consulate for such a cancellation, but it was done as a punishment now! I have learnt about the fact from the *New York Times*, where it was presented as a tragedy of sorts happening to me. But I made it very clear to the reporters telephoning me on that day, that I was not upset about it at all. To commemorate the event, I went to New York with a friend and we went to the very top of the Empire State Building just for the fun of it.'[2]

Having commenced her new life in the USA, Svetlana declared that she was now, 'recognised as a writer'; 'had been making friends rapidly amongst my readers'; and was 'enjoying freedom as I never before had'. If anyone had told her that this would one day happen she said, 'I would certainly not have believed that,' and 'Oh, no! I would only have laughed.'[3]

Did Svetlana have a religious faith? Unlike her father, yes, she did. Said she, 'I have been finding greatest consolation, support, and strength in my own brand of religion – ecumenical brand, should we say – which did not close me to the doors of ANY denomination. I needed inner strength badly for my day-to-day activities with my little daughter, and an outlet on Sunday: a church. ANY church, indeed. The one which would give me more peace, and faith in myself and in my Creator, my loving Creator, who would not drop me altogether in the midst of my confusion.'[4]

Svetlana concluded her chapter 'The Faraway Music: A Trap' by saying, 'I always know, I feel it – how deeply, after all, do I appreciate and love America.'[5]

Chapter 56

Stalin: An Explanation

In 2016 a book entitled, *Raised to Rage: The Politics of Anger and the Roots of Authoritarianism* by US psychology professors Michael Milburn and Sheree D. Conrad was published.[1] Within its pages are to be found clues as to the likely reason why a physically abused and terrified little boy, Ioseb Besarionis dze Dzhugashvili, metamorphosed, step by step, into becoming the homicidal maniac Joseph Stalin.

Denial

The authors defined 'Denial' as 'a psychological defence mechanism … an unconscious mental manoeuvre that cancels out or obscures painful reality'[2] viz. for Stalin, the terrible beatings that he sustained as a small child.

The stifling of emotions

'It is not uncommon for children to respond to beatings by attempting to control the only thing left under their control – their emotions. They may stifle their tears and pain under orders from adults, or because the emotional pain is so great, or because they sense that withholding an emotional response preserves their last shred of autonomy.' And most importantly, denial of one's emotions, 'is one way to avoid being overwhelmed by terrible experiences'.[3]

How denial leads a child to idealise its parents

Said the authors, 'The parents' punitiveness produces rage that the child dare not feel – or at least, must not attribute to the parents' behaviour.[4]

The child denies the reality about his or her parents – their rigidity, their punitiveness – and idealises them, often holding them up as models.'[5]

There is no doubt that Stalin was devoted to his mother, Ekaterina. And of her and his father, Besarion, he declared, 'My parents were uneducated people, but they treated me not at all badly.'[6]

How denial provides only temporary relief

Said the authors, 'Denial may allow a person to cope successfully over the short term, but evidence from numerous studies shows that the long-term consequences of denial are dangerous. People who deny traumas they have experienced, and the pain associated with them, or who block out the truth about their childhood or present circumstances pay a price in impairment of mental and physical health, ability to cope with new stresses, and even the ability to think clearly.'[7]

Fear of what the future holds

'Denial of childhood abuse leaves grown children with feelings that are mysterious in the context of seemingly benign everyday life: terror, hypervigilance, a feeling of impending doom. Even when they deny what they have suffered in childhood – thus disconnecting these feelings from the events of the past – they must try to make sense of their experience. So, they project their feelings into the future and come to believe that they will suffer some terrible fate.'[8]

Said Golden, Adverse Childhood Experiences (ACEs), 'contribute to a lowered "set point" for experiencing a threat; a sensitivity to experience threat, even when none exists'.[9]

This was certainly the case with Stalin, who was ultra-sensitive to threats, whether real or imagined, and saw demons everywhere!

Aggression

The correlation between Adverse Childhood Experiences (ACEs) and aggression in the adult had already been discussed.

Authoritarianism

Adorno and his colleagues 'theorised that children raised by rigid and punitive parents develop a personality they called *authoritarian.*[10] Authoritarians displace their anger toward parents onto substitute targets defined by the prejudices of parents and their society.'[11]

The 'Projection' of ACE induced anger onto others and their victimisation

US psychologist Professor Amy Marcus-Newhall and colleagues stated that subjects who were provoked and unable to retaliate are significantly more likely to behave aggressively towards an innocent target than individuals who were not provoked.[12]

The physically abused child, said Milburn and Conrad, 'has to split off and deny those aspects of the self [which] the parents scorn – childishness, selfishness, sexuality, and primarily, anger and aggressive impulses towards the parents. That "bad self" is attributed unconsciously, through the defence mechanism of *projection* [transfer of emotions] to others, usually members of minority groups in the society, who are then despised as evil, inferior, and dangerous.'[13]

The authors 'found, specifically, that men with a history of being brutalised in childhood seemed to both deny the pain of their own experience and their anger at the perpetrators, while simultaneously displacing that anger onto political issues that involved an element of punishment'.[16] 'The child denies the parents' abusiveness and idealises them while displacing the rage onto the despised minority group.' This is called 'projection'.[14]

'When children deny that their parents are harsh, even abusive, they repress their anger toward them, as well as their fear and sadness. Once they are no longer burdened with an accurate perception of what is going on around and within them, they can act out their rage and feelings of helplessness by picking on someone weaker.'[15]

Viz. The colossal number of innocent, defenceless victims tortured, starved, incarcerated, and murdered under Stalin's direction runs into tens of millions and is beyond human comprehension.

A failure to develop a sense of morality

According to US psychologist Richard M. Merelman, 'Children whose behaviour is strictly controlled by external sanctions have no opportunity to develop their own internalised sense of morality.'[16]

Irrational behaviour

'A crucial aspect of the politics of denial is the pursuit of irrational policies, despite overwhelming evidence that they are at best failing, and at worst, exacerbating problems.'[17] Viz. Stalin's purges, for example of the Red Army during the Second World War.

To summarise:

'Traumatic emotion from childhood … can produce increased support for punitive, authoritarian, and irrational policies.'[18] The likely sequence of events, as far as Stalin was concerned, is as follows:

Childhood Brutalisation › Denial › Suppression of Anger and Stifling of Emotions › Terror, Hypervigilance, A Sense of Impending Doom › A Failure to Develop Morality › Irrational Behaviour › Authoritarianism › Anger Projection and Victimisation.

Here then, is the likely explanation of why Stalin the terrified toddler, who lived in mortal fear and dread of his parents and particularly of his father who might easily have killed him when he hurled his little son to the floor, grew up to become, not caring and compassionate, but a 'Man of Steel' responsible for the deaths of millions of people, the overwhelming majority of whom were perfectly innocent citizens.

In a paper entitled 'Child Abuse may Change Brain Structure and Make Depression Worse', Swedish psychiatrist Nils Opel and colleagues of the University of Münster, Germany, referred to the fact that 'abuse during childhood is linked to changes in brain structure', and that these changes may persist into adulthood. 'Statistical analysis revealed that those who experienced childhood abuse were more likely to have a smaller insular cortex – a brain region involved in emotional awareness.'[19]

***

The notion that what Stalin's paranoia and authoritarianism can be accounted for by the severe physical and emotional abuse that he suffered in childhood, leading to actual physical changes in his brain of the kind referred to by Nils Opel above, is therefore compelling. In 1865 US poet of Scots descent, William Ross Wallace, composed a poem that every parent would do well to heed. Entitled, 'The Hand That Rocks the Cradle Rules the World', it includes the verse:

Infancy's the tender fountain,
  Power may with beauty flow,
Mothers first to guide the streamlets,
  From them souls unresting grow –
Grow on for the good or evil,
  Sunshine streamed or evil hurled,
For the hand that rocks the cradle
  Is the hand that rules the world.

Woe betide those who desecrate and defile the cradle, instead of rocking it!

In 1988, Stalin's daughter, Svetlana, declared, 'I dream about the time when the heavy burden of Lenin's Party of liars and murderers will finally be lifted off the shoulders of the great multi-millions of people, and they can finally breathe freely. My granddaughters, I do not doubt, will see that day. For me, there is the dream, the vision, the anticipation.'[20]

Svetlana died on 22 November 2011. Some might say that the day of which she had dreamed has not yet dawned!

Chapter 57

Russia Today

The experience of Alexei Navalny indicates the impossibility of a person being elected to the Russian parliament, forming his or her own political party without the consent of the Kremlin, or being allowed to criticise the government in any way. In the course of his political activities, Navalny was arrested on several occasions, on spurious charges of embezzlement and fraud.

Alexei Anatolyevich Navalny was born on 4 June 1976 in Butyn, some 20 miles south-west of Moscow. His father Anatoly, a former military officer, and his mother, Lyudmila, (née Navalnaya) owned a basket-weaving factory.

Navalny graduated in commercial law from the Peoples' Friendship University of Russia in 1998 and from 1999 to 2001 he attended the State Finance Academy. Meanwhile, in 2000, he married economist Yulia Abrosimova.

Cable News Network (a US cable television channel specialising in news coverage) gives a timeline of events leading up to Navalny's incarnation in a Russian prison:

2000: 'Joins Yabloko, the Russian United Democratic Party.'

2007: 'Launches the National Russian Liberation Movement ("NAROD", the Russian word for "People").'

November 2010: 'Blows the whistle on a $4 billion embezzlement scheme at the state-run oil pipeline operator, Transneft, by posting leaked documents on his blog.'

5 December 2011: 'Takes part in protests following Vladimir Putin's December 4 election win. Is arrested but is released after 15 days.'

2011: 'Founds the Anti-Corruption Foundation (FBK). The organisation investigates corruption in the Russian government and posts supporting documentation.'

27 April 2017: 'Navalny is splashed in the face with an antiseptic green dye. The attack causes vision damage in one eye.'

29 July 2019: 'Suffers an "acute allergic reaction" while serving a 30-day sentence in police custody.'

20 August 2020: 'Feels sick during a return flight to Moscow from the Siberian city of Tomsklin and falls into a coma from suspected poisoning.'

22 August 2020: 'Arrives at the Charité Hospital in Berlin in Germany.'

2 September 2020: 'In a statement, the German government reports that Navalny was poisoned with a chemical nerve agent from the Novichok group. Novichok was used in a March 2018 attack on former Russian spy Sergei Skripal and his daughter, Yulia Skripal, in the English cathedral city of Salisbury.'

The would-be assassins were Alexander Mishkin and Anatoliy Chepiga, who travelled to the UK on false passports under the names Alexander Petrov and Ruslau Boshirov respectively. Both are agents of the GRU, the Foreign Military Intelligence Agency of the General Staff of the Armed Forces of the Russian Federation (created by Stalin in February 1942).

23 September 2020: 'Is discharged from the hospital.'

21 December 2020: 'CNN reports that Konstantin Kudryavtsev, an agent who belonged to an elite toxins team in Russia's FSB, revealed

during a debriefing details about how Navalny was poisoned, but didn't realise he was speaking to Navalny himself.'

In other words, Navalny tricked Kudryavtsev into confessing to the Russian authority's involvement in the crime.

17 January 2021: 'Navalny is detained moments after arriving in Moscow.'

2 February 2021: 'A Moscow court sentences Navalny to prison for more than two and a half years for violating probation terms from 2014 while he was in Germany.'

The irony and absurdity of this will not be wasted on the reader!

3 March 2021: 'Navalny's lawyer Vadim Kobzev tells CNN that Navalny is being held in "Detention Center 3" in Kolchugino in the Vladimir region east of Moscow. Navalny will be held temporarily before being moved to a penal colony.'

31 March 2021: 'Navalny, who is imprisoned in "Penal Colony No. 2" in Pokrov [60 miles or so east of Moscow], says he is going on a hunger strike to protest against prison officials' refusal to grant him access to proper medical care.'

23 April 2021: 'Navalny announces that he is ending his hunger strike after receiving medical attention.'

26 April 2021: 'Moscow's chief prosecutor freezes Navalny's political movement by suspending activities at his offices across the country.'[1]

In respect of the Russian Secret Services' practice of chemically poisoning its political opponents, surely the Soviet authorities realise that such chemicals can be detected by forensic examination and the source usually identified? The conclusion is, therefore, that the assassins and their superiors act with a sense of total impunity, knowing that on their return home, they will be treated as heroes, rather than the criminals that they are.

In 2021 BBC News sent its Moscow correspondent Steve Rosenberg to the city of Novosibirsk in south-west Siberia. This was in order to see what the local people thought about the forthcoming Russian legislative elections, to be held from 17 to 19 September 2021, for 450 seats in the State Duma, the lower house of the Federal Assembly.

Sergei Boiko, a city councillor who headed the local office of opposition politician Alexei Navalny, spoke to the reporter:

Rosenberg: 'Is there any real opposition on the ballot?'

Boiko: 'No.' He laughed.

Rosenberg: 'Boiko had plans to run for parliament but under a new law, he was banned from participating in elections for a period of five years because of his association with Navalny, who was currently in prison. In respect of the ballot papers [which contained a dozen or more names of candidates], voters here have a choice, but critics say all the parties have been vetted by the Kremlin who approve opponents in a stage-managed vote.'

Meanwhile, in Bulgaria, Rosenberg met Dmitry Gudkov, a Russian opposition politician who had fled to that country.

Rosenberg: 'His problems began when he announced that he was running for Parliament.'

Gudkov: 'There were 15 raids; 200 officers raced to my parents' house, my brother's apartment, and my own apartment. It was a signal that I can't participate in the elections. They wanted to get rid of me.'

Rosenberg: 'What kind of message were they sending?'

Gudkov: 'That if Dmitri stays in Russia, he and his aunt will be sent to jail. The second message was that the jail is not the worst thing that can happen with Dimitri.'

Rosenberg: 'To what extent has democracy been destroyed in Russia?'

Gudkov: 'I would say 100 per cent. Everything's destroyed. We have no democracy in this country. It's a dictatorship.'

Rosenberg pointed out to Olga Blago, Chairman of the Novosibirsk Election Commission, that Article 32 of the Constitution states that citizens of the Russian Federation have the right to elect and to be elected to state bodies of power. To this, she replied, 'In every country, including yours, there are legal restrictions on certain categories of citizen, including who can take part in elections. Our restrictions are in the interests of society and the state. Democracy isn't absolute freedom. Democracy is about order and procedure.'

Daria Atamonova, a 19-year-old, was Independent Candidate for the city council of Berdsk, Novosibirsk, in central Russia. 'But she's received threats,' said Rosenberg. 'Her parents were sent a funeral wreath with Daria's name on it.'

Daria: 'I'm used to this. In the Sverdlovsk region, one candidate was sent a tombstone. What do you make of this?', Daria asked a middle-aged lady and prospective voter.

Voter: 'It means they [the authorities] are afraid of you. If they weren't afraid, they wouldn't have done this. Well done, and carry on with a smile!'

Rosenberg: 'It's not best time to be in politics, is it?'

Daria: 'If not now, then when?'

Rosenberg: 'Politics isn't dead?'

Daria: 'No, absolutely not. They're trying to kill it, but they won't succeed. You can't silence everyone.'[2]

Clearly, Russian President Vladimir Putin maintains a stranglehold over the electoral system. It should be remembered, however, that just as Stalin was able to stay in power by the grace and favour of the secret police (NKVD), so the same applies to Putin, who relies on the current secret police – the KGB – of which, appropriately enough, he is a former agent!

Nonetheless, what is so extraordinary is the resilience of the Russian people; their refusal to give up hope, despite all.

What kind of leader or member of the Russian government could condone such Stalin-type persecution on the part of the authorities? The answer? One who could sleep soundly in his (or her) bed without his conscience being in any way troubled. An unkind person; one without human decency and compassion; one with no respect for human life. In short, one without any shred of empathy.

By contrast, the great and revered Russian poet Leo Tolstoy, declared that, 'There is only one enduring happiness in life: to live for others,'[3] indicating that he possessed an entirely different set of values.

Chapter 58

Putin and Stalin: Two of a Kind!

On 24 February 2022 forces of Russia (the Russian Federation) invaded Ukraine. The incredibly brave resistance put up by Ukrainians indicates that they valued their freedom as much as life itself, and that they had no desire whatsoever to join Russia.

Vladimir Putin is Russia's President, and he must therefore bear full responsibility for sanctioning the innumerable crimes committed in his name. By now, his methods are all too familiar. Ignore the Geneva Convention and human rights; pulverise residential areas with cruise missiles, artillery shells, chemical weapons, cluster bombs, and barrel bombs. Make a special point of targeting hospitals, schools, kindergartens, high-density apartment blocks, and markets where people go to stock up on essential provisions.

This is not to say that similar barbaric tactics have not been used previously in modern times. For example, the bombing of British cities by the Luftwaffe, or of German cities by the RAF and US Air Force during the Second World War; the Nazi Holocaust; the use of napalm by the US in Vietnam (1955–75); the Rwandan Genocide (1994).

The invasion of Ukraine, a sovereign, democratic, peace-loving country by a totalitarian regime under the leadership of Putin, has been met with horror and disbelief the world over. To witness it is to be reminded of the forcible annexation of Eastern Europe by the Soviet Union under the leadership of Stalin, following the Allied victory in the Second World War. So, are there similarities between Putin and Stalin?

Putin is an anachronism, a throwback to the dark ages of the 'Iron Curtain' and the 'Cold War', when the rest of the world has long since moved on into a new era of freedom and prosperity. Having witnessed the dissolution of the Soviet Union on 26 December 1991, Putin (who has been in power as President of Prime Minister of Russia since August 1999) has been fretting and sulking ever since. He is now hell-bent on putting matters right, as he sees it, by expanding the 'Russian Empire'.

Attitude to dissent

Just as Stalin would not tolerate the slightest dissent, neither will Putin, either at home or abroad. For example, just as Stalin had exiled communist theorist and revolutionary Leon Trotsky murdered in Mexico City in August 1940, so Russian secret agents travelled to the English cathedral city of Salisbury in March 2018 in order to poison former Russian military intelligence officer Sergei Skripal and his daughter, Yulia; and in August 2020 the opposition leader Alexei Navalny, who still languishes in a Russian jail, was poisoned on home soil.

Ukraine

From demonstrations on the streets of Moscow and in many cities across Russia it is clear that thousands if not millions of Russians are bemused, horrified, and sickened by the invasion of Ukraine, whose people they have so much in common with, such as ethnicity and religion. As for language, although the Russian and Ukrainian languages are different, Russian is widely spoken in Ukraine. But what of these dissenters? Today, Putin's police are busy arresting and imprisoning anyone who dares to raise a voice against the Kremlin and mighty 'Czar' Putin by speaking up against the war in Ukraine.

The pursuit of power: absolute rule

As with Stalin, the words 'debate', 'discussion', 'compromise', and of course 'democracy', are absent from Putin's vocabulary. Like Stalin, Putin's goal (and that of his military, secret service chiefs, and Russian oligarchs) is to remain in power at all costs, and thereby hold on to his luxurious palace on the Black Sea coast, his superyacht, and untold wealth that he has no doubt salted away in foreign bank accounts – monies siphoned off from the Russian economy and stolen from the Russian people.

Putin and Stalin: 'Confirmation Bias' and sycophancy respectively

Putin has now been in power for 23 years, compared with Stalin's 24. Just as Stalin was surrounded by sycophants who rushed to fulfil his every wish and to satisfy his every whim, so Putin is surrounded by 'Yes Men' who share and confirm him in his views. ('Confirmation Bias' is defined as the tendency to interpret new evidence as confirmation of one's existing beliefs or theories.) And as a result, he has lost his grip on reality and overestimates his capabilities.

Putin and Stalin: both pathological liars

Stalin was pathologically dishonest, encouraging his henchmen to fabricate evidence against his opponents in order to give him a pretext to persecute them. Similarly, Putin, through his Foreign Minister Lavrov, perpetrates lie after lie, saying, for example, that Ukraine is a threat to Russia and that the Ukrainian Government is a Nazi regime. Such remarks are frankly risible and no one is taken in by them.

Had Western governments shown more willingness from the beginning to address Putin's concerns about the possibility of Ukraine joining NATO, the present catastrophe might have been avoided. However, the three Baltic States joined NATO in March 2004, and Estonia and Latvia border Russia, yet neither has proved to be any threat whatsoever. As for the 'Nazi' smear, it should be pointed out that Ukraine's president Volodymyr Zelensky is Jewish and that his family members died in the Holocaust.

Reigns of terror

Just as Stalin unleashed a reign of terror on his people, with endless 'purges', so Putin, realising that the brave Ukrainians have brought his invasion to a standstill, has now adopted the coward's way out by raining down missiles on innocent civilians. What Putin describes as a 'precision-guided' attempt to destroy Ukraine's infrastructure is in fact genocide, as collateral damage is unavoidable. Of this, he is only too well aware, and film and video footage relayed from Kiev and Kharkiv confirm this, but he remains unmoved.

Putin and Stalin: Paranoia

In an article entitled 'Vladimir Putin: The Security Men, Officials, and Friends who are in the Russian President's Inner Circle', published online on 28 February 2022, Diana Magnay, Moscow correspondent for Sky News, stated as follows in respect of Putin: 'His close associates include the Siloviki ['Strongmen'] – the security men around Putin, most of whom rose up through the ranks of the KGB as he did, and have a hawkish, Cold War mindset.' She then proceeded to mention 8 people who were especially close to the President: 'Perhaps the most powerful of them all is Nikolai Patrushev, Head of Russia's Security Council.' Aged 70, Patrusshev was recruited by the KGB in 1975.

'Alexander Bortnikov is the current Director of the FSB, Russia's domestic intelligence agency and successor to the Soviet spy agency, the KGB.' Aged 70, Bortnikov was also recruited by the KGB in 1975.

'Sergei Naryshkin is the head of the SVR, Russia's Foreign Intelligence Agency.' Aged 67, Naryshkin was a fellow student with Putin at the KGB Higher School, Moscow, in the late 1980s.

'Sergei Shoigu is Russia's Defence Minister and a close associate of Putin. They go on widely publicised hunting and shooting expeditions to Siberia together.' Aged 66.

'Army General Valery Gerasimov is Chief of the General Staff.' Aged 66.

'Anton Vaino is Chief of Staff of the Presidential Executive Office and will therefore spend a substantial amount of time with the Russian president.' Aged 50.

'Sergei Lavrov has been the foreign minister since 2004.' Aged 71.

'Yuri Kovalchuk is a Russian oligarch with family and personal ties to the President.' Aged 70.

All but one of the above were born within three years of the President, who is aged 69. Three of the eight have strong KGB connections. Magnay continued: 'They believe themselves in an existential battle with the West where the ultimate goal of the US vis-a-vis Russia is regime change. In the last few years, their influence has grown as Putin has shifted his focus from economic and social issues towards perceived security-related threats, including the crushing of civil society and internal dissent.'

This again is all too reminiscent of Stalin, and just as his acolytes fed his paranoia, so one may imagine Putin's acolytes doing the very same thing. After all, when the average age of the eight 'close associates' of Putin is 67+ years, from where are fresh, new, and enlightened ideas to come from?

As Magnay said, most of the security men around Putin, 'rose up through the ranks of the KGB as he did and have a hawkish, Cold War mindset'.[1]

Conclusion

With the dawn of the new millennium, people might have been forgiven for thinking that the age of gangster dictators like Stalin and Hitler, with no moral compass, no human decency or humanity, who ruled by brutality, bribery, corruption, misinformation, and the establishment of a police state, were gone forever. And those who thought that the likes of Putin had been consigned to the dustbin of history, how wrong they were, for as with Stalin and Hitler in the twentieth century, the problem of the inhumane dictator is still with us.

The new millennium was hoped to bring a new dawn, where such events could not happen, where such people could not come to power. But so far a fifth of the twenty-first century has elapsed, and the sad conclusion is that nothing has changed for the better.

But in the hearts and minds of Ukrainians and of peace-loving people everywhere, hope still springs eternal and the desire for freedom is unquenchable.

Chapter 59

Epilogue

One final mystery remains. Why did many Russians idolise Stalin during his lifetime, and why do they continue to idolise him after his death?

For Stalin, substitute his parents, and in particular his father Besarion; and for the Russian people, substitute the terrified little boy Josef Dzhugashvili, later known as Stalin. Just as the abused and brutalised Josef went into denial, which meant a) that he displaced his anger onto others and b) that he idolised his abusive parents, rather than blaming them, so, many people in the Soviet Union were in denial about their oppressor Stalin and instead projected their anger elsewhere. And convenient targets for their displaced anger were Stalin's innocent victims, those whose 'crimes' he fabricated, who were murdered in their millions.

Averaging out the various estimates of how many deaths Stalin was responsible for (excluding in wars) as 41.5 million, this was equivalent to 22 per cent of the population of the Soviet Union who were alive in 1953, the year of Stalin's death, when the census was taken.

Just as estimating the number of deaths attributable to Stalin is problematical, so also is estimating the number of Soviet deaths, both military and civilian, in the Second World War. A figure approaching 30 million dead is likely. Therefore, Stalin had proved himself to be *an even greater existential threat to the Russian people than Hitler*, who between them, accounted for the deaths of 70 million or so Russians!

What is Stalin's legacy? To preside over a thirty-one-year-long dictatorship in the Soviet Union; to expand and preside over the largest prison system in the world, in which his political opponents made up a large proportion of the prisoners; to orchestrate the murder and torture of *tens of millions* of Soviet citizens; to carry through the Five-Year Plans, which made Russia's industrial revolution possible; to convince the Russian people that Hitler could be defeated, and to offer them an inspiring, 'Man of Steel'-type leadership throughout the Second World War; to create a culture of terror, which persists to this day.

Bibliography

Adorno, T. W., Frenkel-Brunswik, E., Levinson, D. J., & Sanford, R. N., *The Authoritarian Personality* (Harper & Row, New York, 1950).

Alexandrov, G. F., M. R. Galaktionov, V. S. Kruzhkov, M. B. Milkin, V. D. Mochalov, P. N. Pspelov, *Joseph Stalin: A Short Biography* (Foreign Language Publishing House, Moscow, 1949).

Alliluyeva, Svetlana, 'A Book for Granddaughters', 1988 (Churchill Archives Centre: The Papers of Svetlana Alliluyeva).

Alliluyeva, Svetlana, 'The Faraway Music: A Trap, 1970–1972', *Memoirs 1986–1989* (Churchill Archives Centre: The Papers of Svetlana Alliluyeva).

Alliluyeva, Svetlana, 'Faraway Music: A Sad Decade, 1972–1982, *Memoirs 1986–1989* (Churchill Archives Centre: The Papers of Svetlana Alliluyeva).

Alliluyeva, Svetlana, 'The Faraway Music: 1983–1986: England-USA', *Memoirs 1986–1989* (Churchill Archives Centre: The Papers of Svetlana Alliluyeva).

Alliluyeva, Svetlana, 'The Lovely and Trustful: 1967–1970', *Memoirs 1986–1989* (Churchill Archives Centre: The Papers of Svetlana Alliluyeva).

Alliluyeva, Svetlana, *Only One Year* (Harper Perennial, New York, 1969).

Alliluyeva, Svetlana, *Twenty Letters to a Friend* (Harper Perennial, New York, 2016).

Baron-Cohen, Simon, *Zero Degrees of Empathy: A New Theory of Human Cruelty and Kindness* (Penguin Books, London, 2012).

Beer, Daniel, *The House of the Dead: Siberian Exile under the Tsars* (Allen Lane, London, 2016)

Bowlby, John, *Child Care and the Growth of Love* (Penguin Books, London 1990).

Davrichewy, Josef, *Ah! Ce qu'on rigolait bien avec mon ami Staline!* (Jean-Claude Simoen, Paris, 1979).

Diagnostic and Statistical Manual of Mental Disorders, Fifth Edition, DSM-5th (American Psychiatric Association, Washington DC and London, 2013).

Iremashvili, Joseph, *Stalin und die Tragödie Georgiens: Errinerungen von seinem langjahrigen Freund* (Verfasser, Berlin, 1932).

Kotkin, Stephen, *Stalin: Paradoxes of Power 1878–1928* (Penguin, London, 2015).

Lenman, Bruce P. (Consultant Editor), *Chambers Dictionary of World History* (Chambers Harrap, Edinburgh, 2000).

Milburn, Michael, and Sheree D. Conrad, *Raised to Rage: The Politics of Anger and the Roots of Authoritarianism* (The MIT Press, Cambridge, Massachusetts and London, England, 2016).

Montefiore, Simon Sebag, *The Court of the Red Tsar* (Weidenfeld & Nicolson, London, 2003).

Montefiore, Simon Sebag, *Young Stalin* (Weidenfeld & Nicolson, London, 2007).

Murphy, J. T., *Stalin: 1879–1944* (John Lane the Bodley Head, London, 1945).

Norman, Andrew, *Hitler: Dictator or Puppet?* (Pen & Sword, Barnsley, Yorkshire, UK, 2011).

Pohl, J. Otto, *The Stalinist Penal System* (McFarland, Jefferson, NC, USA, 1997).

Polian, Pavel, *Against Their Will* (Central European Press, Hungary, 2004).

Radzinsky, Edvard, *Stalin* (Anchor Books, New York, 1996).

Rummel, R. J., *Death by Government* (Transaction Publishers, New Brunswick, NJ, 1994).

Soanes, Catherine and Angus Stevenson (Editors), *Oxford Dictionary of English* (Oxford University Press, Oxford, New York, 2005).

Stevenson, Angus and Maurice Waite, *Concise Oxford English Dictionary*, (Oxford University Press, Oxford and New York, 2011).

Suny Richard Grigor, *Stalin: Passage to Revolution* (Princeton University Press, Princeton and Oxford, 2020).

Talbott, Strobe (Translator and Editor), *Khrushchev Remembers* (Little, Brown, Boston, MA, USA, 1970).

Tutaev, David (Translator and Editor), *The Alliluyev Memoirs: Recollections of Svetlana Stalin's Maternal Aunt Anna Alliluyeva and her grandfather Sergei Alliluyev* (Michael Joseph, London, 1968).

Film Documentaries

Kawczak, Andrew, Katyn (1940), History Presentation, 2018.

By the Same Author

By Swords Divided: Corfe Castle in the Civil War. Halsgrove, 2003.
Thomas Hardy: Christmas Carollings. Halsgrove, 2005.
Enid Blyton and her Enchantment with Dorset. Halsgrove, 2005.
Tyneham: A Tribute. Halsgrove, 2007.
Agatha Christie: The Finished Portrait. Tempus, 2007.
The Story of George Loveless and the Tolpuddle Martyrs. Halsgrove, 2008.
Father of the Blind: A Portrait of Sir Arthur Pearson. The History Press, 2009.
Agatha Christie: The Pitkin Guide. Pitkin Publishing, 2009.
Arthur Conan Doyle: The Man behind Sherlock Holmes. The History Press, 2009.
HMS Hood: Pride of the Royal Navy. The History Press, 2009.
Purbeck Personalities. Halsgrove, 2009.
Bournemouth's Founders and Famous Visitors. The History Press, 2010.
Thomas Hardy: Behind the Mask. The History Press, 2011.

Bibliography

A Brummie Boy goes to War. Halsgrove, 2011.
Winston Churchill: Portrait of an Unquiet Mind. Pen & Sword Books, 2012.
Charles Darwin: Destroyer of Myths. Pen & Sword Books, 2013.
Beatrix Potter: Her Inner World. Pen & Sword Books, 2013.
T.E. Lawrence: Tormented Hero. Fonthill, 2014.
Agatha Christie: The Disappearing Novelist. Fonthill, 2014.
Lawrence of Arabia's Clouds Hill. Halsgrove, 2014.
Jane Austen: Love is Like a Rose. Fonthill, 2015.
Kindly Light: The Story of Blind Veterans UK. Fonthill, 2015.
Thomas Hardy at Max Gate: The Latter Years. Halsgrove, 2016.
Corfe Remembered. Halsgrove, 2017.
Thomas Hardy: Bockhampton and Beyond. Halsgrove, 2017.
Mugabe: Monarch of Blood and Tears. Austin Macauley, 2017.
Making Sense of Marilyn. Fonthill, 2018.
Hitler's Insanity: A Conspiracy of Silence. Fonthill, 2018.
The Unwitting Fundamentalist. Austin Macauley, 2018.
Robert Mugabe's Lost Jewel of Africa. Fonthill, 2018.
Hitler: Dictator or Puppet? Pen & Sword, 2011.
Halsewell: A Shipwreck that Gripped the Nation. Fonthill, 2020.
Beatrix Potter: Her Inner World, Pen & Sword Books, 2020.
The Amazing Story of Lise Meitner: Escaping the Nazis and becoming the World's Greatest Physicist, Pen & Sword Books, 2021.
The Real Peter Sellers, Pen & Sword Books, 2021.

Author's website: www.andrew-norman.co.uk
Amazon.co.uk: Andrew Norman: Books, Biography, Blogs

Notes

Introduction

1. Norman, Andrew, *Hitler: Dictator or Puppet?*
2. Alliluyeva, Svetlana, *Only One Year*, p.359.

Chapter 1: Joseph Stalin (Born 18 December 1878): The Early Years: A Cherished Child

1. Murphy, J. T., *Stalin: 1879–1944*, p.6.
2. Dzhugashvili, Keke, 'My Dear Son: The Memoirs of Stalin's Mother', Archive of the Central Committee of the Communist Party of Georgia, f.8, op.2, d.15.
3. Radzinsky, Edvard, *Stalin*, p.61.
4. Dzhugashvili, Keke, op. cit.
5. Murphy, J. T., op. cit., p.14.
6. Ibid., p.15.

Chapter 2: How Stalin Became a Battered Child

1. Alliluyeva, Svetlana, *Twenty Letters to a Friend*, p.211.
2. 'USSR: Joseph Stalin': Svetlana Alliluyeva interview, 1980s, Thames TV.
3. Radzinsky, Edvard, *Stalin*, p.25.
4. Alliluyeva, Svetlana, *Only One Year*, pp.360–1.
5. Radzinsky, Edvard, op. cit., pp.24, 585–594.
6. In researching his biography of Stalin, author Edvard Radzinsky was fortunate enough to be granted access to the President's Archive in the Kremlin, which included Stalin's personal archive. 'I sit under Stalin's ceiling and look through his personal papers,' he said. Radzinsky, Edvard, Ibid., p.22. Radzinsky also had access to the Russian Centre for the Preservation and Study of Documents Relating to Modern History (formerly the Central Party Archive); books from I. V. Stalin's private library with his annotations; the State Archive of the Russian Federation (formerly the Central State Archive of the October Revolution; together with many of other primary and secondary sources. Radzinsky, Edvard, Ibid., pp.585–594.
7. Alliluyeva, Svetlana, *Only One Year*, p.366.

8. Iremashvili, Joseph, *Stalin und die Tragödie Georgiens: Errinerungen von seinem langjahrigen Freund*, p.12.
9. Dzhugashvili, Keke, 'My Dear Son: The Memoirs of Stalin's Mother', Archive of the Central Committee of the Communist Party of Georgia, f.8, op.2, d.15.
10. Ibid.
11. Suny Richard Grigor, *Stalin: Passage to Revolution*, p.709.
12. Montefiore, Simon Sebag, *Young Stalin*, p.2.
13. Davrichewy, Joseph, *Ah! Ce qu'on rigolait bien avec mon copain Staline*, Jean-Claude Simoën, Paris, 1979. In Lafferiere, pp.36–7.
14. Montefiore, Simon Sebag, op. cit., p.29.
15. Kotkin, Stephen, *Stalin: Paradoxes of Power 1878–1928*, p.116.
16. Iremashvili, Joseph, op. cit., p.12.

Chapter 3: Was Besarion Stalin's Real Father?

1. Davrichewy, Josef, *Ah! Ce qu'on rigolait bien avec mon ami Staline!*
2. Letter from N. Goglidze, Kiev, in Radzinsky, Edvard, *Stalin*, pp.21–2.
3. Montefiore, Simon Sebag, *Young Stalin*, Young Stalin, p.17.
4. Ibid., p.18.
5. Kotkin, Stephen, *Stalin: Paradoxes of Power 1878–1928*, p.20.
6. Ibid., p.20.
7. Kanazawa, Satoshi, 'Why Are Stepparents More Likely to Kill Their Children? Are Stepfathers more likely to be Criminal in general?' *Psychology Today*, 9 January 2011.

Chapter 4: Dr John Bowlby: The Importance of a Loving Childhood

1. Bowlby, John, *Child Care and the Growth of Love*, p.13.
2. Ibid., p.13.
3. Ibid., p.15.
4. Ibid., p.220.

Chapter 5: The Tiflis Seminary (1894–99)

1. 'The Tiflis Theological Academy and Seminary', *Wikipedia.*
2. Tutaev, David (Translator and Editor), *The Alliluyev Memoirs: Recollections of Svetlana Stalin's Maternal Aunt Anna Alliluyeva and her grandfather Sergei Alliluyev*, p.228.
3. Alliluyeva, Svetlana, *Only One Year*, p.361.
4. Murphy, J. T., *Stalin: 1879–1944*, p.17.
5. Ibid., p.18.
6. Ibid., p.19.
7. Alexandrov, G. F., et al., *Joseph Stalin: A Short Biography*, p.7.
8. Ibid., p.7.
9. Murphy, J. T., op. cit., p.19.

10. Dzhugashvili, Keke, 'My Dear Son: The Memoirs of Stalin's Mother', Archive of the Central Committee of the Communist Party of Georgia, f.8, op.2, d.15.
11. 'Unpublished Materials from the Biographer of Comrade Stalin', p.19. Grisha Glurjidze, *Memories*, SShSSA, f.8, op.2, ch.1, d.9II, pp.159–160, in Suny Richard Grigor, *Stalin: Passage to Revolution*, p.43.
12. Alliluyeva, Svetlana, *Only One Year*, pp.361–2.
13. Stalin, I. V., *Sochineniya*, XIII, Moscow, 1952–4, pp.113–4.
14. Alliluyeva, Svetlana, *Only One Year*, pp.376–7.
15. Alexandrov, G. F., op. cit., p.9.
16. Ibid., pp.9–10.
17. Dzhugashvili, Keke, 'My Dear Son: The Memoirs of Stalin's Mother', Archive of the Central Committee of the Communist Party of Georgia, f.8, op.2, d.15.

Chapter 6: Stalin the Revolutionary: Exile

1. Alliluyeva, Svetlana, *Twenty Letters to a Friend*, p.68.
2. Alliluyeva, Svetlana, 'The Faraway Music: A Trap, 1970–1972', pp.218–9.
3. Alliluyeva, Svetlana, *Only One Year*, p.362.
4. 'USSR: Joseph Stalin': Svetlana Alliluyeva interview, 1980s, Thames TV.
5. Murphy, J. T., *Stalin: 1879–1944*, p.38.
6. Tutaev, David (Translator and Editor), *The Alliluyev Memoirs: Recollections of Svetlana Stalin's Maternal Aunt Anna Alliluyeva and her grandfather Sergei Alliluyev*, pp.28–9.
7. Ibid., p.30.
8. Alexandrov, G. F., et al., *Joseph Stalin: A Short Biography*, p.12.
9. Tutaev, David, op. cit., p.51.
10. Alexandrov, G. F., op. cit., p.13.
11. Murphy, J. T., op. cit., pp.39–40.
12. Ibid., p.40.
13. Ibid., p.40.
14. Tutaev, David, op. cit., p.135.
15. Murphy, J. T., op. cit., p.41.
16. Alexandrov, G. F., op. cit., p.16.
17. The NKVD was the People's Commissariat for Internal Affairs, the interior ministry of the Soviet Union. Established in 1917 as the NKVD of the Russian Soviet Federative Socialist Republic, the agency was originally tasked with conducting regular police work and overseeing the country's prisons and labour camps. *Wikipedia*.
18. 'Special settlements in Soviet Russia in the 1930s–50s', The Free Library by Farlex, 1 January 2007.
19. Alexandrov, G. F., op. cit., pp.16–17.
20. Murphy, J. T., op. cit., p.42.
21. Alliluyeva, Svetlana, *Twenty Letters to a Friend*, p.68.
22. Alliluyeva, Svetlana, 'The Faraway Music: A Trap, 1970–1972', pp.218–9.

23. Alexandrov, G. F., op. cit., pp.20–21.
24. Murphy, J. T., op. cit., p.42.
25. Alexandrov, G. F., op. cit., p.36.
26. Ibid., p.19.
27. Murphy, J. T., op. cit., p.47.
28. Ibid., p.47.
29. Ibid., p.47.
30. Alexandrov, G. F., op. cit., p.30.
31. Murphy, J. T., op. cit., p.50.
32. Ibid., p.57.
33. Alexandrov, G. F., op. cit., p.32.
34. Murphy, J. T., op. cit., p.58.

Chapter 7: Lenin and his Wife, Nadezhda

1. BBC History: Vladimir Lenin (1870–1924), online.
2. 'Nadezhda Konstantinovna Krupskaya: Soviet Politician', Britannica, online; and 'Nadezhda Krupskaya', *Wikipedia*.
3. Alexandrov, G. F., et al., *Joseph Stalin: A Short Biography*, p.28.

Chapter 8: 'Tishka': Stalin's Beloved Companion in Siberia

1. Tutaev, David (Translator and Editor), *The Alliluyev Memoirs: Recollections of Svetlana Stalin's Maternal Aunt Anna Alliluyeva and her grandfather Sergei Alliluyev*, pp.216–7.

Chapter 9: Stalin's Marriage to Ekaterina Svanidze (15 July 1906)

1. 'Alexander Svanidze', *Wikipedia*.
2. Montefiore, Simon Sebag, *Young Stalin*, pp.66–7.
3. Svanidze, Alexander Semyonovich, Hrono.ru.
4. Montefiore, Simon Sebag, op. cit., p.144.
5. Ibid., p.144.
6. Radzinsky, Edvard, *Stalin*, p.63.
7. Montefiore, Simon Sebag, op. cit., p.160.
8. Kotkin, Stephen, *Stalin: Paradoxes of Power 1878–1928*, p.105.
9. Montefiore, Simon Sebag, op. cit., p.165.
10. Kotkin, Stephen, op. cit., p.105.
11. Radzinsky, Edvard, op. cit., p.64.
12. Ostrovskii, Aleksandr V., 'Who Stood Behind Stalin's Back?' Tsentropoligraf-Mim Delta, Moscow, 2004, p.253, in Kotkin, Stephen, *Stalin: Paradoxes of Power 1878–1928*, p.105.
13. Montefiore, Simon Sebag, op. cit., p.165.
14. Ibid., p.174.
15. Radzinsky, Edvard, op. cit., p.64.

16. Montefiore, Simon Sebag, op. cit., p.200.
17. Ibid., pp.67, 201.
18. Ibid., p.201.
19. Ibid., pp.202–3.

Chapter 10: For Stalin the Work Goes On

1. Murphy, J. T., *Stalin: 1879–1944*, p.61.
2. Alexandrov, G. F., et al., *Joseph Stalin: A Short Biography*, p.35.
3. Murphy, J. T., op. cit., p.62.
4. Alexandrov, G. F., et al., op. cit., p.35.
5. Russian, Soviet, and CIS History: Biographies: Leon Trotsky, ENCYCLOpedia.com, online.
6. Deutscher, Isaac, *The Prophet Armed*, Oxford University Press, London, 1954, p.103.
7. 'Alexander Parvus', *Wikipedia*.
8. Trotsky, Leon, 'Three Conceptions of the Russian Revolution', Summer 1939, The Trotsky Internet Archive, online.
9. Stevenson, Angus and Maurice Waite, *Concise Oxford English Dictionary.*
10. 'Duma': *Wikipedia*.
11. Murphy, J. T., op. cit., p.62.
12. Ibid., p.63.
13. Ibid., p.67.
14. Alexandrov, G. F., op. cit., p.39.
15. Ibid., p.40.
16. Ibid., p.41.
17. Murphy, J. T., op. cit., p.69.
18. Alexandrov, G. F., op. cit., p.42.
19. Murphy, J. T., op. cit., p.69.
20. Ibid., p.69.
21. Ibid., p.70.
22. Alexandrov, G. F., op. cit., p.43.
23. Ibid., pp.43–4.
24. Ibid., p.45.
25. Tutaev, David (Translator and Editor), *The Alliluyev Memoirs: Recollections of Svetlana Stalin's Maternal Aunt Anna Alliluyeva and her grandfather Sergei Alliluyev*, p.228, Note 2.
26. 'Suren Spandari Spandaryan', *Wikipedia*.
27. Alexandrov, G. F., op. cit., p.46.
28. Murphy, J. T., op. cit., p.77.
29. Alexandrov, G. F., op. cit., p.47.
30. Tutaev, David, op. cit., p.189.
31. Ibid., p.189.
32. Alexandrov, G. F., op. cit., p.47.
33. Murphy, J. T., op. cit., p.86.

34. 'Old Bolshevik', *Wikipedia.*
35. Alexandrov, G. F., op. cit., p.48.
36. Ibid, p.50.
37. Tutaev, David, op. cit., pp.194–5.
38. Alexandrov, G. F., op. cit., p.52.
39. Murphy, J. T., op. cit., p.98.
40. Ibid., p.100.
41. Ibid., p.101.
42. Ibid., p.102.
43. Ibid., p.109.
44. Ibid., p.137.

Chapter 11: The Revolution is Successful: Stalin's Dream Comes True!

1. Alexandrov, G. F., et al., *Joseph Stalin: A Short Biography*, p.56.
2. 'Smolny Institute', *Wikipedia.*
3. Alexandrov, G. F., op. cit., p.56.
4. Murphy, J. T., *Stalin: 1879–1944*, pp.110–111.
5. Ibid., p.111.
6. Ibid., p.115.
7. Ibid., p.118.
8. 'Nadezhda Konstantinovna Krupskaya: Soviet Politician', Britannica, online; and 'Nadezhda Krupskaya', *Wikipedia.*
9. Alexandrov, G. F., op. cit., p.75.

Chapter 12: Civil War

1. *Britannica* online.
2. 'Brest-Litovsk Treaty', *Wikipedia.*
3. 'White Movement', *Wikipedia.*
4. *Britannica* online.
5. Alexandrov, G. F., et al., *Joseph Stalin: A Short Biography*, pp.60–1.
6. Ibid., p.62.
7. Ibid., p.63.
8. Voroshilov, K. E., *Stalin and the Red Army*, Moscow 1940, p.6, in Alexandrov, G. F., et al., *Joseph Stalin: A Short Biography*, p.69.
9. *Britannica* online.
10. Alexandrov, G. F., op. cit., p.58.
11. Ibid., p.75.

Chapter 13: Stalin and the Alliluyev Family

1. Murphy, J. T., *Stalin: 1879–1944*, p.137.
2. Tutaev, David (Translator and Editor), *The Alliluyev Memoirs: Recollections of Svetlana Stalin's Maternal Aunt Anna Alliluyeva and her grandfather Sergei Alliluyev*, p.17.

3. Alliluyeva, Svetlana, 'Faraway Music: A Sad Decade, 1972–1982', p.218.
4. Kotkin, Stephen, *Stalin: Paradoxes of Power 1878–1928*, p.53.
5. Tutaev, David, op. cit., p.27.
6. Ibid., pp.32–34.
7. Ibid., p.90.
8. Ibid., p.119.
9. Ibid., p.124.
10. Ibid., p.111.
11. Ibid., p.124.
12. Ibid., pp.131,133.
13. Ibid., p.136.
14. Ibid., p.139.
15. Ibid., p.140.
16. Ibid., pp.151–3.
17. Ibid., p.144.
18. Woods, Alan, and Ted Grant, 'In Defence of Marxism: Marxism and the National Question', 25 February 2000, online.
19. Tutaev, David, op. cit., p.145.
20. Ibid., p.211.
21. Ibid., pp.202–3.
22. Ibid., p.207.
23. Ibid., p.212.
24. Ibid., p.186.
25. Ibid., p.188.
26. Ibid., p.189.
27. Ibid., p.192.
28. Ibid., pp.218–9.
29. Ibid., p.219.

Chapter 14: Stalin's Writings

1. J. V. Stalin: Works by Decade, MIA Stalin Archive online.
2. Soanes, Catherine and Angus Stevenson (Editors), *Oxford Dictionary of English*.
3. Alexandrov, G. F., et al., *Joseph Stalin: A Short Biography*, p.85.
4. Murphy, J. T., *Stalin: 1879–1944*, p.71.
5. Soanes, Catherine and Angus Stevenson (Editors), *Oxford Dictionary of English*.
6. Zhukov, G. K., *Vospominaniya I razmyshleniya*, 5th Edition, Moscow, 1963, Volume 2, p.95.
7. Vasilievsky, A. M., *Delo vsei zhizni*, 3rd Edition, Moscow, 1978, p.501.
8. Churchill, W., *History of the Second World War*, Volume 4, p.434.
9. Soanes, Catherine and Angus Stevenson (Editors), *Oxford Dictionary of English*.

Chapter 15: Stalin's Marriage to Nadezhda Alliluyeva (24 March 1919)

1. Alliluyeva, Svetlana, *Twenty Letters to a Friend*, p.125.
2. Ibid., p.97.
3. Ibid., p.99.
4. Alliluyeva, Svetlana, *Only One Year*, p.144.
5. Alliluyeva, Svetlana, *Twenty Letters to a Friend*, pp.25–6.
6. Alliluyeva, Svetlana, *Only One Year*, pp.367–8.
7. Alliluyeva, Svetlana, 'A Book for Granddaughters', p.107.
8. Alliluyeva, Svetlana, *Twenty Letters to a Friend*, p.36.
9. Alliluyeva, Svetlana, *Only One Year*, pp.367–8.
10. Alliluyeva, Svetlana, *Twenty Letters to a Friend*, p.30.
11. Ibid., p.105.
12. Alliluyeva, Svetlana, *Only One Year*, p.144.
13. Alliluyeva, Svetlana, *Twenty Letters to a Friend*, p.105.
14. Ibid., pp.111–2.
15. Alexandrov, G. F., et al., *Joseph Stalin: A Short Biography*, p.78.
16. Ibid., p.87.
17. Ibid., pp.94–6.

Chapter 16: Leon Trotsky: His Banishment (1928)

1. 'Leon Trotsky', *Wikipedia*.
2. 'Socialism in One Country', *Wikipedia*.
3. Leon Trotsky, *The Permanent Revolution*, Chapter 10, 'What is the Permanent Revolution?' Basic Postulates, 1930, The Trotsky Internet Archive, online.

Chapter 17: Nadezhda's Disillusionment with her Husband Stalin

1. Alliluyeva, Svetlana, *Twenty Letters to a Friend*, pp.111–2.
2. Alliluyeva, Svetlana, *Only One Year*, pp.367–8.
3. Ibid., p.369.
4. Alliluyeva, Svetlana, *Twenty Letters to a Friend*, pp.111–2.
5. 'USSR: Joseph Stalin': Svetlana Alliluyeva interview, 1980s, Thames TV.
6. Alliluyeva, Svetlana, *Twenty Letters to a Friend*, pp.111–2.

Chapter 18: The Death of Nadezhda (9 November 1932)

1. Alliluyeva, Svetlana, *Twenty Letters to a Friend*, p.119.
2. Ibid., pp.25–6.
3. Ibid., p.24.
4. Ibid., p.30.

Chapter 19: Nadezhda's Death: The Truth at Last!

1. Alliluyeva, Svetlana, *Twenty Letters to a Friend*, p.176.

2. Alliluyeva, Svetlana, *Only One Year*, pp.148–9.
3. Intrepid Adventure: Exploring the World, 'Stalin's Secret Bunker', online.
4. Alliluyeva, Svetlana, *Only One Year*, pp.148–9.
5. Ibid., p.364.

Chapter 20: Nadezhda's Death: The Aftermath

1. Alliluyeva, Svetlana, *Twenty Letters to a Friend*, pp.118–9.
2. 'USSR: Joseph Stalin': Svetlana Alliluyeva interview, 1980s, Thames TV.
3. Alliluyeva, Svetlana, 'A Book for Granddaughters', p.95.
4. Alliluyeva, Svetlana, *Only One Year*, pp.367–8.
5. Ibid., p.369.
6. Ibid., p.373.

Chapter 21: Stalin's Early Kindness to his Daughter, Svetlana

1. Alliluyeva, Svetlana, *Twenty Letters to a Friend*, p.30.
2. Ibid., pp.35–6.
3. Ibid., p.103.
4. Ibid., p.31.
5. 'Kuntsevo Dacha', *Wikipedia*.
6. Alliluyeva, Svetlana, *Twenty Letters to a Friend*, pp.149–50.
7. Ibid., p.151.
8. Ibid., p.152.
9. Ibid., pp.155–6.
10. Alliluyeva, Svetlana, *Only One Year*, p.368.
11. Ibid., pp.368–9.
12. Alliluyeva, Svetlana, *Twenty Letters to a Friend*, p.70.
13. Ibid., pp.70–1.
14. Ibid., p.102.

Chapter 22: Stalin's Unbelievable Cruelty to his Relatives

1. Alliluyeva, Svetlana, *Twenty Letters to a Friend*, p.81.
2. Ibid., pp.79.
3. Svanidze, Alexander Semyonovich, Hrono.ru.
4. Ibid.
5. Alliluyeva, Svetlana, *Twenty Letters to a Friend*, pp.75–6.
6. Ibid., p.76.
7. Svanidze, Alexander Semyonovich, op. cit.
8. Ibid.
9. Alliluyeva, Svetlana, *Twenty Letters to a Friend*, p.37.
10. Ibid., pp.75–6.
11. Ibid., p.82.
12. Ibid., p.82.

13. Alliluyeva, Svetlana, *Twenty Letters to a Friend*, p.37.
14. 'GPU', *Wikipedia*.
15. 'OGPU', *Wikipedia*.
16. Redens, Stanislav Frantsyevich, Hrono.ru.
17. 'Stanislav Redens', *Wikipedia*.
18. Soanes, Catherine and Angus Stevenson (Editors), *Oxford Dictionary of English*.
19. Alliluyeva, Svetlana, *Twenty Letters to a Friend*, p.61.
20. Ibid., pp.79–80.
21. Alliluyeva, Svetlana, *Only One Year*, pp.147–8.
22. Alliluyeva, Svetlana, *Twenty Letters to a Friend*, p.61.
23. Montefiore, Simon Sebag, *The Court of the Red Tsar*, p.498.
24. Alliluyeva, Svetlana, *Twenty Letters to a Friend*, p.63.
25. Alliluyeva, Svetlana, *Only One Year*, p.154.
26. Alliluyeva, Svetlana, *Twenty Letters to a Friend*, p.52.
27. Ibid., p.66, Note.
28. Alliluyeva, Svetlana, *Only One Year*, p.374.
29. Alliluyeva, Svetlana, *Twenty Letters to a Friend*, p.57.
30. Ibid., p.37.
31. Ibid., p.61.
32. Alliluyeva, Svetlana, *Only One Year*, p.374.
33. Ibid., p.374.
34. Ibid., p.154.
35. Ibid., p.154.
36. Alliluyeva, Svetlana, *Twenty Letters to a Friend*, pp.77–8.
37. Ibid., p.82.
38. Ibid., pp.80–81.

Chapter 23: Others Known to Svetlana who 'Disappeared'

1. Alliluyeva, Svetlana, *Twenty Letters to a Friend*, pp.144–5.
2. Ibid., p.144.
3. Ibid., p.145.
4. Ibid., p.81.
5. Ibid., p.63.
6. Ibid., p.204.
7. Ibid., p.205.
8. Alliluyeva, Svetlana, *Only One Year*, p.385.
9. 'Leningrad Affair', *Wikipedia*.
10. Ibid.
11. Alliluyeva, Svetlana, *Twenty Letters to a Friend*, p.6.
12. Montefiore, Simon Sebag, *The Court of the Red Tsar*, p.643.
13. Alliluyeva, Svetlana, *Twenty Letters to a Friend*, p.231.

Chapter 24: Stalin's Sons, Yakov and Vasily

1. Alliluyeva, Svetlana, *Twenty Letters to a Friend*, p.36.
2. Ibid., pp.166–7.
3. Ibid., pp.166–7.
4. Ibid., p.165.
5. Ibid., pp.106–7.
6. Ibid., pp.166–7.
7. Ibid., pp.106–7.
8. Ibid., p.165.
9. Ibid., pp.168–9.
10. Ibid., p.177.
11. Ibid., pp.168–9.
12. Ibid., p.193.
13. Ibid., p.169.
14. Ibid., p.170.
15. Ibid., p.193.
16. Alliluyeva, Svetlana, *Only One Year*, p.370.
17. Alliluyeva, Svetlana, *Twenty Letters to a Friend*, pp.112–3.
18. 'Vasily Stalin', *Wikipedia*.
19. Alliluyeva, Svetlana, *Twenty Letters to a Friend*, p.193.
20. Ibid., p.222.
21. Ibid., p.223.
22. Ibid., p.223.
23. Ibid., pp.221–2.
24. Ibid., pp.224–5.
25. Ibid., pp.225–6.
26. Ibid., pp.225–6.
27. Ibid., p.227.
28. Ibid., p.229.
29. Ibid., p.230.
30. Ibid., p.230.

Chapter 25: Empathy: Simon Baron-Cohen

1. Baron-Cohen, Simon, *Zero Degrees of Empathy: A New Theory of Human Cruelty and Kindness*, p.ix.
2. Soanes, Catherine and Angus Stevenson (Editors), *Oxford Dictionary of English*.
3. Baron-Cohen, Simon, op. cit., p.13.
4. Soanes, Catherine and Angus Stevenson (Editors), *Oxford Dictionary of English*.
5. Baron-Cohen, Simon, op. cit., p.11.
6. Ibid., p.15.

7. Ibid., p.16.
8. Ibid., pp.16–17.
9. Ibid., p.20.
10. Ibid., p.30.
11. Ibid., p.45.

Chapter 26: For Svetlana the World Closes in

1. Alliluyeva, Svetlana, *Twenty Letters to a Friend*, pp.127–8.
2. Ibid., p.139.
3. Ibid., p.129.
4. Ibid., p.134.
5. Ibid., pp.136–7.
6. Ibid., p.135.
7. Ibid., p.130.
8. Ibid., p.237.
9. Ibid., p.131.
10. Ibid., p.180.
11. Ibid., p.184.
12. Ibid., p.181.
13. Ibid., pp.186–7.
14. Ibid., pp.188–9.
15. 'Svetlana Talks About Her Father, Joseph Stalin, 1967', historycomestolife.
16. Alliluyeva, Svetlana, *Twenty Letters to a Friend*, p.194.
17. Ibid., p.195.
18. Ibid., pp.196–7.
19. Ibid., p.205.
20. Ibid., p.207.
21. Alliluyeva, Svetlana, 'The Lovely and Trustful', p.28.
22. Talbott, Strobe (Translator and Editor), *Khrushchev Remembers*, pp.309–10.
23. Ibid., p.223.
24. Alliluyeva, Svetlana, *Twenty Letters to a Friend*, pp.190–1.
25. Ibid., p.181.

Chapter 27: For Svetlana the Light Dawns

1. Alliluyeva, Svetlana, *Only One Year*, p.142.
2. Ibid., pp.147–8.
3. Ibid., pp.141–2.
4. Alliluyeva, Svetlana, *Twenty Letters to a Friend*, p.147.
5. Alliluyeva, Svetlana, *Only One Year*, p.364.
6. Ibid., p.148.
7. Ibid., p.150.
8. Alliluyeva, Svetlana, *Twenty Letters to a Friend*, p.121.
9. Alliluyeva, Svetlana, *Only One Year*, pp.140–1.

10. Ibid., pp.142–3.
11. Ibid., p.143.
12. Alliluyeva, Svetlana, 'A Book for Granddaughters', p.105.
13. Alliluyeva, Svetlana, 'The Faraway Music: 1983–1986: England-USA'.
14. Ibid., p.175.
15. Ibid., p.220.
16. Ibid., p.221.

Chapter 28: Professor Vladimir Bekhterev and Stalin's Paranoia

1. Moroz, Oleg (1989), 'The Last Diagnosis: A Plausible Account That Needs Further Verification', *Psychology*, Volume 27, Issue 5, 189, pp.82–102.
2. Soanes, Catherine and Angus Stevenson (Editors), *Oxford Dictionary of English.*
3. Radzinsky, Edvard, *Stalin*, p.30.
4. *Vestnik Znaniya*, 1927, No. 24.
5. Ibid.
6. *Psychology*, Volume 27, Issue 5, 1989.
7. Moroz, pp.82–102.
8. PsychiatryOnline, American Journal of Psychiatry, Vladimir Bekhterev, 1857–1927.

Chapter 29: Suppression of the Kulaks (1929–32)

1. 'Dekulakization', *Wikipedia.*
2. Alexandrov, G. F., et al., *Joseph Stalin: A Short Biography*, p.109.
3. Joseph Stalin, Speech on Agrarian Policy, 27 December 1929, Hanover College, Hanover, IN, USA.
4. Alliluyeva, Svetlana, *Only One Year*, pp.376–7.
5. Talbott, Strobe (Translator and Editor), *Khrushchev Remembers*, p.70.

Chapter 30: A Purge of Politicians (1936–38)

1. Talbott, Strobe (Translator and Editor), *Khrushchev Remembers*, p.80.
2. Montefiore, Simon Sebag, *The Court of the Red Tsar*, p.151.
3. Talbott, Strobe, op. cit., p.79, note 9.
4. Ibid., p.89.
5. Ibid., pp.74, 77.
6. Ibid., p.78.
7. Ibid., pp.81–4.
8. Ibid., pp.43–4.

Chapter 31: Alexander Solzhenitsyn: The Inhumanity of the Gulag System

1. Hardy, Dale, 'Solzhenitsyn in Confession', Simon Fraser University, 2006, p.23.

2. Solzhenitsyn, Alexander, *One Day in the Life of Ivan Denisovich*, Sphere Books, London, 1970.
3. *One Day in the Life of Ivan Denisovich*, Preface.
4. Ibid., p.7.
5. Ibid., p.12.
6. Ibid., p.47.
7. Ibid., pp.156–7.

Chapter 32: Stalin and his Mother Ekaterina: His 'Rock'

1. Alliluyeva, Svetlana, 'A Book for Granddaughters', p.95.
2. Ibid.
3. Dzhugashvili, Keke, 'My Dear Son: The Memoirs of Stalin's Mother', Archive of the Central Committee of the Communist Party of Georgia, f.8, op.2, d.15.

Chapter 33: Elections to the Supreme Soviet (December 1937)

1. Alexandrov, G. F., et al., *Joseph Stalin: A Short Biography*, pp.137–8.
2. '1937 Soviet Union Legislative Election', *Wikipedia*.

Chapter 34: Stalin's Purges of the Red Army (1937–39 and 1940–42)

1. '1937–1941: Military Purges', GlobalSecurity.org online
2. Osborn, John W. Jr, 'Joseph Stalin's Paranoid Purge', Warfare History Network online.
3. Talbott, Strobe (Translator and Editor), *Khrushchev Remembers*, p.85.
4. Ibid., p.87.
5. 'Taman Army', *Wikipedia*.
6. Talbott, Strobe, op. cit., p.87.
7. Ibid., p.88.
8. '1941 Red Army Purge', *Wikipedia*.
9. Talbott, Strobe, op. cit., p.89.
10. Radzinsky, Edvard, *Stalin*, pp.369–70.
11. Ibid., p.371.
12. Ibid., p.372.
13. Ibid., pp.372–3.

Chapter 35: Lavrenti Beria

1. Khrushchev, Nikita, 'On the Cult of Personality and Its Consequences', speech delivered at the Twentieth Party Congress of the Communist Party of the Soviet Union, 25 February 1956. From the Congressional Record: Proceedings and Debates of the 84th Congress, 2nd Session (22 May 1956–11 June 1956), C11, Part 7 (4 June 1956), pp.9389–9403. Wilson Centre, Digital Archive, International History Declassified.
2. Talbott, Strobe (Translator and Editor), *Khrushchev Remembers*, pp.335–6.

3. Alliluyeva, Svetlana, 'A Book for Granddaughters', p.105.
4. Alliluyeva, Svetlana, *Twenty Letters to a Friend*, p.81.
5. Ibid., p.80.
6. Ibid., p.143.
7. Alliluyeva, Svetlana, *Only One Year*, p.374.
8. Ibid., p.374.

Chapter 36: The Second World War: Stalin as a Wartime Leader

1. Chadaev, Y. E., *V Groznoye Vremya*, 'In a Terrible Time', Ms. I State Archive Collection, in Radzinsky, Edvard, *Stalin*, pp.464, 587.
2. Alexandrov, G. F., et al., *Joseph Stalin: A Short Biography*, p.154.
3. Ibid., p.157.
4. Ibid., p.159.
5. Khrushchev, Nikita, 'On the Cult of Personality and Its Consequences', speech delivered at the Twentieth Party Congress of the Communist Party of the Soviet Union, 25 February 1956. From the Congressional Record: Proceedings and Debates of the 84th Congress, 2nd Session (22 May 1956–11 June 1956), C11, Part 7 (4 June 1956), pp.9389–9403. Wilson Centre, Digital Archive, International History Declassified.
6. Alexandrov, G. F., op. cit., pp.160–2.
7. Ibid., pp.162–3.
8. Ibid., p.167.
9. 'USSR: Joseph Stalin': Svetlana Alliluyeva interview, 1980s, Thames TV.
10. Alexandrov, G. F., op. cit., p.126.
11. Ibid., p.126.
12. Joseph Stalin: Speech at an Election Meeting Stalin Election District, Moscow 9 February 1946.

Chapter 37: The Katyn Atrocity

1. Kawczak, Andrew, Katyn (1940), History Presentation, 2018.
2. Engel, David (1993). *Facing a Holocaust: The Polish Government-in-Exile and the Jews, 1943–1945*. UNC Press Books. p.71.
3. Rees, Laurence (4 May 2010). *World War II Behind Closed Doors: Stalin, the Nazis and the West*. Random House Digital, Inc. pp. 243–246.
4. 'Excerpts: Beria letter to Stalin on Katyn', BBC News Channel, 28 April 2010 online.
5. Radzinsky, Edvard, *Stalin*, p.499.
6. Kawczak, Andrew, Katyn (1940), History Presentation, 2018.

Chapter 38: Stalin's Unashamedly Violent Tendencies

1. 'Behind Closed Doors', BBC Four, Episode 3, 2008.
2. Joseph Stalin: Speech at an Election Meeting Stalin Election District, Moscow 9 February 1946.

Chapter 39: From Battered Child to Angry and Violent Adult

1. Adorno, T. W., Frenkel-Brunswik, E., Levinson, D. J., & Sanford, R. N., *The Authoritarian Personality*, in Milburn, Michael and Sheree D. Conrad, *Raised to Rage: The Politics of Anger and the Roots of Authoritarianism*, p.4.
2. Milburn, Michael and Sheree D. Conrad, op. cit., pp.4, 51.
3. 'Promises: Behavioral Health: Anger and Trauma', 25 November 2020, online.
4. Baron-Cohen, Simon, *Zero Degrees of Empathy: A New Theory of Human Cruelty and Kindness*, pp.49–50.
5. 'Promises: Behavioral Health: Anger and Trauma', op. cit.
6. Fox, B. H., et al., 'Trauma Changes Everything: Examining the Relationship between Adverse Childhood Experiences and Serious, Violent and Chronic Juvenile Offenders', 'Child Abuse & Neglect', 1 January 2021.
7. Win, Emma, Nur Hani Zainal, and Michelle Gayle Newman, 'Trait Anger Expression Mediates Childhood Trauma Predicting for Adulthood Anxiety, Depressive, and Alcohol Use Disorders', *Journal of Affective Disorders*, March 2021.
8. Zhu, Wenfeng, et al., 'The Role of Metacognitive Beliefs and Anger Rumination, Aggressive Behavior, 10.1002/ab.21878, 46, 2, pp.162–169, 2020. In Golden, Bernard, 'How Adverse Childhood Experiences Impact Adult Anger: Adverse Childhood Experiences Influence Cognitive and Emotional Development', 6 June 2021 online.
9. Sukhodolsky, D. G., A. Golub, and E. N. Cromwell, 'Development and Validation of the Anger Rumination Scale, *Personality and Individual Differences*, 31, 2001, pp.689–700.
10. 'Promises: Behavioral Health: Anger and Trauma', op. cit.
11. Ibid.
12. Ibid.

Chapter 40: Stalin's Anti-Semitism

1. Talbott, Strobe (Translator and Editor), *Khrushchev Remembers*, p.279.
2. Ibid., p.278.
3. Alliluyeva, Svetlana, *Twenty Letters to a Friend*, p.167.
4. Ibid., pp.204–5.
5. Alliluyeva, Svetlana, *Only One Year*, p.154.

Chapter 41: Trotsky's Criticisms of Stalin

1. Leon Trotsky, 'Stalin's Political Biography', 1932, The Trotsky Internet Archive, online.
2. Soanes, Catherine and Angus Stevenson (Editors), *Oxford Dictionary of English*.
3. Trotsky, Leon, 'Leon Trotsky on Hitler's Victory', March 1933, The Trotsky Internet Archive, online.

4. Soanes, Catherine and Angus Stevenson (Editors), *Oxford Dictionary of English*.
5. Trotsky, Leon, 'Latest Lies About the Moscow Trials Serve Stalin's New Diplomatic Needs', 5 July 1937, The Trotsky Internet Archive, online.
6. Trotsky, Leon: 'Stalin: An Appraisal of the Man and his Influence', Introduction, 1940, The Trotsky Internet Archive, online.
7. Ibid.
8. Soanes, Catherine and Angus Stevenson (Editors), *Oxford Dictionary of English*.
9. Trotsky, Leon: 'Stalin: An Appraisal of the Man and his Influence', Introduction, 1940, The Trotsky Internet Archive, online.

Chapter 42: Stalin's Persecution of Trotsky

1. 'Lev Sedov', *Wikipedia*
2. Trotsky, Leon, 'Leon Sedov: Son, Friend, Fighter, The Trotsky Internet Archive, online.
3. Trotsky, Leon, 'Trotsky Letter Exposes Stalin's Role in Recent Assassination Attempt', 24 May 1940, The Trotsky Internet Archive, online.
4. Trotsky, Leon, 'Stalin Seeks My Death', Coyoacán, Mexico City, 8 June 1940, The Trotsky Internet Archive, online.
5. 'This Day In History: Stalin Orders Trotsky Into Internal Exile (1928)', 11 January 2017.

Chapter 43: Stalin Versus Trotsky

1. Trotsky, Leon, 'The Permanent Revolution', Chapter 2. 'The Permanent Revolution is Not a 'Leap' by the Proletariat, but the Reconstruction of the Nation under the Leadership of the Proletariat', 1931, The Trotsky Internet Archive, online.
2. Soanes, Catherine and Angus Stevenson (Editors), *Oxford Dictionary of English*.
3. Trotsky, Leon, 'The Principles of Democracy and Proletarian Dictatorship', 1918, The Trotsky Internet Archive, online.
4. Trotsky, Leon, *My Life*, Chapter 34, 'The Train', The Trotsky Internet Archive, online.
5. Trotsky, Leon, 'Their Morals and Ours', 1938.
6. Soanes, Catherine and Angus Stevenson (Editors), *Oxford Dictionary of English*.
7. Trotsky, Leon, *The Revolution Betrayed*, Chapter 11, 'Whither the Soviet Union?', The Trotsky Internet Archive, online.

Chapter 44: Did Stalin Ever Show Remorse or Insight into his Condition?

1. Alliluyeva, Svetlana, 'A Book for Granddaughters', p.94.
2. Montefiore, Simon Sebag, *The Court of the Red Tsar*, pp.455–6.

Chapter 45: Stalin and his Paranoia

1. *Diagnostic and Statistical Manual of Mental Disorders, Fifth Edition, DSM-5th*, pp.649–651.
2. Shakespeare, William, Banquo, *Macbeth*, Act 1, Scene 3.

Chapter 46: Stalin's Jealousy: Georgy Zhukov

1. Hiroyaki Kuromiya, *Stalin: Profiles in Power* (Pearson Longman, Harlow, UK, 2005), pp.42–3. In Gregory, Paul R., *Politics, Murder, and Love in Stalin's Kremlin*, pp.37–8.
2. Montefiore, Simon Sebag, *The Court of the Red Tsar*, p.436.
3. Talbott, Strobe (Translator and Editor), *Khrushchev Remembers*, pp.605–6.
4. Stalin: The Nazis and The West', WW2 Behind Closed Doors, a BBC/KCET Hollywood co-production, BBC Four, 2008, Episode 5.
5. Montefiore, Simon Sebag, op. cit., pp.436–7.
6. Stalin: The Nazis and The West', op. cit.
7. Kornukov, A. M., 'Chief Marshal of Aviation A. A. Novikov: His 100th Birthday', Warheroes.ru
8. Montefiore, Simon Sebag, *The Court of the Red Tsar*, p.487.
9. Zhukov, Georgy Konstantinovich, Biographical Index, Hrono.ru
10. Montefiore, Simon Sebag, op. cit., pp.487–8.
11. 'Georgy Zhukov', *Wikipedia*.
12. Ibid.
13. Stalin: The Nazis and The West', op. cit.

Chapter 47: A Purge of Doctors

1. 'Doctors' Plot', *Wikipedia*.
2. Montefiore, Simon Sebag, *The Court of the Red Tsar*, pp.514–5.
3. Talbott, Strobe (Translator and Editor), *Khrushchev Remembers*, p.304.
4. 'Andrei Zhdanov', *Wikipedia*.
5. Brent, Jonathan, 'Doctors' Plot', *The Yivo Encyclopedia of Jews in Easter Europe*, Yivo Institute for Jewish Research, online.
6. Talbott, Strobe, op. cit., pp.303–4.
7. Alliluyeva, Svetlana, *Twenty Letters to a Friend*, p.216.
8. Brent, Jonathan, 'Doctors' Plot', *The Yivo Encyclopedia of Jews in Easter Europe*, Yivo Institute for Jewish Research, online.
9. 'Doctors' Plot', *Wikipedia*.
10. Khrushchev, Nikita, 'On the Cult of Personality and Its Consequences', speech delivered at the Twentieth Party Congress of the Communist Party of the Soviet Union, 25 February 1956. From the Congressional Record: Proceedings and Debates of the 84th Congress, 2nd Session (22 May 1956–11 June 1956), C11, Part 7 (4 June 1956), pp.9389–9403. Wilson Centre, Digital Archive, International History Declassified.

11. Talbott, Strobe, op. cit., pp.305–6.
12. Ibid., p.305.
13. Ibid., p.306.
14. Ibid., p.305.
15. Ibid., p.301.
16. 'Doctors' Plot', *Wikipedia*.
17. Khrushchev, Nikita, op. cit.

Chapter 48: Stalin is Rewarded

1. Alexandrov, G. F., et al., *Joseph Stalin: A Short Biography*, p.152.
2. Ibid., p.152.
3. Ibid., p.173.
4. Ibid., p.187.

Chapter 49: Stalin's Final Years

1. Alliluyeva, Svetlana, 'A Book for Granddaughters', p.95.

Chapter 50: Stalin's Death (5 March 1953): Aftermath

1. 'Gulag': History.com editors, 21 August 2018.
2. Alliluyeva, Svetlana, *Twenty Letters to a Friend*, p.161.
3. Ibid., p.10.
4. Ibid., p.15.
5. Alliluyeva, Svetlana, *Only One Year*, p.166.

Chapter 51: February 1956: Khrushchev Acknowledges Stalin's Crimes

1. Wolfe, Bertram, *Khrushchev and Stalin's Ghost*, in Talbott, Strobe (Translator and Editor), *Khrushchev Remembers*, p.4.
2. Khrushchev, Nikita, 'On the Cult of Personality and Its Consequences', speech delivered at the Twentieth Party Congress of the Communist Party of the Soviet Union, 25 February 1956. History and Public Policy Program Digital Archive, From the Congressional Record: Proceedings and Debates of the 84th Congress, 2nd Session (May 22, 1956–June 11, 1956), C11, Part 7 (June 4, 1956), pp. 9389–9403. Wilson Centre, Digital Archive, International History Declassified.

Chapter 52: Excess Mortality in the Soviet Union under Joseph Stalin

1. Polian, Pavel, *Against Their Will*, p.313.
2. Pohl, J. Otto, *The Stalinist Penal System*, McFarland, 1997, p.148.
3. Haynes, Michael, *A Century of State Murder? Death and Policy in Twentieth Century Russia*, Pluto Press, London, 2003, pp.214–5.
4. Healey, Dan, 'Illness and Inhumanity in Stalin's Gulag', *The American Historical Review*, 1 June 2018, 123, pp.1049–51.
5. Polian, Pavel, op. cit., p.313.

6. Pohl, J. Otto, op. cit., p.58.
7. '1937–1941: Military Purges', GlobalSecurity.org online
8. '1941 Red Army Purge', *Wikipedia.*
9. Kużniar-Plota, Małgorzata, 'Decision to Commence investigation into Katyn Massacre', Departmental Commission for the Prosecution of Crimes against the Polish Nation, 30 November 2004.
10. 'Excess Mortality in the Soviet Union under Joseph Stalin', *Wikipedia.*
11. Kondrashin, Viktor, 'Was the 1932–33 Famine in Ukraine 'an act of genocide against the Ukrainian people'? My response to S. V. Kulchytsky', 1 April 2019 online.
12. Ellman, Michael, 'The 1947 Soviet Famine and the Entitlement Approach to Famines', Cambridge Journal of Economics 24, 2000, pp.603–30.
13. Rummel, R. J., 'How Many Did Communist Regimes Murder', Unpublished essay, November 1993.
14. Ghosh, Palash, IBT World: 'How Many People Did Joseph Stalin Kill?', 3 May 2013, online.

Chapter 53: Was Stalin the Twentieth Century's Bloodiest Dictator?

1. Rummel, R. J., 'How Many Did Communist Regimes Murder', Unpublished essay, November 1993.
2. Ibid.
3. Ibid.
4. Ibid.

Chapter 54: Was Communism a Greater or Lesser Evil than Tsarism?

1. 'Comparison of Tsar and Communist Rule', Politics, UKEssays.com, 13 August 2018 online.
2. Beer, Daniel, *The House of the Dead: Siberian Exile under the Tsars.*
3. Lauchlan, Iain, 'Security Policing in Late Imperial Russia', published in *Late Imperial Russia: Problems and Prospects* by Ian Thatcher (editor), Manchester UP, 2005, pp.22–3.
4. Rummel, R. J., *Statistics of Democide*: Genocide and Mass Murder Since 1900, Center for National Security Law, School of Law, University of Virginia, Charlottesville, Virginia, USA, 1997.
5. 'Cheka', *New World Encyclopedia.*
6. Lenman, Bruce P. (Consultant Editor), *Chambers Dictionary of World History,* p.721.
7. 'Politics of Russia', *Wikipedia.*

Chapter 55: The Fate of Svetlana

1. Alliluyeva, Svetlana, *Only One Year,* p.3.
2. Alliluyeva, Svetlana, 'The Lovely and Trustful', p.62.
3. Ibid., pp.67–8.

4. Alliluyeva, Svetlana, 'The Faraway Music: A Trap, 1970–1972', p.169.
5. Ibid., p.214.

Chapter 56: Stalin: An Explanation

1. First published as *The Politics of Denial* in 1996.
2. Milburn, Michael and Sheree D. Conrad, *Raised to Rage: The Politics of Anger and the Roots of Authoritarianism*, p.3.
3. Ibid., p.41.
4. Ibid., p.56.
5. Ibid., p.4.
6. Stalin, I. V., *Sochineniya*, Moscow, Volumes 13, p.113. In Volkogonov, p.6.
7. Milburn, Michael and Sheree D. Conrad, op. cit., p.31.
8. Ibid., p.82.
9. Golden, Bernard, 'How Adverse Childhood Experiences Impact Adult Anger: Adverse Childhood Experiences Influence Cognitive and Emotional Development', 6 June 2021 online.
10. Milburn, Michael and Sheree D. Conrad, op. cit., p.55.
11. Ibid., p.181.
12. Marcus-Newhall, Amy, William C. Pedersen, Mike Carlson, and Norman Miller, 'Displaced Aggression Is Alive and Well: A Meta-Analytic Review', *Journal of Personality and Social Psychology*, 1 Apr 2000, 78(4), pp.670–689, in Milburn, Michael, and Sheree D. Conrad, op. cit., p.xvi.
13. Milburn, Michael and Sheree D. Conrad, op. cit., p.4.
14. Ibid., p.56.
15. Ibid., p.5.
16. Merelman, R. M., 'The Development of Political Ideology: A Framework for the Analysis of Political Socialization', *American Political Science Review* 63, pp.750–67, in Milburn, p.181.
17. Milburn, Michael and Sheree D. Conrad, op. cit., p.xviii.
18. Ibid.
19. Scully, Ruby Prosser, 'Child Abuse may Change Brain Structure and Make Depression Worse', MIND, *New Scientist*, 21 March 2019.

Chapter 57: Russia Today

1. 'Alexey Navalny Fast Facts', CNN Editorial Research, CNN World, 2 May 2021, online.
2. 'Russian Elections: How Democratic Are They?', BBC News, 2021, You Tube.
3. Tolstoy, Leo, 'Family Happiness', *The Russian Messenger*, No. 7–8, April 1859.

Chapter 58: Putin and Stalin: Two of a Kind!

1. Magnay, Diana, Moscow Correspondent, 'Vladimir Putin: The Security Men, Officials, and Friends who are in the Russian President's Inner Circle', Sky News, 28 February 2022, online.

Index